For Mum and Dad

More Than A Shirt

MORE THAN A SHIRT

How Football Shirts
Explain Global Politics,
Money and Power

JOEY D'URSO

SEVEN DIALS

First published in Great Britain in 2025 by Seven Dials,
an imprint of The Orion Publishing Group Ltd
Carmelite House, 50 Victoria Embankment
London EC4Y 0DZ

An Hachette UK Company

1 3 5 7 9 10 8 6 4 2

Copyright © Joey D'Urso 2025

The authorised representative in the EEA is Hachette Ireland,
8 Castlecourt Centre, Dublin 15, D15 XTP3,
Ireland (email: info@hbgi.ie)

The moral right of Joey D'Urso to be identified as
the author of this work has been asserted in accordance
with the Copyright, Designs and Patents Act of 1988.

The names of some individuals in this book have been
changed to protect their identity and privacy.

All rights reserved. No part of this publication may be
reproduced, stored in a retrieval system, or transmitted
in any form or by any means, electronic, mechanical,
photocopying, recording, or otherwise, without the
prior permission of both the copyright owner and the
above publisher of this book.

A CIP catalogue record for this book is
available from the British Library.

ISBN (Hardback) 978 1 3996 2280 6
ISBN (Trade Paperback) 978 1 3996 2281 3
ISBN (eBook) 978 1 3996 2283 7
ISBN (Audio) 978 1 3996 2284 4

Typeset by Input Data Services Ltd, Bridgwater, Somerset

Printed in Great Britain by Clays Ltd, Elcograf, S.p.A.

CONTENTS

Introduction   1

1. Putin's Wars
FC Schalke 04 & Red Star Belgrade   17
2. Criminal Connections
Envigado FC & Parma FC   46
3. The Global Gamble
FC Goa & Nottingham Forest   74
4. World on the Move
Changing Lives FC & France National Football Team   106
5. American Exceptionalism
Houston Dash & Inter Miami   134
6. Beyond Oil and Gas
FC Barcelona & Real Madrid   166
7. Democracy's Limits
Prisoners of Robben Island & Newcastle United   196
8. China's Rise and Retreat
West Bromwich Albion & Guangzhou Evergrande   226
9. The Other Half
England Women's Goalkeeper Shirt & SC Corinthians SP   255
10. Borders
Rangers FC & Club Deportivo Palestino   284

11. Financial Times
Beşiktaş J.K. & Australia Women's Training Shirt 312

Postscript 342
Acknowledgements 348
Endnotes 351
Picture Credits 370

INTRODUCTION

I hope this book changes the way you see the world. If that sounds a pretentious goal, allow me to be a little more specific. I hope this book changes the way you see the world when it comes to the football shirts you see out and about. There is more to them than meets the eye. Every shirt tells a deeper story about the world we inhabit.

This book has taken me on a journey to a dozen countries on five continents to tell the story of twenty-two different football shirts, enough for two teams of eleven players. I have travelled from Colombia to Cape Town, from Texas to Qatar, from Germany to India. Each chapter tells the story of two shirts which give a window into a big global topic, from geopolitics to immigration, nationalism to oil and gas. Wherever you live in the world you likely see football shirts worn by people on the street, or by footballers themselves as you watch games on TV, either intentionally or by catching a glimpse in the corner of a room somewhere. Spotting shirts in the wild is more common in some parts of the world than others, but the world's most popular sport is ever-growing in popularity, and will be bigger when you come to read this paragraph than when I sat down to write it. Soon after reading this you will spot a football shirt in the wild. It may be the next time you leave the house. You may even be able to spot one from where you are reading this right now, perhaps in a cafe or on public transport. After finishing this book I hope you will see something deeper in every shirt you see. I hope this book gives you the tools to learn something new from every shirt. It may only become clear after some extra research, but there will be something, because every football shirt tells a story.

For billions of us, some of life's most powerful memories are footballing ones. These may be jumping up and down in the stands, being drenched with beer in the pub, or hugging relatives in front of the television. Football shirts can do more than just inspire sporting memories or teach us about the game itself. They can also be a device to better understand the world around us beyond football, giving an insight into things that initially appear unrelated. A German shirt sporting the logo of a Russian gas company can be a way of telling one of the century's biggest stories: how Russia slid into dictatorship under Vladimir Putin, reawakening conflicts that were thought long finished. In Medellín in Colombia, a football shirt featuring the silhouetted face of a drug warlord is a way of understanding that country's fraught history as well as highlighting why football around the world is so often associated with organised crime. In England's post-industrial north-east, the local team Newcastle United have worn a shirt in the green of Saudi Arabia's flag, paying homage to the authoritarian state which bankrolls their club. This tells a bigger story about the oil and gas that powers our world and what may happen when it all runs out.

I am not arguing that football is the main force behind all these global trends. The sport is one narrative strand among countless others. But it is one that is perhaps more likely to engage and intrigue us than dry economic statistics, or news stories about distant politicians with names that are hard to remember. Of course not *everything* important can be explained by football

INTRODUCTION

shirts. Finding a shirt to explain the rise of artificial intelligence or the dangers of antibiotic resistance feels a stretch at the time of writing this book, although things could change. Yet as the game becomes ever more global with the proliferation of satellite television and high-speed internet, the world's biggest sport looms larger in international affairs than ever before, and the game's links to politics are growing deeper and more numerous. Football can provide a way into understanding things that are otherwise too abstract, too big or too distant to fully grasp. Football shirts can help us think about topics that may be more life and death than football, but are not *bigger* than football – because nothing in the world is bigger. Nothing can be truly universal in a world divided by language, religion and geography, but football comes pretty close, closer than anything else. The football shirt in all its varieties, is close to a universal object, one which we can use to help understand the world.

We all remember our first football shirt. Since the age of four I have been going to watch Aston Villa in my home city of Birmingham in England. My first game was a 2–2 draw with Arsenal in 1996. I still have the programme, its cover featuring future England manager Gareth Southgate who played for Villa back then. My childhood photos are full of all sorts of claret-and-blue paraphernalia, the club's colours dating back to 1888 when chairman William McGregor founded the world's first-ever football league. I never had an actual replica shirt until the age of ten. That changed when my grandmother moved house after my grandfather died, freeing up some cash. She gave each of her grandchildren £100 with the stipulation that, rather than it being sensibly saved somewhere, we should be allowed to spend it on whatever we wanted. I was old enough to know exactly what that was.

Aston Villa's 2002–03 shirt was claret with blue sleeves and a claret-and-blue striped V-neck. The shorts were white and the socks, unusually that season, were claret rather than blue. I bought the full kit and barely took it off. The logo on the front of the shirt was for Rover, the iconic car company based in Longbridge, just a couple of miles from where I grew up in Bournville, which is the home of Cadbury's chocolate, another great British industry. Rover and Villa were a perfect brand match, representing Birmingham's role as the centre of the UK's motor industry which was famous around the world in the twentieth century. That season's white away shirt featured the logo of MG, another famous British car manufacturer and part of the MG Rover Group. At the time of the Villa deal, Rover was the last UK-owned car manufacturer catering to the masses. It didn't last much longer, though. Over decades, manufacturing jobs had been drifting eastwards to places like Eastern Europe and Asia where labour was cheaper. The Longbridge factory could not survive. In 2005, after lengthy takeover negotiations, Rover went into liquidation, a year after the company's logo was replaced on Villa's shirts by German finance firm DWS Investments. For the first time in decades cars were no longer being made at Longbridge, with 6,000 MG Rover employees losing their jobs alongside many more job losses in the supply chain.

At the time, I played football in a junior league not far from Longbridge, wearing my Villa kit whenever I could for training. The sense of loss hung over the entire place. A few years later there was a similar feeling in Bournville. Cadbury's was founded by benevolent Victorian capitalists who constructed my home neighbourhood as a 'model village', with greenery and other amenities for workers at a time when such conscientiousness was uncommon. In 2009, the company was sold to an American conglomerate.

INTRODUCTION

Chocolate was still made in Bournville under the Cadbury's name, and the area has fared far better than Longbridge, but things feel a little different now. These things changed in my city but Aston Villa, in its essence, did not. Football clubs provide many of us with a constant in a world where everything else seems to change – companies rise and fall, relatives live and die, houses are bought and sold. No family member of mine lives in the same house as they did when I was born, but Villa Park is still there, the only geographical constant in my life. Even when clubs move stadiums the team remains, a North Star in an ever-changing world. The changes in my own team's claret-and-blue shirts over my lifetime tell stories about the place where I grew up, and some bigger global stories too, but this is just my own niche example. You will have your own.

Fans have only been able to buy replica shirts for around half a century. In October 1973, John Griffiths was managing director of British sports manufacturer Admiral. One day he drove 100 miles from his factory in Leicestershire for a morning meeting at a mail-order catalogue company on the outskirts of Leeds. The meeting was not a success but following a consolation breakfast, Griffiths and his colleague spotted some footballers training across the road. The team was Leeds United, at that time in their heyday under legendary manager Don Revie. Griffiths collared Revie, showed off some shirt samples in his office over a cup of tea and came up with a revolutionary idea.[1] Before this meeting, football clubs simply bought generic kits 'off the peg' from retailers in a preferred colour. Griffiths suggested that Admiral and Leeds work together on a kit. Revie made clear that Leeds' all-white home kit, copied from Real Madrid, was sacrosanct, but he said the company could do what they liked with the club's yellow away kit, and training jerseys. Griffiths proposed a bespoke Leeds kit made by Admiral, which could be sold to fans as well as being worn by players. He came up with a yellow design with an Admiral logo on the chest on the opposite side to the Leeds badge, as well as a training top with 'Admiral' emblazoned on it, which players would wear before kick-off. The deal was a huge success, with replica shirts flying off the shelves in West Yorkshire and beyond. For a while, football-mad English children could only buy the shirts of Leeds United, but other clubs and the rest of the sportswear industry quickly copied the idea.

Many but not all of the shirts in this book tell a story because of the sponsor's logo they carry. When it comes to sponsors as opposed to kit manufacturers, Uruguayan club Peñarol are thought to be the first club to carry a logo on their shirts back in 1950, but this was swiftly discontinued.[2] For most of the twentieth century, many countries had bans on sullying shirts with anything as grubby as a corporate logo. Football back then was hugely popular but not nearly as slick and corporate as it is today. The first definitively established sponsorship deal came in 1973, the same year that Leeds partnered with Admiral to make their kits, when German club Eintracht Braunschweig started carrying the logo of local spirit manufacturer Jägermeister – the spirit served alongside Red Bull to make a Jägerbomb cocktail.[3] Red Bull is now a key player in football, not just sponsoring but owning teams in Leipzig in Germany and Salzburg in Austria, as well as New York City, and having a minority stake in Leeds United.

These days, alcohol sponsors are common in South America, but no major European club has a booze brand on the front of their shirt. It brings up awkward questions regarding advertising to children, and football is far more globalised now. Liverpool's star player in recent years has been Mohamed Salah, an Egyptian and a proud Muslim. This could have caused issues if he had scored his countless Liverpool goals while wearing the logo of Carlsberg, the Danish beer brand that sponsored the club's shirts between 1992 and 2010, and still has a commercial deal with Liverpool.

During the 1970s, sponsorships continued to take off in Germany with Bayern Munich, the country's best-supported team, signing a deal with Adidas which became both kit manufacturer and shirt sponsor. In England, there was some resistance when Derek Dougan, the bombastic chairman of little Kettering Town, reached a deal for a 'four-figure sum' with local automotive firm Kettering Tyres. Kettering played Bath City in the lowly Southern League in January 1976 with the offending two words written across their chests. A stern letter from the FA led to the club changing the logo and dropping some letters so the shirt read 'Kettering T', which Dougan claimed stood for 'Town'. Eventually, with the threat of a fine, he backed down.

Dougan and others made the case that continental clubs were benefiting from this cash while English sides were leaving money on the table. A couple of years later the FA relented and dropped the ban. In 1979, Liverpool became the first top-flight club to get a shirt sponsor, with Japanese electronics manufacturer Hitachi paying £100,000 over two years.[4] Other clubs soon followed despite a ban on showing shirts with sponsors on the BBC, a restriction that soon fell by the wayside. If you watch the weekly highlights show *Match of the Day* these days, you will see hundreds of sponsors' logos, not just on shirts but on billboards around stadiums as well as on the walls in front of which managers and players are interviewed. This is all despite the BBC's strict domestic ban on TV advertising in the conventional sense.

The rise of shirt sponsors was slow and uneven. Aston Villa became champions of Europe in 1982, sadly a decade before my birth. In the photos of the club's greatest ever night, in Rotterdam, when captain Dennis Mortimer lifted the trophy after a surprise 1–0 win over Bayern Munich, neither Villa's nor Bayern's shirts had commercial logos despite the German side being sponsorship trailblazers. The following season the new European champions were sponsored by local Birmingham brewery Davenports. Sponsors in those days were often very local and many deals were for a relative pittance in an era when there was little football on TV and far less cash flowing through the game in general. Club chairmen were grateful for anything to boost the coffers.

After the Davenports deal expired, Villa went sponsor-less for a couple of seasons which happened a lot in the early days of shirt sponsorship. Deals were worth relatively little, so it did not matter hugely either way. The club's first long-term deal, lasting from 1984 to 1993, was with Mita Copiers, a Japanese electronics company. This was an era when such firms played a huge role in English football, from Sharp at Manchester United, JVC at Arsenal, and Brother at Manchester City. The Japanese economy was booming at the time and exporting electronic goods around the world. This slowed by the middle of the 1990s, known as the 'Lost Decade' for the Japanese economy, and the Premier League deals duly dried up. Villa then cycled through a series of sponsors including Müller, a German yoghurt company, AST, a US computer firm, and the telecoms firm NTL at the dawn of a new millennium when UK consumers were first getting broadband connections and mobile phones.

After Rover, then DWS Investments, and a couple of years with the 32Red online casino, Villa's next sponsor was an oddity that went against the tide of an increasingly commercialised game. Eccentric American chairman Randy Lerner decided to forgo a traditional sponsor and carry the logo of Acorns, a local children's

INTRODUCTION

hospice, between 2008 and 2010. This shirt is fondly remembered by fans, not only for its wholesome sponsor, but because it was worn through a successful period that included three successive sixth-place finishes, plus Europa League football and a League Cup final. I still have mine although the Acorns logo has largely rubbed off after fifteen years of sweat and washing powder. Villa was the first English club to carry a charity rather than a regular sponsor, emulating Barcelona who had done so a year earlier by putting a logo on their famous red-and-blue shirts for the first time – that of UNICEF, the United Nation's children's charity. They later replaced UNICEF with Qatar Airways, a rather less virtuous sponsor – more on that later.

This bout of altruism did Villa no good on the pitch. Lerner had spent hundreds of millions without Villa breaking into the elite and he soon turned off the spending taps, starting a slow and steady period of decline. Villa realised they needed sponsorship cash and, like many Premier League clubs, had a succession of gambling sponsors, including the period of time when the club dropped into the Championship, England's second division, between 2016 and 2019. Gambling sponsors have become increasingly prevalent in the Premier League and other parts of Europe and have remained on Villa's shirts through the club's remarkable resurgence since 2018 which included qualifying for the Champions League in 2023–24 for the first time in four decades. In October 2024, I was at Villa Park for a repeat of that famous scoreline: Aston Villa 1–0 Bayern Munich, the best memory of my life as a football fan. Through most of my adult life, proudly supporting an underachieving provincial team has been a core part of my identity while working in London. Villa becoming suddenly brilliant upon the arrival of Spanish manager Unai Emery was magical, if a little discombobulating at times. Wearing a Villa shirt in a

London gym, as I have done often, represented something very different compared to a few years earlier.

Two years after I finished university I moved to the city of Lyon for a few months, where I studied French while working part-time. At one point my classmates included a fellow Brit, a couple of Germans, lots of South Koreans, two Japanese people, and those of various South American nationalities. One day, we played a game probably familiar to you. One person writes a celebrity's name on a note and sticks it to another's forehead. That person then asks the other players 'yes or no' questions. *Is it a man? Are they a singer?* You keep going like this until you get the answer.

Such an international crowd made this game tough. There were few common references. Even names I thought would be universal – Beyoncé, Madonna, Tom Cruise – faced the barrier of producing all their work in a language that most of the world does not speak. Queen Elizabeth II, US president Barack Obama and then-presidential candidate Donald Trump were truly universal names. But beyond that auspicious trio there were two more: Lionel Messi and Cristiano Ronaldo. Both men stand a good claim to being not just the best footballers of all time, a debate Messi surely won with his World Cup win in 2022, but the most famous humans to have ever lived. It is hard to appreciate music in a foreign language, even harder with TV and films, but football can transcend this as one of the world's few true universal interests. Messi has now become a huge celebrity in the USA despite not speaking English in public. It is hard to think of anyone else who has managed this. In the USA football has long lagged behind the country's domestic sports while in India, cricket is dominant, but the picture is changing fast in both those countries. Globally, no sport comes remotely close to football. Wherever you go in the

INTRODUCTION

world there are not many things that you will see almost everywhere. The Coca-Cola logo is one. The Monobloc, the white plastic chair with curved arms and vents down the back, is another. And then there are football shirts. They are usually made of cheap polyester sold to consumers in the West for upwards of $100 but made (or illegally copied) for a fraction of that, often by workers earning a pittance in parts of the world where labour laws are limited.

The idea behind this book – using football shirts as a tool to explain the world around us – is one that has been brewing in my head for a long time. After beginning a career in 2016 as a journalist covering British politics, I started a new role four years later as an investigative reporter at sports media website *The Athletic*, now owned by the *New York Times*. Digging into football's grubby side, I uncovered wrongdoings in the sport, from Premier League clubs advertising illegal gambling in Asia, to the embrace of cryptocurrency products which were fleecing fans. Often an idea for an article was sparked by looking up a curious sponsor I had spotted on a TV screen, shirt or a billboard, the money sloshing through the game telling deeper stories about our world. Since then I have moved to *The Times* and *Sunday Times*, where I work as a data journalist, still writing about politics, sport and other topics, using numbers to tell stories.

This book is intended for football obsessives, those who have deep emotional attachments to particular shirts and want to understand some of the bigger forces behind the global game. It is also intended for those with a keen interest in politics and international affairs who don't necessarily follow football closely, but know that it is more than just a game these days. I hope this book is of interest to people who want to understand more about what the World Cups in Qatar and Saudi Arabia mean for the geopolitics of the Middle East, about China's efforts to use football as a foreign policy tool, and about football's role in the story of immigration and integration in Europe. Sometimes it is not a sponsor but something else about a shirt which makes it tell a wider story, such as the blue of France representing that country's uneasy relationship with the immigrant communities who now dominate the national team, or what the unsponsored England women's goalkeeper shirt tells us about changing gender roles around the world. As someone obsessed with both football and politics, I hope to write for an audience with an interest in either subject, but not necessarily both.

A paradox of football's rise to world domination is that despite the ever-increasing popularity of the game globally, the attention and the money is flowing mainly to a small group of clubs based in Western Europe. Several of them infamously attempted to peel off in April 2021 to form the European Super League, which imploded on launch after a furious backlash from fans. These clubs' shirts can be spotted on streets around the world, though often the garments are of dubious authenticity.

Another common sight these days, and a booming global industry, is retro shirts. Just as there is nostalgia for the designs and bright colours of an earlier period of football, there is nostalgia for sponsors which seem more tangible, more grounded in the communities where the teams are from, compared to the modern era where several Italian clubs have been sponsored by cryptocurrency companies which have gone bust. This nostalgia can be rose-tinted. Italian club Parma are a plucky underdog of Italian football who had a great spell of success around the time of the new millennium, but these glory years are inextricably linked to fraud by the dairy company that owned the club and sponsored its shirts. The logos on the front of football shirts continue to tell stories of financial scandals as well as geopolitical ructions.

INTRODUCTION

In October 2021, Saudi Arabia's Public Investment Fund bought Newcastle United, then an underachieving English side with a big fanbase. A struggling club suddenly became the world's richest, on paper at least. Although Premier League spending rules complicate the picture, Newcastle, Abu Dhabi's Manchester City and Qatar's Paris Saint-Germain could at some point in the future be battling it out in what is effectively a Middle Eastern proxy war, the rivalries and alliances of that desert region playing themselves out on muddy football pitches in the northern European winter as part of these energy superpowers' attempts to 'diversify' away from fossil fuels in a world where natural resources are finite, and burning them is damaging the climate. Football shirts can have a role in global power games playing out thousands of miles away.

When I tell people I am writing a book about the football shirts that explain the world, they sometimes assume this means the most famous shirts worn by the biggest European heavyweights. This is not the approach I have taken though. I have chosen some big names, like the iconic blue and red of Barcelona and the all-white of Real Madrid, as well as the blue of the French national team, the most successful national side of modern times. But there are also shirts from Serbia, Chile and India. There is a shirt worn by South African political prisoners decades ago, and one that tells the story of Australia's women's team having a branded nickname. I have tried to choose shirts that tell stories. It is possible to make the case for all sorts of other football shirts that tell stories about the world we live in. This is a book written from my own vantage point. I tell these stories as someone who understands football in England better than anywhere else, so England is discussed the most, woven in with travels around the world. This is not the worst thing given the Premier League's global dominance, but people from other places would see some of these stories differently and would pull out different meanings from different shirts. Every football fan could come up with a different list. If you have a drawer of football shirts, riffle through it and have a go at this yourself. Look at the badges, the colours and the sponsors, and find out why your shirt looks exactly the way it does. Every shirt tells a story.

This book will grapple with many weighty topics, including the power structures of football itself and the decisions taken by men in suits that can make football feel increasingly removed from the game we learned to love as children. Frankly, some of it is a bit depressing. But I want to end on a note of optimism before we begin. Football is brilliant. In the past, I have been asked why I love it so much, and I have a simple answer.

You know that feeling when your team scores a last-minute winner? There is nothing else like it in the world. The pure elation that makes you scream yourself hoarse, punch the air while sat alone on the sofa, or hug strangers in the row in front of you. I have been writing about football for a while now, but generally watch games from the stands rather than the press box, and have rarely had to exercise the professional detachment necessary for the full-time match-going journalist. I love supporting my club and my country and making strange noises when I do. Nothing is quite like the emotion of watching football. All sorts of other things give pleasure and joy in life – romantic love, the warmth of family, a brilliant piece of art, the taste of wonderful food and drink. These things are all great, but are pleasurable in a different way to that back-of-the-net euphoria. Nobody ever punched the air and shouted 'Come on!' after a delicious glass of wine, or even the birth of a baby. Football gives access to a whole plane of emotions that are otherwise not part of the human experience. I'm sure this can exist in other sports too, but there are far fewer people to share it with.

INTRODUCTION

Different people appreciate different aspects of football. For some it is about family, belonging and emotion, others love analysing tactics and quoting statistics. The thing that most grips me about football is the *culture* of it. I love speaking to people from faraway places about what football means to them, and how it interacts with weighty topics as well as daily life. I have grown up pickled in the brine of football culture, which now increasingly plays out on social media as much as in pubs or workplaces. It is a shared language – I once spent several hours in a bar in Armenia at the time Leicester City were surprisingly running away with the Premier League in 2016. We had virtually no shared language but could repeat the words 'Jamie Vardy' and 'Riyad Mahrez' while looking at clips on a mobile phone.

What is so special about football culture is that it is becoming more universal while culture more broadly is not. In most countries a handful of terrestrial channels have declined in importance as a web of streaming services has emerged. Curated music playlists mean the biggest pop songs are less well known than they once were. The biggest TV series, films and albums are appreciated by fewer people. Football, though, is getting ever-more popular. Around the world the game is conquering new territories, spreading its wings, penetrating the rare gaps where it is not already loved, as I understood when researching this book, spotting shirts everywhere and speaking to people about Premier League ups and downs, from the seafront of Cape Town in South Africa, a slum in Medellín in Colombia to the back streets of Goa in India. 'The game has a global audience,' football writer David Goldblatt wrote of football in the mid-1980s, 'but one restricted in number and reach by the absence of television sets and signals in much of the rural, global south, especially China and India.'[4] These constraints are disappearing. When I visited India in 2023, I heard about the breakneck speed that cheap mobile internet is reaching the country's rural areas. There are people who lack safe sanitation facilities but can stream the latest football highlights on their phone.

I am a football optimist. This is in many ways a golden age for a sport which is more and more popular around the world. Where I live in England more people are attending matches every week than ever before, not just in the Premier League but way down the divisions. The game is becoming increasingly inclusive and diverse on and off the pitch. The women's game no longer feels like an afterthought; it is here to stay as a key part of the global game, growing at a breakneck pace. The world's only truly global sport is more global than it has ever been, but less global than it will be tomorrow. It is the biggest thing and it is growing ever bigger. Yes, the money sloshing around it, and where it comes from, has its negatives. But it also means the quality of the product is incredibly high. It is a privilege to be able to watch the likes of Lionel Messi, Erling Haaland and Kylian Mbappé play a sport that is an intricate battle of talent and tactics, where shocks frequently can and do happen. Modern football is flawed for sure, but it is wonderful and constantly changing, while remaining fundamentally the same game invented a century-and-a-half ago, that billions of people have since fallen in love with. It is the most popular thing on the planet and still growing in popularity because it is so brilliant. It is a privilege to write a book about football.

Let's talk about some shirts.

1

PUTIN'S WARS

FC Schalke 04 & Red Star Belgrade

'Listen, you have to stop. I'm not a politician. I have never experienced war. Even to talk about it I feel bad because I'm very privileged. I sit here in peace, and I do the best I can, but you have to stop asking me these questions, I have no answers for you.'

Chelsea manager Thomas Tuchel, February 2022[8]

'There were yellow balloons everywhere,' recalls Roman Kolbe, pointing into the middle distance at the sky above the shallow hills that surround the German city of Gelsenkirchen. It is October 2023, and we are standing on the steps of the Veltins Arena, home of Roman's beloved FC Schalke 04, one hour before a match kicks off. Kolbe is wearing a blue-and-white Schalke scarf with the club badge and an image of a smashed swastika. He is the editor of *Schalke Unser*, a fan publication which has long been a vocal voice not only on tactics and team selections, but also the politics of this club – of which there are a lot.

Those yellow balloons were released into the sky back in 2010, when the Ruhr region in the west of Germany was recognised by the European Union as its Capital of Culture, at a time when Schalke were flying high in the German Bundesliga. The award was a big deal for this unfashionable industrial heartland area of five million people scattered across several towns and cities including Dortmund, Essen and Duisburg, as well as Gelsenkirchen. Those balloons hovered above the region's 350 mineshafts, the holes in the ground where workers once crawled in the dark and the dirt to haul up the coal which powered Germany's industrial revolution from the mid-nineteenth century onwards. The balloons were a recognition of what the mines had done for this region.[1]

But since the 1950s, the number of people working in the Ruhr coalfield has fallen from almost half a million to virtually nobody. It is now far cheaper to import coal and other forms of energy from elsewhere. The last two mines closed in 2018. The region has pivoted to new industries, such as financial services and clean energy, but Gelsenkirchen remains an unflashy place, a far cry from the slick offices of Frankfurt, the hipster cafes of Berlin or the wealthy industrial parks of Munich. It is a place that has seen better times and there is not a great deal going on in town as I get a pizza and a beer on Friday evening ahead of Schalke's game the following day against FC Hannover 96 in the Bundesliga 2, Germany's second division. In 2021, Schalke were relegated for the first time in thirty years. They bounced back up but were immediately relegated again in 2023.

When I watch them, Schalke are in the process of setting an unfortunate world record. The club's average attendance during the 2023–24 season was the highest in history for any club in the world outside their country's top division, beating fellow German side Hamburg who set the record the previous season. The Veltins Arena is an incongruous venue, designed for the pinnacle of elite entertainment rather than Germany's second tier. It has a retractable roof and capacity of 62,000 and hosted the 2004 UEFA Champions League final and a World Cup quarter-final two years later, and more recently concerts by the likes of Taylor Swift, U2 and the Rolling Stones. For football, fans flood into Gelsenkirchen from all over Germany and even further afield, desperate to experience the atmosphere at one of the country's most historic and best-supported clubs, with strong fan traditions and deep roots in the Ruhr coalfield communities. Not long ago, Schalke were regulars in the Champions League, reaching the semi-finals in 2011, and won several domestic trophies in the early twenty-first century as well as heartbreakingly losing the Bundesliga on the final day of the 2006–07 season. But all that feels a distant memory now.

When Schalke are playing well, it's almost impossible to get a ticket here. On this occasion, it isn't, because things are going badly – very badly. Not only are the club competing in the second tier, but Schalke have won only one of their first nine games and hover above the relegation zone, with fans seriously starting to worry about dropping down to Germany's third division. It is early in the season, but the fear is real. Another relegation would threaten Schalke's very existence.

Nevertheless, the stadium is almost full, meaning the Veltins Arena hosts one of the biggest crowds in European football that weekend despite being outside the top flight. Despite the 12 p.m. kick-off time a couple of thousand fans have travelled from Hanover, three hours to the north-east. Germany's football culture runs deep, only rivalled by England for travelling away fans and high attendances below the first division. Many Schalke fans wear the iconic German terrace gear of sleeveless denim jackets covered in pin badges. Although the coal mines are no more, heavy industry is still a deep part of the club's identity, and some fans walk around in white hard hats as a tongue-in-cheek nod to the Ruhr's roots. The reason I am here is not coal, though. This story is about a different natural resource that has also powered German homes and businesses: gas. Gas from Russia.

As blue-and-white replica shirts stream past me on all sides on my way into the stadium, many carry a familiar logo, written in white, alongside a picture of a gas flame. The Russian gas company Gazprom sponsored Schalke's shirts between 2007 and 2022, a period in which the company became ubiquitous in European football through a long-running sponsorship deal with the UEFA Champions League, club football's most-watched competition. The Gazprom logo is a visual accompaniment to some of modern football's most iconic memories, plastered across stadium billboards throughout the extended brilliance of Cristiano Ronaldo at Real Madrid and Lionel Messi at Barcelona, as well as the long-awaited lifting of the trophy by global powerhouses like Bayern Munich, Liverpool and Inter Milan. UEFA and Schalke both dramatically ditched their deal with Gazprom in February 2022 when Vladimir Putin's Russia invaded Ukraine. Putin and Russia became international pariahs overnight with Gazprom suddenly viewed for what it was – an arm of the Russian state. Ordinary people from Germany and other countries realised that, by importing Russian gas, they were indirectly funding Putin's war machine.

The story of Gazprom goes back to the early 1990s when the Soviet Union collapsed and split into fifteen successor states, of which Russia was by far the biggest and most populated. At the top of the to-do list for the new Russia, led by the charismatic but erratic Boris Yeltsin, was dealing with the USSR's vast state-run industries. Yeltsin and his advisers' solution was to end Soviet nationalisation through a voucher system. One-third of the oil and gas industry was immediately privatised and each Russian citizen given a voucher that could be used to buy stakes in industries, a version of the shareholder capitalism that had caught on in Western countries in the 1980s, with the masses supposedly profiting from the shift in public to private ownership. But Russia's scheme was bungled and ordinary people, desperate for cash as the economy imploded all around them with alcoholism and violent disorder ravaging the country, sold their shares for vastly less than what they were worth. Although the USSR had been an oil and gas powerhouse, few ordinary Russians appreciated the sheer scale of the country's natural resources and how valuable the oil and gas fields would become when combined with investment and technical expertise. The average voucher was sold for $20 and some for as little as $7, the price of two bottles of cheap vodka. Others were put into 'voucher funds' which turned out to be shams. Others were sold in rigged auctions.[2]

The privatisation of Gazprom, the USSR's state gas company which owned one-third of the world's natural gas reserves at the time, was particularly egregious, writes journalist Peter Conradi. 'Those who wanted to buy shares could do so only in the tiny Siberian and Arctic villages where the company had its energy deposits. The management also reserved the right to buy outsiders' shares at a price it dictated. The result was that only Gazprom people ended up buying the company, with the managers, who were the only ones with any money, benefiting from the auction.'[3] When Gazprom issued its shares, the company was valued at $250 million, but three years later, the stock market valued the company at $40.5 billion. This was widely seen as a lowball figure given the sheer scale of Russian reserves but nevertheless meant a 16,192 per cent rate of profit for the lucky and well-connected few who hoovered up cheap shares at the right time. The voucher system proved to be 'one of the most unfair that could have been chosen,' says Peter Conradi. 'The state effectively sold off a large chunk of its assets for a fraction of its market price.' This meant a massive redistribution of wealth from the state to a tiny number of men who would come to be known as the oligarchs. One of them was Roman Abramovich, later owner of Chelsea, who acquired a controlling interest in oil company Sibneft for $250 million in 1995. He would later sell it back to the Russian government for $13 billion a decade later.

After the chaos of the 1990s, the relatively unknown Vladimir Putin replaced Boris Yeltsin as president of Russia on New Year's Eve, 1999. He moved quickly to bring the oil and gas industries under direct state control, shifting away from a system where oligarchs operated beyond the power of the state. While the structure of the oil industry was complex, the gas industry was more straightforward – a state-controlled monopoly straddling the biggest gas reserves on the planet. The chief executive of Gazprom was Rem Vyakhirev and on his watch huge sums of money were plundered from the company and syphoned into the pockets of board members. Putin did not like this. Little more than a year after taking office he summoned Gazprom bosses to the Kremlin for a meeting which his biographer Philip Short describes:

> [Putin] had no intention of interfering in the affairs of a private company, he said, but Gazprom played an exceptional role in Russia's economy and, if nobody objected, he would like a few words with Rem Vyakhirev before the meeting took place. They spend about an hour together. When Vyakhirev emerged, he told his colleagues that he had decided to step down.[4]

In his place, Putin would appoint Alexei Miller as CEO of Gazprom while Igor Sechin became chair of state oil firm Rosneft. Both were close Putin allies dating back to his days as mayor of Saint

Petersburg, a theme for many of those who became fantastically wealthy in the new Russia. 'It was blatant cronyism, but it meant that Putin had men he trusted in charge of the state enterprises which generated the biggest financial flows,' says Short. 'Putin had moved quickly to bring Gazprom to heel because of its importance to the economy and as an instrument of foreign policy.'[5]

This allowed Putin's inner circle to gain huge profits at the state's expense. It meant Gazprom could no longer be seen as just a private company and it became a tool of the state under the de facto control of President Putin. By 2005, the Kremlin directly controlled the company – it was effectively renationalised. Gazprom had long given Russia influence over its Soviet neighbours, particularly Georgia and Ukraine, which did not have gas reserves of their own. In the mid-2000s these countries were diplomatically and culturally moving out of Russia's orbit and towards the EU and US. 'For the most part, Gazprom had doled out gas at heavily discounted prices, just as it had when they were part of the Soviet empire,' explains Catherine Belton in *Putin's People*, her forensic account of Putin's inner circle. 'Ukraine, above all, stood out as a vital transit corridor for the continent's needs. But now that its leadership had taken a westward tilt, the Kremlin indicated that it intended to put an end to any more subsidies.'[6] Gazprom became a foreign policy tool. Ukraine's gas was switched off on New Year's Day 2006 after brinkmanship over prices. A deal was eventually reached but sparked corruption allegations, sowing discord among Ukraine's pro-Western leadership and giving a boost to Viktor Yanukovych, a former prime minister who was closer to Putin than his rivals. He would later become president before being toppled by the Euromaidan protests of 2013–14, which was followed by Putin's invasion of Crimea.

The link between German football and Russian gas also began in 2006, a time when Vladimir Putin had a better reputation in Western capitals than would later be the case. That year, out of nowhere, news emerged that Schalke had received a lucrative offer from a prospective new shirt sponsor. A curious image was published showing Putin holding up a blue Schalke shirt with a Gazprom logo, in a boardroom full of men in dark suits. The meeting took place in the German city of Dresden, east of the former Iron Curtain, where Putin had served as a KGB spy for five years in the 1980s. These years gave him a deep understanding of Germany and fluency in the language. One of the men in the photo was Schalke president Clemens Tönnies who had his own reasons for building a relationship with Putin. He was keen for his meat processing company, Tönnies Holding, to make inroads to the east. Incomes in Russia were rising as the country rode the wave of a commodities boom. After trying a few people who worked for Schalke during this era, I managed to speak to one who was well placed to comment on the unusual link between a German football club and the Russian state. The photo of Putin and Tönnies has aged badly, said this person, who spoke to me on condition of anonymity. 'In hindsight, it was quite strange that the head of the Russian state would be in that picture. It's even stranger now than it was then. Schalke, being a very famous club, was a symbol of this German–Russian business relationship.' A news report from the time said the deal was worth 20 million euros, eclipsing Bayern's with Deutsche Telekom.[7]

Back to 2023 and many of the Schalke fans streaming past on the way into the stadium wear the club's latest shirt which carries the logo of Veltins, a local brewery which also gives its name to the Veltins Arena. Many others are wearing older shirts featuring the logo of Gazprom, which sponsored the club for sixteen years. A small number of fans in these older shirts have taped over the Gazprom logo with stickers in a matching shade of blue. These stickers were handed out by fan groups in the aftermath of the Ukraine invasion in 2022, when Schalke shirts became an unwitting symbol of Putin's war crimes. Many fans had long felt uncomfortable with the sponsorship deal forged by Clemens Tönnies, unpopular for presiding over a period of on-field decline and financial mismanagement, as Russia's actions in Europe were becoming increasingly objectionable. In 2008, tanks rolled into Georgia and six years later, coinciding with the Winter Olympics in the Russian city of Sochi, Russia annexed the Ukrainian province of Crimea. Both events sparked outcry but no changes to Schalke's shirts.

In a bar inside the Veltins Arena, over a late-morning beer and bratwurst sausage, fanzine editor Roman Kolbe tells me his fellow supporters were bemused and confused when Gazprom came along to replace a local insurance company on Schalke's shirts. Most advertising deals follow a simple logic: a company wants to sell a product. In general, companies market their product in a way which they think will boost sales, be that through TV advertising, social media banners or plastering their logo on a football shirt. Look at other sponsors of the UEFA Champions League in recent years – McDonald's, Heineken, PlayStation – all tangible consumer products that a football fan watching in the stands or on the sofa might go out and purchase. The same is also true for companies offering less tangible services like insurance, banking or online gambling. Nobody watching a Champions League or FC Schalke match is going to go out and buy a cubic metre of Gazprom gas, though. Nobody, that is, beyond a small circle of powerful people who were working to open the German market to Russian gas on a massive scale. 'In the beginning, we thought [Gazprom] wanted to get to the end customer, but I don't think this was ever the game,' says Kolbe. 'I think they wanted to get a platform to talk to politicians and to "greenwash,"' he says, using a word to describe polluting companies attempting to deceptively bolster their public image.

The relationship between German politics and Russian gas goes back a long way. Back in the 1970s when the Soviet Union was at the peak of its powers, Russian gas started flowing in big volumes. Back then, extraction methods were rudimentary and the Cold War barriers limited trade. During that time there was a quid pro quo. Russia was offering gas to heat German homes and businesses at a time when the Ruhr coalfields in places like Gelsenkirchen were in terminal decline. In return, Germany could offer investment, as well as talent and expertise, to help the USSR efficiently extract gas and sell it to the world.

From 1969, West German chancellor Willy Brandt embarked on *Ostpolitik*, the normalisation of relations with the Soviet Union and the Soviet-allied state of East Germany. Governments subsequently viewed close relations with Russia as necessary to prevent another war in Europe, underpinned by the belief that this would lead to a more democratic Russia and a more peaceful continent. This was accompanied by deepening economic links and the notion of change through trade – *Wandel durch Handel* – an idea that assumed Russia's economy would become ever more closely entwined with those of Germany and the rest of Europe. After the Berlin Wall came down in 1989, leading to the union of communist East Germany with its confidently capitalist Western neighbour, the gas-fuelled bond between Russia and Germany deepened. 'Germany's stance towards Russia has long been influenced by its guilt over the death and destruction caused by the Nazi invasion of the Soviet Union, and by gratitude for [last Soviet leader Mikhail] Gorbachev's role in allowing reunification,' writes Peter Conradi.[8]

Relations deepened further in the 1990s and 2000s, and, in Putin, the Germans thought they had found someone they could work with. 'With hindsight, the notion of ever-closer economic ties with Russia was the Achilles heel of *Ostpolitik*,' says Bernhard Blumenau, a lecturer in international relations at the University of St Andrews. 'Trade was meant to deter Putin from aggressive power politics, but it increased Germany's dependence on cheap Russian gas and other raw materials. The heyday of European–Russian relations ended in 2006. From then on, the prospect of Russia using Europe's huge dependency on its gas as a potential instrument of blackmail loomed ever more threateningly.'[9]

Constantin Zerger is an energy expert and lapsed Schalke fan. When I spoke to him over the phone from his home in the German capital, he was getting ready to go and watch his adopted local team FC Union Berlin, who have had a remarkable rise in the past few years from playing in the fifth tier of German football in 2005 to Champions League matches against Real Madrid in the 2023–24 season. His day job is as an expert and campaigner in the field of German energy and how it relates to politics. He told me that Germany's core policy was 'buying cheap gas from Russia and using this to create a competitive advantage against other industries and other countries', adding that reliance on Russian gas became even deeper from 2011 when Chancellor Angela Merkel dramatically announced Germany would be winding down its nuclear power plants in response to the Fukushima disaster in Japan. This sent Germany on an opposite trajectory to many of its neighbours. In France, a huge proportion of energy – around 70 per cent in 2024 – comes from nuclear power, which is very clean in terms of carbon emissions and does not rely on foreign powers.

Germany went in another direction and, in the years leading up to the Ukraine war in 2022, the proportion of German energy coming from natural gas rose steadily to around 55 per cent of the total. This amounted to about €200 million, or $220 million, in energy payments sent *every single day* from German households and businesses to Russia, via Gazprom and other companies directly or indirectly controlled by the Russian state. Zerger says politicians from both the left-wing Social Democrats and right-wing Christian Democrats were responsible for this situation.[10] After the Ukraine invasion, it is a source of embarrassment, he says. 'Nobody really wants to talk about it. It's, like, let's look ahead, not at the mistakes of the past.'

Germany is, of course, not the only country to have made moral compromises to keep the lights on, and Schalke is not the only football shirt with moral complexities, otherwise this would be a short book. The UK and USA have given little in the way of pushback on human rights abuses in countries like the United Arab Emirates, Qatar and Saudi Arabia, which have vital reserves of oil and gas. There's a football link to all this, which we will come back to. In defence of the German public and political class, they reacted swiftly and decisively once Putin launched an outright invasion of the whole of Ukraine in February 2022. A few days later German chancellor Olaf Scholz, who had replaced Angela Merkel two-and-a-half months earlier, gave one of the most consequential speeches in modern German history. He ripped up decades of *Ostpolitik* and *Wandel durch Handel* in one go. The speech has become known as the *Zeitenwende*, or 'historic turning point', referencing Scholz's description of Putin's invasion. Germany had had an ultra-cautious defence policy since the shame of the Second World War, its small military rarely engaging in overseas operations. This was upended in 2022, with Scholz pledging €100 billion to modernise the German Army. He vowed that Germany would increase defence spending above NATO's target of spending 2 per cent of gross domestic product.[11] The USA, in particular President Trump in his first term, had long been frustrated at Germany for undershooting this, accusing them of freeriding, but 2022 changed everything. 'We are living through a watershed era and that means that the world afterwards will no longer be the same as the world before,' Scholz told the German parliament in Berlin.

With public mood shifting quickly, Schalke ditched their deal with Gazprom. UEFA did too. More significantly the gas taps from Russia to Germany were switched off. 'People became aware that Germany was basically funding the Ukrainian war through this, because it's directly feeding Putin's budget,' energy expert Constantin Zerger told me. 'There was a huge consensus that gas should not be imported from Russia any more. For the first time, energy poverty became a real issue and not just a theoretical debate for many households.' He says Schalke's deal always felt strange because Gazprom did not have any connection to German consumers. 'They were only doing business-to-business stuff. For them, it was only about image. The return on investment was that Gazprom was seen as the friendly neighbour,' he says. 'It was a mind-fuck to have a Russian company that's fuelling Putin's budget after he attacked Crimea. To see that on television in Germany and no one's really asking questions . . . It normalises it.'

The links between Gazprom and Schalke went deeper than the former paying the latter to carry its logo. A Reuters investigation into Clemens Tönnies alleged that the club's owner was 'at the centre of Gazprom's influence campaign' in Germany, his relationship with Putin and other officials ensuring 'red carpet treatment' for his meat firms in Russia: 'Executives at Gazprom's Berlin office collected names of politicians and businesspeople to invite to Schalke's VIP box at home matches'.[12] There was lucrative business to be done.

In the early 1990s, shortly after German reunification, transporting gas from Russia to Germany was a long and expensive ordeal, with canisters loaded on the back of lorries which drove through many other countries, throwing up a host of logistical and political complications. Solutions included the Yamal–Europe pipeline, which took gas overland from Russian gas fields in Siberia, through Belarus to the European Union. Another set of pipelines passed through Ukraine.

In 1997, Germany and Russia began exploring an even more direct solution, a 1,200km (750-mile) underwater pipeline. The Nord Stream pipeline would go underneath the Baltic Sea from Vyborg in Russia's far west, close to the border with Finland, all the way to Lubmin, a seaside resort on Germany's Baltic Coast. This had the advantage of transporting gas directly from Russia to Germany, bypassing political instability in other countries at a time many former Soviet states were in varying situations of chaos. The pipeline was not popular with many in the United States and Ukraine as well as Poland – in 2006 the country's defence minister Radek Sikorski angered German politicians by likening the pipeline to the 1939 Nazi–Soviet pact. Opponents feared that getting Germany hooked on Russian gas would create a security problem in Europe, and that bypassing Ukraine would diplomatically isolate the country, meaning Russia would lose a reason to maintain good relations with the West. Germany had a much more receptive attitude to Russia though, and this came right from the very top.

At a game between Schalke and Duisburg in 2011, German president Christian Wulff and his successor Frank-Walter Steinmeier were in the VIP area often frequented by Gazprom officials. In July 2014, a few months after Russia annexed Crimea and was well on its way to becoming a pariah state, Schalke played a friendly match in the German state of Mecklenburg-Vorpommern where the Nord Stream pipeline made landfall. Gazprom officials were in attendance, as was the region's interior minister who later said the match was to raise money for a local anti-hooliganism campaign and that, if Gazprom saw the match as a lobbying opportunity, he was not aware. Mecklenburg-Vorpommern, a rural state in Germany's far north-east bordering Poland and the Baltic Sea, is a key part of the Gazprom story. The island of Rügen was represented in the German parliament by Angela Merkel for three decades. Russians were regular visitors to the state in the early twenty-first century.

Gerhard Schröder was Germany's chancellor from 1998 to 2005 before Angela Merkel's sixteen-year stint in charge. Just ten days before he was voted out of office in 2005, Schröder agreed a deal for the first Nord Stream pipeline, known as Nord Stream 1, signing a €1 billion loan guarantee with state funds. Remarkably, within weeks of being replaced by Merkel, Schröder was directly advising the Nord Stream project as chair of its shareholders' committee. Opposition politicians in Germany, and critics overseas, especially in the US, condemned the move. But the gas issue was not a big deal at the time, with Russia edging closer to the West diplomatically, and Cold War rivalries fading away. In 2009, Schröder joined the board of TNK-BP, a Russian oil company which four years later was acquired by oil firm Rosneft, owned by the Russian state. He later became a director of the board at Rosneft and remarkably in early 2022, just a few weeks before the invasion of Ukraine, joined the board of directors of Gazprom, the company whose little flame logo was on Schalke shirts for sixteen years, as well as the billboards of thousands of Champions League games.

After war broke out in 2022 the *New York Times* reported on how Schröder, 'Putin's man in Germany', got a phone call after leaving office in 2005 from his 'friend' the Russian president, offering him the role at Nord Stream which would net him more than $1 million a year lobbying for Russian gas interests in the country he recently led.[13] Catherine Belton describes Schröder as the Russian president's 'staunch ally' and not just on energy issues, explaining that he has been 'richly rewarded for his labours defending Putin's actions in Ukraine and Syria, and (Putin's) clampdown on democracy at home'.[14] The Nord Stream 1 pipeline was eventually completed in 2011 and Schröder attended the ceremony at Vyborg in Russia with Putin, and in Lubmin in Germany alongside his successor Angela Merkel. Eleven years later, when full war broke out, the outcry against Schröder was swift. His entire twenty-person staff resigned, and his hometown of Hanover stripped him of his honorary citizenship. Schröder was criticised when he left office for signing up to work for a foreign company so quickly, but the Nord Stream project itself was uncontroversial, he accurately pointed out. 'The next government continued with it seamlessly. Nobody in the first Merkel government said a word against it. No one.' Schröder has been unrepentant, saying the gas deals benefited both countries. '[Others in Germany] all went along with it for the last thirty years,' he said. 'But suddenly everyone knows better.'

The Revierderby, Schalke vs Borussia Dortmund, is one of the spiciest head-to-heads in world football. It has taken on a rather one-sided nature in recent years as Dortmund have chased titles and gone deep into European competitions while Schalke have fallen into the second division. Nevertheless, as Schalke crowds stream past on their way to the Hannover game there are plenty of badges and shirts sporting the phrase 'Dortmund *scheisse*' (shit) or depicting a cartoon man in the blue-and-white of Schalke urinating on the black-and-yellow shirt of their rivals. Like many of the world's great football rivalries, Schalke and Dortmund fans have more in common than they might care to admit. In 2024, Dortmund fans used the biggest club football game in the world, the Champions League final which they lost 2–0 against Real Madrid, to protest their team's sponsorship deal with arms manufacturer Rheinmetall AG. 'Rheinmetall's 2024 deal with as romantic a club as Borussia Dortmund was a naked attempt to normalise an arms manufacturer, because of the realistic prospect of war with Russia,' writes journalist Miguel Delaney. 'Club chief executive Hans-Joachim Watzke . . . defended the sponsorship out of concern for how "freedom" itself must be protected in Europe.'[15]

Both Dortmund and Schalke come from the Ruhr region and champion their industrial heritage proudly. Germany has always been relatively resource-poor compared to its neighbours, a problem which became more acute in the second half of the twentieth century as the coalfields became uneconomic, the industry that gave the Ruhr its identity gradually disappearing. Germany's status as a big manufacturer and exporter required lots of energy. This meant a reliance on Russian gas, something Putin was well aware of as the drumbeats to war grew louder in early 2022. 'Let German citizens open their purses, have a look inside and ask themselves whether they are ready to pay three to five times more for electricity, for gas and for heating,' Putin said in a press conference with Olaf Scholz in the frantic days of shuttle diplomacy just before war broke out. 'If they are not, they should thank Mr Schröder because this is his achievement, a result of his work.'[16]

Gerhard Schröder is a lifelong Borussia Dortmund fan, but a

few days after the Ukraine war broke out the club cancelled his honorary membership with immediate effect, describing his role at Russian companies as 'unacceptable against the background of the Russian war of aggression against Ukraine'. Despite Schröder's footballing affiliation to Schalke's fierce rivals, he played a hand in the club's deal with Gazprom by working closely with Clemens Tönnies according to the Reuters investigation which quoted a former Gazprom executive as saying the Schalke deal was inspired by Russian oligarch Roman Abramovich's purchase of Chelsea.[17]

Nord Stream 2 is a second pipeline, running parallel to the first, designed to increase the vast quantities of gas funnelling from Russia to Germany every day in return for cash flowing in the other direction, from wealthy Germany to less wealthy Russia. Gerhard Schröder was a well-remunerated manager of the project. Construction began in 2018 and was completed in 2021, but never entered service after war got in the way. Mecklenburg-Vorpommern saw lots of lobbying in favour of the pipeline, by Gazprom and other Russian companies. The region's volleyball team, one of the best in Germany, had 'Nord Stream 2' on their orange jerseys. After the fallout of Putin's invasion of Ukraine it was reported that Russians had been pumping cash into the region for years, including setting up an innocuous-sounding 'foundation' which served as a conduit for at least €165 million in lobbying, including the hosting of a 'Russia Day' in the former communist region.[18]

Far from where the Nord Stream pipeline makes landfall, a thousand miles to the south-west and far closer to Germany's borders with the Netherlands and Belgium than with Poland, kick-off is approaching in Gelsenkirchen. I speak to die-hard fan Susanne Hein-Reipen and her husband Gunter about their beloved FC Schalke, or 'Null-Vier' (zero-four) as many fans call their club, referring to the year the club was founded. Susanne wears a branded Schalke puffer coat, is putting a brave face on the club's dire predicament by explaining that she and her husband remember following Schalke in the second division in 1980, when things were even worse. Like every other Schalke fan I speak to, Susanne is highly knowledgeable about the financial situation of the club, from the controversial loans taken out by Clemens Tönnies to the Gazprom issue. She says she supported the sudden binning of the Gazprom sponsorship, but believes suddenly removing a huge chunk of revenue at a time when the club was already struggling created a 'domino effect', directly contributing to Schalke's second relegation and making it harder for the club to bounce back. Susanne and Gunter are typical of German fans in being deeply engaged in the idea of their club as a social institution with responsibilities far beyond winning on the pitch.

I make it inside the stadium and sit high up in the western stand with an excellent view of Schalke's Nordkurve, the famous terrace behind one goal where the club's hardcore supporters stand for the entire ninety minutes making lots of noise. Susanne and Gunter used to have seats there but, now older, have moved elsewhere so they can sit down. In true European style, there is a drummer at the front of the Nordkurve who faces away from the pitch and towards the stands, never taking a glance behind him even when a goal is scored, focused only on setting the rhythm for his fellow fans. The crowd's ramshackle homemade banners are a striking contrast to the slick modern stadium.

Hovering just above the relegation zone after about a quarter of the season, the home fans are hoping for a win to lessen the alarming possibility of relegation to the third division. Moments before half-time, Schalke take the lead and the mood becomes raucous despite the early kick-off time. With the score 1–0 at half-time, I get a reasonably priced beer and enjoy it in my seat, a pleasant change from watching professional football in England where drinking alcohol anywhere in view of the pitch has been prohibited for decades as a measure against crowd trouble. After the game kicks off for the second half, the noise comes from the far corner of the ground when Hannover equalise, but Schalke then hit two more in quick succession. The Nordkurve roars and the fans, spurred on by the beat of the drum, don't stop bouncing until the end. A late Hannover consolation does little to dampen the spirits of fans who have had little reason to cheer in recent months. It ends 3–2 to Schalke.

After each Schalke goal, a picture of the scorer is flashed up on the stadium's giant 'video cube', a vast box hovering over the centre of the pitch with screens on all sides, a common feature of relatively tiny basketball venues but uncommon in football where the technology needed for such a structure is very expensive. It is on this video cube where the likes of Taylor Swift and Ed Sheeran have been beamed to tens of thousands of concert-goers. Schalke fanzine editor Roman Kolbe has another anecdote about the video cube. In the later years of the Gazprom sponsorship the video cube carried the logo of Nord Stream 2. Pitch-side advertising, too, began to promote the pipeline during televised Schalke games at a time when the pipeline had not yet received final regulatory approval. The club was playing a major role in the lobbying effort to build a new pipeline to pump more gas to Germany from Russia, which had already invaded Crimea at this point.

Back in the mid-2000s, the Gazprom deal tangibly transformed Schalke's fortunes, explained the anonymous former Schalke employee I spoke to. 'We at least doubled our sponsorship income.

That had a great financial impact. We had €10 million a year extra to spend on players'. Almost immediately after signing the deal, the club signed Raúl from Real Madrid, one of the greatest Spanish players of all time and for many years was the Champions League's record goalscorer, though he has since been overtaken by Cristiano Ronaldo, Lionel Messi, Robert Lewandowski and Karim Benzema. Raúl scored five of his seventy-one goals in the competition for Schalke, including both home and away in the thrashing of Inter – 7–3 over two legs – in the 2011 Champions League quarter-finals, one of the greatest results in the club's history. I saw several fans in the stadium wearing 'half-and-half scarves' from that epic occasion 12 years earlier. In 2011's 5–0 victory over Duisburg in the German cup final, Schalke's line-up featured Manuel Neuer, Julian Draxler and Benedikt Höwedes – all World Cup winners with Germany in 2014 – as well as Klaas Jan-Huntelaar and Joël Matip, who have both played for some of Europe's biggest clubs.

Any photos of these glory years are accompanied by an advert for Gazprom on the front of players' shirts. In the years immediately after the deal, Schalke were regularly competing against Europe's best and receiving a sizable share in the vast TV revenues that the Champions League generates. Doing well on the pitch always helps minimise issues off it, and the former Schalke employee explains that although there was some criticism of the deal in those glory days, it wasn't particularly noisy or widespread. 'The club always argued [Gazprom] is a normal supplier, so it can't be a bad company. Schalke would argue "OK, this isn't Oxfam or Médecins Sans Frontières or something, but other companies aren't always that good either".' The former employee claims Tönnies used to say Putin would ask him about Schalke's results, although others were sceptical of this.

There were even discussions at one point about the club visiting Putin in Moscow, an idea that went down badly with fans' groups. In 2021, Schalke did play a summer friendly in Austria against Zenit Saint Petersburg, Putin's hometown club which is owned by Gazprom. Criticism of the Schalke deal grew in intensity after the war with Georgia in 2008 and the Crimean invasion of 2014, but it still all felt rather abstract and remote to many Germans. This was true across Europe. Roman Abramovich had owned Chelsea since 2003 and had long held ties to Russia's president, acting as a public face of the successful 2018 World Cup bid. In 1999, he vetted Putin's cabinet candidates in meetings at the Kremlin. 'I respect him a lot,' Abramovich said of Putin. 'In my opinion, everything that Putin does, he does without making any mistakes.'[19] Drawing a direct link between the two proved difficult, and Abramovich was highly litigious in chasing after those who pointed out what seemed obvious. It was only in the aftermath of the 2022 invasion that he was sanctioned by the UK government and forced to sell the club, with the proceeds intended to go to a foundation to help those impacted by the Ukraine war.

A cash boost can only help so much against a backdrop of financial mismanagement in a league in which Bayern Munich were becoming increasingly dominant, and Schalke squandered a lot of the Gazprom windfall, the former employee says. 'They invested a lot in players with money they didn't have.' The club borrowed cash trying to chase a high position in the league table with the aim of qualifying for the Champions League, which would lead to more revenue. But the plan didn't work. The club's transfer policy of signing young players and developing them was unsuccessful, wasting huge sums on players who flopped like Ukrainian winger Yevhen Konoplyanka, Nabil Bentaleb who signed from Tottenham Hotspur, and record-signing Breel Embolo, a Swiss striker. As a team with a modern stadium, high gate receipts and additional money from concerts and other events, the Covid pandemic hit the club particularly badly. Relegation in 2021 was the culmination of a protracted period of decline. The Gazprom deal had helped Schalke, but there is a limit to the benefits of a simple sponsorship deal, as opposed to a takeover situation where an entity with almost bottomless pockets can finance a club like Abramovich did at Chelsea, and Middle Eastern states have done at Paris Saint-Germain, Newcastle United and Manchester City. Abramovich once met Jeffrey Lurie, owner of American football team the Philadelphia Eagles, who asked the Russian about his 'EBITDA', a measure of operating profits. Abramovich was baffled by the question.[20] He spent, or more accurately lost, more than £2 billion in his nineteen years owning the London club. Owning an NFL team can be a licence to print money if run effectively, but owning a top European football team is almost always a shortcut to losing cash. People do it for other reasons. Owning Chelsea elevated Abramovich from yet another businessman to an internationally famous figure, helpful for building contacts, or perhaps warding off potential antagonists who would rather not pick a fight with – or seek to harm – someone so well known. Schalke has always been fully owned by its fans. Germany's '50+1 rule' mandates that the majority of a club's shares must be owned by fans, effectively banning outside investors becoming majority owners. German football fans vociferously defend this arrangement, despite the view in some quarters that it reinforces Bayern's dominance and makes it increasingly hard for German clubs other than Bayern to compete in Europe, particularly against state-run clubs in other countries.

The former employee I spoke to told me that, in Schalke's heyday, the media were often curious about whether Gazprom was meddling in the club's internal matters and if Vladimir Putin or one of his henchmen were ultimately pulling the strings at this historic German institution. They explain this was not the case at all. 'They were hardly interested. We always thought maybe they won't renew their sponsorship because they show little interest, usually sponsors show more interest. There were always rumours they would rather be on the shirt of Bayern.' They speculate Gazprom chose the club because it has a good image of a 'very local club with die-hard fans', lending a slice of Ruhr authenticity to the company selling Russian gas to the Germans. 'Within the club, we were sometimes a bit puzzled . . . it must have something to do with higher politics that we don't understand.' While it all looks terrible in hindsight, there was little vocal criticism before the Ukraine invasion. The company also boosted its image by donating money to local charities, admirable in isolation but a classic tactic of a company under scrutiny. 'Our financial situation was always very difficult. We always had high debt, so "Shut up we need the money" was the message to the fanbase of Schalke. What really changed it was the Ukraine war.'

Back in February 2020, I visited the Serbian capital of Belgrade, speaking at a conference for my old employer BBC News before making the switch to covering football full-time. As I travelled back to England to watch Aston Villa lose the EFL Cup final 2–1 to Manchester City at Wembley, there was an odd sight on my plane – lots of passengers wearing medical-style face masks. Many appeared to have travelled from East Asia. I thought it somewhat strange, an overreaction to the 'coronavirus' I had been reading about in the news. Little did I know this would be my last plane ride for a long time. I didn't watch a football match on my trip to Belgrade but had always wanted to visit the city because of the

Partizan vs Red Star Belgrade rivalry, a staple of 'world's fiercest derbies' articles and YouTube videos.

Fast-forward three years to my trip to Gelsenkirchen and, a few weeks later, I spent a Tuesday evening at home flicking between the various UEFA Champions League matches on different channels. I settled on TNT Sports' *Goals Show*, where pundits discuss the evening's games while showing the goals from different matches as they go in. I spotted a familiar logo, white on blue, a flickering flame. The Gazprom logo had long been removed from the stadium billboards of UEFA Champions League matches by this point. But there was still a team wearing it – Red Star Belgrade, or FK Crvena Zvezda as they prefer to be called these days, to the horror of tongue-tied English commentators. Red Star are thirty-four-time Serbian league winners and won the European Cup in 1991 the year before it was rebranded as the Champions League. In the decade before that, European Cup winners included Nottingham Forest, Aston Villa, Hamburg, PSV Eindhoven and Steaua Bucharest. Since then, Europe's footballing elite has become ever richer and the likelihood of a team like Red Star winning again is very low. These days Red Star are relative minnows who routinely qualify for the Champions League group stage but go no further. On this occasion, as I was watching from my sofa, they were visiting reigning European champions Manchester City. They gave City a minor scare by leading at half-time but were predictably beaten 3–1. The return leg was played a couple of months later in Red Star's intimidating home ground, known as the Marakana after Brazil's national stadium, the English side winning 3–2, a surprisingly close and entertaining contest explained by City heavily rotating their squad having already won the Champions League group. In the stadium in Serbia, the Gazprom logo was visible everywhere.

The invasion of Ukraine in 2022 was received differently in Serbia to elsewhere in Europe. Serbia is not part of the European Union, an entity which has heavily backed Ukraine. Serbia has signed up to the official process to join in the future although this doesn't look likely any time soon, despite heavily relying on the bloc economically and sharing a border with loyal EU members Czechia and Romania, as well as the more pro-Russian Hungary.[21] With its history of Orthodox Christianity and experience of communism under the state of Yugoslavia, Serbia has long had close political and cultural ties to Russia and has looked both ways on the Ukraine war. Three months after the invasion the country signed a three-year deal on advantageous terms to keep the country warm through the winter with – you guessed it – Gazprom.[22]

To understand more about the connection between Gazprom and the football club that has long had ties to the country's government, I spoke to Nebojša Marković, a football journalist based in Belgrade. He told me that Red Star's deal with Gazprom ultimately comes down to cold hard cash. Red Star have gone from being European Champions in 1991, to continental also-rans three decades later. This is because teams in Western Europe, especially England and Spain, have secured huge TV deals which pay the wages of the world's best players. 'It's not easy finding sponsorship in the Serbian league,' Marković told me. 'In other leagues, it's much easier to get visibility to sell your products.' This means the Gazprom deal, in place since 2010, has been 'very important' for Red Star. 'Back then Red Star were not in a great situation, not only financially but also results-wise.' Bitter rivals Partizan Belgrade won six titles in a row from 2007–08 onwards, while Red Star barely competed in Europe. 'With the help of Gazprom, it became easier,' says Marković. Red Star won the league every season bar two between 2013 and 2024, including a run of seven consecutive titles. In recent years the club has also enjoyed some better results in Europe, beating Liverpool and drawing with AC Milan, meaning not just UEFA prize money but also making themselves more attractive to sponsors. Marković says their last Gazprom deal was worth around €5 million per season, on a par with the lowest deals in the Premier League, while being ten times smaller than deals signed by England's best teams who Red Star come up against in Europe, but giving them a huge advantage over domestic rivals.

Marković says this dependence means Gazprom is viewed favourably by Serbians and Red Star fans, with many of his countrymen taking a far more pro-Russian view of the conflict than fans in Germany or elsewhere. Red Star general manager Zvezdan Terzić has said the club owes its continued survival to Gazprom. 'If it wasn't for Gazprom, the question is whether there would be a Red Star,' he remarked when asked if the club would keep the deal in February 2022 after Russia invaded Ukraine. 'People who love Red Star will never forget what Gazprom did for the club'.[23]

Just like at Schalke before the invasion, many Red Star fans would rather talk about the football than sponsorship deals and dismiss the idea that there is anything political going on. But Marković tells a tale that suggests this might be naive. 'In 2011, Vladimir Putin visited Belgrade. He was here for some political matters, but he also visited Red Star's stadium. Red Star's under-19 team played Zenit Saint Petersburg in a friendly. Putin came and was in the VIP lounge for a game that ended 1–1. It was a big deal for Red Star to get such a huge political figure in the stadium.' At the time he was Russia's prime minister, not president, having swapped roles in 2008 for a four-year period to comply with constitutional term limits. His stooge Dmitry Medvedev took the top job before the two swapped back in 2012. Grainy YouTube footage of the game in

Belgrade shows Putin taking his seat in a noisy Marakana stadium surrounded by flares and red-and-white banners.[24]

More recently there is plenty of YouTube footage, less grainy as camera phone technology has improved, of Red Star fans chanting 'Ross-i-ya' (Russia) and waving banners of a half-and-half Serbian and Russian flag. This happened in the immediate aftermath of the invasion of Ukraine as the spotlight fell on the club's deal with Gazprom. After the invasion, Russia was suspended from UEFA as other countries refused to play them in qualifiers for the upcoming FIFA World Cup. 'There is anti-Russian hysteria across Europe now,' said manager Zvezdan Terzić. 'Politics interfered beyond any reason in sports. The Russian people are close to the Serbian people and always will be.'[25]

The Nord Stream 2 pipeline was finished in September 2021, but did not enter service because of wider events. A year later, following the Ukraine invasion, a series of underwater explosions hit both pipelines at a time when Nord Stream 1 was still sending some gas from Russia to Germany. It was initially assumed Russia was to blame while others suggested the American intelligence services were involved. More recently, credible reports in the *New York Times* and the *Wall Street Journal* reported that a group of Ukrainian divers blew up the pipeline, with German authorities issuing an arrest warrant for a Ukrainian national, though details remained hazy.[26,27] Gazprom and Russia still have pariah status in Germany and energy prices have got far more expensive, and Schalke got a new sponsorship deal with the shallower-pocketed Veltins brewery. As for the UEFA Champions League, Crypto.com, an online exchange, was lined up as a replacement before the deal fell through at the last moment. But then in August 2024 the deal was revived and the logo of a cryptocurrency company can be seen on the billboards at Champions League games – more on that industry later. With a string of other big money sponsors too, Europe's premier club competition could cope without Gazprom's millions, though a separate deal with Qatar Airways means the big questions about energy politics have not gone away.

    The desire for politics to stay out of sport is understandable. Unfortunately, the people running Schalke and Red Star Belgrade, not to mention the Champions League, made the choice to link the fate of their clubs and competition to continental geopolitics by welcoming money from Russia's state gas company. Schalke's blue shirt is now shorn of the Gazprom logo. The club survived that 2023–24 season in mid-table in Germany's second division but the heights of the early Gazprom years feel a million miles away. Red Star's red shirt, meanwhile, was carrying the Gazprom name long after Putin's invasion of Ukraine made that flame logo unacceptable in Western Europe. These two shirts tell us how Russia's natural resource wealth, and territorial aggression, have upended politics across Europe. A fragile status quo that lasted three decades after the end of the Cold War has been ripped up, a knotty story that a couple of football shirts can help us make a little more sense of.

2

CRIMINAL CONNECTIONS

Envigado FC & Parma FC

'We Catholics believe that football can be a vehicle of love for one's neighbour and respect for one's rival. An antidote to the bad education, racism and violence that have taken over this beautiful sport.'
  Gabriel García Márquez, Colombian writer and winner of the Nobel Prize in Literature

It would be an exaggeration to say I travelled all the way from England to Colombia to see if I could find anyone wearing one specific football shirt. But when I went there in March 2024 and spotted the shirt in the wild, I was pretty pleased. The shirt in question was worn between 2012 and 2014 by Envigado FC, one of the smaller clubs in the Colombian Premier League, based in the southern suburbs of Medellín which is a city that has been transformed in recent decades. In the late 1980s and early 1990s, it was literally the most dangerous city in the world but it is now frequented by international tourists and digital nomads enjoying pleasant green surroundings, year-round sunshine and a party lifestyle.

I watched Envigado play Millonarios on a Sunday lunchtime. While I was taking in the action on a pitch beautifully framed by the mountains behind, my eyes were darting around at the fans, trying to spot that shirt. No luck. When the final whistle blew, I thought I had failed in my mission. And then I saw it. A short, stout man heading out was wearing a white replica shirt. On the back below his neck was a small silhouette of a man's face. It was the face of a murdered former leader of an international drug cartel.

Russia and Qatar have gas. Abu Dhabi and Saudi Arabia have oil. Colombia has another valuable natural inheritance, not fossil fuels but the coca leaf. The Andes region, which also includes Peru and Bolivia, produces almost all the world's crop.[1] The leaf has psychoactive properties which have been used for millennia by indigenous people for medical and recreational purposes and by the twentieth century it was widely used in medicine as well as in the early version of Coca-Cola, hence the name. In the 1970s it became apparent that, through a relatively low-cost industrial process, the bulky coca leaves could be transformed into an easily transportable and extremely addictive powder. Cocaine boomed in popularity as a party drug in American cities in the 1970s, particularly Miami and New York City where the disco scene was blossoming. Around the same time, a young man from Envigado with a background in petty crime spotted a business opportunity. By the end of the 1980s, he would be named the world's seventh-richest man by *Forbes* and almost certainly the richest criminal of all time, a man who at one point threatened to overthrow the Colombian state. His name was Pablo Escobar, leader of the Medellín drug cartel which at its height earned billions of dollars a year, tax free of course, by controlling the majority of the cocaine supply to the United States. His motto was *plata o plomo* – silver or lead. Anyone standing in his way faced a choice between taking a bribe or taking a bullet.

The links between Colombian drug gangs and football run deep. One of the earliest signs that the cartels were tightening their grip on Colombian society became apparent during a football match in December 1981. Nacional and América – two of the country's 'Big Three' clubs alongside Millonarios – were playing each other in the city of Cali where América are based. Both clubs were owned by cartels, which had recently decided to work together to stamp out the problem of guerilla groups kidnapping Colombians for ransom. As the match was about to kick off a small aeroplane circled the stadium. When the referee's whistle blew, a crewman opened a hatch and held a bale of leaflets out of it, snipping the string binding them and pushing the leaflets out into the sky. A cloud of paper fluttered towards the centre of the pitch.[2]

The manifesto printed on each leaflet announced a 'general assembly' in which 223 of Colombia's top 'businessmen' said they would no longer put up with the kidnappings, which were being carried out by left-wing groups seeking to earn ransom money to fund their revolutionary politics. These 'businessmen' were drug traffickers with power bases scattered across the country, all cooperating for the first time. All had pledged cash to a new vigilante fund creating an organisation called 'Death to Kidnappers'. Any bemusement the fans in the stadium might have felt at the stunt likely vanished when their eyes moved further down the leaflet. The traffickers offered hard cash in exchange for information leading to the capture of the kidnappers and promised that those found guilty would be 'hung from the trees in public parks or shot and marked with the sign of our group'.[3] The threat extended to the families of those deemed responsible. Stopping the kidnappings was a worthy cause but the cure turned out to be worse. The stadium leaflet drop was the first skirmish in a power shift which would see the chaotic violence of the guerrillas supplanted with the ruthless and systematic violence of the drug traffickers, carried out on a much bigger scale, that came to threaten the viability of the Colombian state.

Escobar started his political career on Envigado town council, where he made football a cornerstone of his campaigns, lobbying for sports facilities, as well as donating lighting and kit. 'Unlike other politicians, there's no delay,' writes David Arrowsmith in *Narcoball*. 'If he promises shirts or balls, the next day one of his men turns up with the gear. If he promises lights or stands, within 24 hours a team of workmen arrive to do his bidding.' An increasingly prominent figure in his hometown, drug lord Pablo Escobar was elected to Congress in 1982. Soon afterwards the justice minister, Rodrigo Lara Bonilla, publicly exposed Escobar by detailing the new politician's links to drug trafficking. Escobar did not appreciate this level of scrutiny and quit frontline politics for good. It was an open secret that he bankrolled his hometown club Atlético Nacional and in 1983 justice minister Bonilla declared that more than half of the fifteen teams in the Colombian professional league were financed by drug traffickers, a pronouncement which kicked off the first of three government investigations into the issue.[4] Bonilla named names: Escobar as well as Hernan Botero, owner of Nacional, Gilberto Rodríguez, who owned América de Cali, and Bogotá kingpin José Rodríguez Gacha, known as 'The Mexican', owner of Millonarios. A month later, the newspaper *El Espectador* published even more details, agitating the cartels which were growing increasingly more powerful as the state struggled to rein them in.[5] The cartels became obsessed with Bonilla, and, in 1984, he was murdered in his car by a hired assassin riding on the back of a moped. Guillermo Cano, the editor of *El Espectador* who had shown great bravery in reporting on the traffickers, was also gunned down in 1986, eventually giving his name to a prestigious international journalism award. Colombia had been scheduled to host the World Cup that year but had withdrawn four years prior, blaming FIFA's excessive and costly demands. Mexico took over at short notice. This was perhaps just as well given what was going on in Colombia by 1986, particularly in Medellín which was a proposed host city. By then it was the world's most dangerous place.

Escobar's wealth and profile grew, gracing the covers of magazines like *Newsweek*, *Time* and *Forbes,* and he felt invincible. However, in 1989 he pushed it too far, ordering the detonation of a bomb on board an Avianca passenger jet in an attempt to kill presidential candidate César Gaviria Trujillo. The politician was not on the flight but 107 innocent passengers died including two US citizens. (Three more civilians on the ground were killed by falling debris.) Although thousands of Colombians had already been killed in the country's bloodthirsty drug wars, the killing of Americans changed the diplomatic picture, explains Mark Bowden in his book *Killing Pablo*. 'It marked Pablo Escobar, José Rodríguez Gacha and other cartel leaders as a direct threat to American citizens. As such, the Narcos were now men who, in the eyes of the [President George H.W. Bush] administration, could legally be killed.'[6]

All this is documented in the Netflix hit series *Narcos*, a thoroughly enjoyable drama for a Westerner trying to get up to speed on what happened in Medellín in the 1980s and 1990s, although locals told me of their discomfort at the way it glamorises the violence that sits in such recent memory, while also humanising Escobar as a thoughtful and even sympathetic figure rather than the sadistic murderer he really was.[7] Colombians also grumble at the fact that the main character is played by a Brazilian actor whose accent sounds nothing like the *'paisa'* Medellín-accented Spanish of locals. Narco-tourism, in which tourists visit Escobar-related sites around the city, is seen as distasteful in a place that has now moved on in an impressive way. One of these sites includes the cushy prison known as La Catedral where Escobar spent time living in comfortable conditions as part of a deal with the Colombian government and played exhibition football matches against professionals including the entire Atlético Nacional team and even a visiting Diego Maradona in 1991.

In Medellín I took a guided tour of Comuna 13, once a very dangerous neighbourhood but now a tourist trap, where foreign visitors pose for Instagram photos in front of colourful street art. It's a fun place to visit and a miracle it exists given what went on here in the very recent past. As well as the narco-violence of the 1980s and 1990s, in 2002 the army raided the district with tanks and helicopters in a move against the FARC left-wing guerilla group. Dozens of locals were killed. These days it feels a bit like a theme park so, wanting to learn more about the real Medellín, I went to a neighbourhood not on the tourist trail – Moravia.

Medellín's population boomed in the middle of the twentieth century after the completion of a railway network connecting the city with remote parts of the province of Antioquia. From 1948 to 1958, the Colombian countryside was plagued by La Violencia, a ten-year civil war between the country's Liberal and Conservative parties estimated to have killed more than 200,000 people, one in fifty Colombians at the time.[8] Many fled the fields for the relative safety of the big city and lots of new arrivals to Medellín settled in the place that came to be known as Moravia along the new railroad. In the 1970s, the city needed somewhere to dump its trash and settled on the new neighbourhood. Some families were moved but many others stayed, resisting relocation as rubbish piled up all around them. Many recycled trash and sold it to get by. After the misery of the 1980s and 1990s, things improved a little in the 2000s, as Moravia was cleaned up and long-term residents allowed to acquire their homes, many of which were built on compressed piles of garbage.

This is not a place you visit without a guide, so I went on a tour led by a grandmother named Gladys whose father fled to the neighbourhood when it was literally a dump. She is a community leader and carries out tours with Milo, a young man from another part of Medellín who speaks excellent English and is deeply engaged in his city's history. Moravia remains a very poor district today and does not attract foreign tourists like other parts of Medellín. They showed me their neighbourhood, ramshackle but much loved. Like everywhere in Colombia, it is hard to escape football. Wherever you look there are children in shirts of Colombian clubs, as well as fake versions of those of European clubs – mostly Real Madrid and Barcelona, with a smattering of English clubs and the odd Atlético Madrid, Inter Milan and Paris Saint-Germain. I find it striking that just about all the foreign replica shirts I see in Moravia, as well as on my other travels around the world researching this book, represent the teams behind the controversial and swiftly aborted European Super League proposals of 2021, in which the owners of several of the continent's biggest clubs attempted to break away from their domestic leagues and create a new competition, plans ditched after almost universal outrage.

The most common English shirt in Colombia was that of Chelsea, a trophy-winning machine in their pomp under former Russian owner Roman Abramovich, but mid-table strugglers at the time I visited. Chelsea's prevalence in Medellín told me something about the Premier League 'Big Six' of Arsenal, Chelsea, Liverpool, Manchester City, Manchester United and Tottenham.

This moniker can feel arrogant when those teams often finish lower than other clubs, including my own team who came fourth in 2023–24. Somewhat gratingly, though, the category is legitimate for two reasons. Firstly, those six teams have far higher revenues than any other clubs, which gives them a safety net. They might have the odd bad season where others finish above them, but they can afford to make mistakes that other clubs cannot. Indeed, a year after my visit Chelsea were in a far better state, thanks in large part to Cole Palmer, a mercurial young English midfielder signed from Manchester City. Secondly, the huge power of a global brand like Chelsea means it will take far more than one or two bad seasons for the club's global popularity to diminish. Chelsea Women also recently bought Mayra Ramírez, the Colombian women's team striker, which may be a significant factor – just as with the Liverpool shirts I saw bearing the name of Colombian forward Luis Díaz.

As we continue the tour, weaving through children in AC Milan, Chelsea and Barcelona shirts, we come to a concrete court packed in among concrete housing blocks, some of which have the roof weighed down with rocks to prevent them blowing off in a storm. We passed several groups of children kicking a ball around. Some wear the colours of the local big clubs, Nacional and Independiente Medellín, universally known as Medellín. None wear the shirt of little Envigado a few miles down the road, the club whose shirt once carried the face of a cartel leader. More on that later.

On either side of the court are two huge murals. One is in the green and white of Nacional, celebrating when they became champions of South America in 2016 after winning the Copa Libertadores, the continent's equivalent of the Champions League. The other mural is the red and blue of Medellín. Without as many honours to shout about, this second mural focuses on family and community, portraying a father taking his young son to a game.

The elite club was on a dismal run of form when I visited, with supporters' anger often taking a dark turn. In December 2023, black-and-white notices were posted around the city carrying the faces of the club's president and vice-president, inviting fans to the two men's 'funerals'. Three months later, the league issued a statement denouncing 'the threats and acts of intimidation that managers, players, referees, officials and various actors' were facing in the Colombian league, sometimes targeted at the families of those involved in football. In a sinister twist, one of those threatened was the referee Carlos Ortega, whose uncle, Álvaro Ortega, also a referee, was murdered in 1989 by Escobar's Medellín Cartel, an event which led to the cancellation of the league that season because it became impossible to find people willing to officiate matches.[9]

(A side note relating to football sponsorship: after this episode, the Colombian league got back off the ground thanks to a sponsorship deal with Mustang cigarettes. Of all the vices to pour money into football, Big Tobacco is not usually one of them, for the obvious reason that the brand does not fit very well with elite sport. The Copa Mustang was a rare example.)[10]

At the end of the tour of Moravia, my guide showed me one of the most startling graphs I have ever seen. It showed Medellín's homicide rate. From a relatively low base, it shot up to 380 per 100,000 in 1991, making Medellín not just the most dangerous city in the world, but the most dangerous place that has ever existed in the era of reliable statistics, as once declared by *Time* magazine.[11] For context, in 2023, the highest murder rate in the world was less than half that, in the city of Colima in Mexico.[12] But since the deadly early-1990s, the homicide rate in Medellín has plummeted, with a couple of minor bumps. The problem hasn't gone away and there has been a small increase in violence in recent years but Medellín is a completely transformed place. By 2023, the rate in Medellín had fallen twenty-fold to fifteen murders per 100,000, significantly lower than many US cities, and less than half that of New Orleans, Baltimore and Detroit.[13]

Crime statistics are influenced by numerous complex social forces, but in Medellín, the death of one man made an instant difference. After Escobar was shot dead in 1993 the power of drug cartels diminished overnight. Medellín is now a pleasant place to visit and is packed with foreign visitors. One of the hottest political issues is that rents are rising quicker than locals' incomes – a serious problem for sure, but one that would have seemed alien in the 1990s when there were no foreign tourists, and locals were chiefly concerned with surviving the day. Hired killings took place throughout the 1980s and 1990s over relatively trivial amounts of cash, and countless Colombians were caught in the crossfire or were victims of mistaken identity. At one point a bounty of $700 was placed on the head of each and every police officer – kill an officer and prove it to Pablo to get paid. I wrote an early draft of this chapter in the sunny cafes of the Poblado district, the buzz of mopeds providing background noise to the tapping of my keyboard. Not long ago, there would have been a genuine fear every time one of those mopeds pulled up, that a man would hop off the back to gun somebody down with an automatic weapon.

The construction of cable cars in the 1990s played a big role in Medellín's transformation, helping to connect the poorest barrios on the city's hillsides – hard to reach by road – with the city centre. I took one to the beautiful Parque Arví, high in the hills above the city, then stayed out late eating traditional Colombian food and drinking beers on streets which felt just as safe as those of any Western city. Tourism is throwing up its own problems. Medellín's reputation for sex, drugs and reggaeton, combined with its low cost of living, means it has become a destination for sex tourism. When I checked into my relatively smart hotel near the party district, the receptionist informed me that I may take up one guest for free, but for an additional overnight visitor, I must pay a charge. I politely made clear that would not be necessary.

On the Saturday evening of my trip, I went to a match at Medellín's main stadium, far bigger than the one in little Envigado. Pablo Escobar helped build this venue as part of his longstanding involvement with Atlético Nacional, and two major events in Colombian history happened in the surrounding streets through which I walked before the game. On 3 December 1992, Escobar was five months into his stint as a fugitive after escaping from prison. At the time Colombia was ravaged by a quasi-civil war, which had multiple participants: Escobar and his supporters, rival drug traffickers, anti-Escobar vigilantes, and the Colombian government. Following a 3–2 Atlético Nacional victory over Junior FC, happy fans were milling around the stadium when a huge car bomb went off, killing ten police officers and four fans.[14] Escobar's repentant son Juan Pablo later noted that his father carried out the attack because he was 'convinced that violence would force the government to grant him the judicial concessions he'd demanded several times ... Over the next week another dozen cars would blow up in Medellín.'[15] Escobar was terrorising his own people, and his feud with the Colombian government was spiralling into all-out war.

Still on the run a year later in the neighbourhood of Los Olivos, a ten-minute walk from the stadium, the fugitive Escobar was finally tracked down. Colombian and American military officers worked together, tracing his phone calls to family members and associates, before eventually pinning down his location. He was gunned down while trying to escape on a rooftop. Soldiers posed with his bloated corpse. While most Colombians celebrated, Escobar still had supporters in those neighbourhoods that he had furnished with money, jobs and social projects as part of his strategy of cultivating loyalty and fear. To this day, souvenir sellers in Medellín still sell Escobar-related merchandise with his face on, particularly the notorious grinning mugshot from his arrest in 1977. Most locals see this as distasteful but, in the barrios, I notice several young children running or cycling around with Escobar T-shirts on.

Before going to the game I visited a park in the Belén district of Medellín. In the park is a statue of a man kicking a football. It is Andrés Escobar, no relation to Pablo. In the summer of 1994, a few days after scoring the own goal that sent Colombia crashing out of the World Cup, he was shot six times in the back after an argument outside a Medellín nightclub.[16] The statue is inscribed with his nickname: Caballero del Fútbol, the gentleman of football. Football in Medellín has seen violence more recently than that. The Medellín derby, the Clásico Paisa, sees Atlético Nacional take on Independiente Medellín in the stadium they share. Atlético Nacional were champions of South America in 1989 and 2016, and are seventeen-time champions of Colombia, while Independiente Medellín have won just six titles. It is one of the most fiercely contested derbies in South America, on and off the pitch. In 2019, videos emerged of rival fans fighting each other with machetes in the middle of the day in a busy Medellín street. A few hours after a derby match ended in 2023, two Independiente Medellín fans were killed in street battles.[17] 'It's the most absurd thing that can happen. They're killing kids over a club badge,' said William Gallego, father of one of the men who died. 'Football is not about killing each other.' Sadly in Colombia it all too often is.

Before the game the Medellín stadium felt lively but not intimidating. There were conspicuous groups of Western tourists, recognisable and not just because of their fair complexions. It was pointed out to me that Colombian men tended to always wear trousers. Only tourists wore shorts out in the evening. There were notably more women than at the matches I go to in England. Many fans were wearing the red shirt of Medellín, and I grabbed one myself on the way in for just a few dollars, another to add to my collection and help my goal of being one of the more esoterically dressed runners in my local south London park. I spotted several fans in Barcelona shirts, perhaps because the similar colour scheme blends in nicely. The game I watched saw Independiente Medellín hosting Once Caldas from the town of Manizales, who brought a noisy away support, despite their home being five hours away to the south. As is traditional around the world, the noisiest home fans were behind the goal while the side stands were more sedate.

The atmosphere slowly built and, by the time the 45,000-seater stadium was almost full, it was positively riotous. Banners in the ground commemorated the most famous of Medellín's six league titles, which came in 2002 after a forty-five-year drought. I was in the corner of the stadium, able to observe the ultras without feeling like I might get in over my head. Red-and-blue banners were draped from front to back, many referencing specific neighbourhoods in the city. Curiously, fans of this club like to replace 's' and 'c' with 'x' in their banners, for example the word 'resistance' becoming 'REXIXTENXIA'. Other banners carried giant faces depicting fellow ultras who have died. The noisy singing began with the Colombian national anthem which precedes each league game, with everyone knowing all the words. Red and blue smoke filled the air before the game kicked off. Shirtless young men, their torsos covered in tattoos demonstrating club or neighbourhood loyalty, grabbed hold of banners and stood on the railings on the upper tier, hanging above the tier below while singing throughout the game. Stewards were nowhere to be seen.

Unlike in England where singing is reactive to events on the pitch and rival fans engage in back-and-forths, here the singing continued with little concern for the onfield action. That was perhaps just as well. The game I saw was low on quality but high on drama. Medellín took an early lead, but the whole outlook changed when they had a player sent off for a high tackle after half an hour. Replays confirmed the red card looked soft. Although Once Caldas were clearly the inferior side, the numerical advantage helped them get a goal back before Dayro Moreno, the 38-year-old all-time top scorer in the Colombian top flight, scored a long-range screamer in the last minute to put them 2–1 ahead. The black-and-white away end erupted at the surprise win. The home fans were finally silenced and slunk off into the night, as I weaved through them heading for the Metro. I was grateful to discover I had not been scammed by a worryingly informal bag drop system, where a shopkeeper stashes your stuff behind a tile in his ceiling in exchange for a modest fee.

The following day at Envigado FC, a twenty-minute cab ride to the south of central Medellín, there were no tourists to be seen. This club has the nickname Cantera de Héroes (Quarry of Heroes), a nod to their reputation as the place from where Colombia's footballing superstars are mined. The team was only founded in

1989 but has produced many big names for the national team including Fredy Guarín, Juan Fernando Quintero and Jhon Durán, the former Aston Villa player whose looping winner I saw in that 1–0 win over Bayern Munich in October 2024. Three months later he was sold to Saudi Arabia to play alongside Cristiano Ronaldo at Al-Nassr. The most notable Envigado product of all is James Rodríguez, the attacking midfielder who was top scorer at the 2014 World Cup, won two Champions Leagues with Real Madrid, and is a strong contender for the greatest Colombian footballer of all time, although Carlos Valderrama, known for his iconic curly hair and for captaining the national team at three World Cups in the 1990s, might just shade it.

In the game I watched, Envigado hosted Millonarios from the capital city Bogotá, a ten-hour drive away. Despite the distance, there were more away fans than home supporters, something I had never encountered at a football match before. The rowdiest Millonarios fans took up one end of the ground, singing, shouting and literally jumping up and down throughout. I had seen many raucous football crowds all around the world, but this coordinated rhythmic jumping was new to me. It looked exhausting. I was also impressed at how varied the songbook was compared to English fans; they seemed to sing for ninety minutes without repeating a tune, with one particularly catchy ditty borrowing the tune of Boney M's 'Rivers of Babylon'. In the main side stand where I was sitting, supporters of both sides were freely mingling. It struck me that, despite Colombia's violent past – and, to an extent, its present – rival fans here could be trusted to sit together, something which does not generally happen in Europe. The stadium only had stands on two sides, giving a clear view to the skyscrapers of nearby Medellín and the mountains beyond.

I spent a lot of time appreciating the view because the match was hardly scintillating. The early kick-off time meant conditions were hot and sweaty and the pace was sluggish. (England's chilly climate is an underrated factor in its fast-paced and aggressive brand of football.) Although both sides had forwards with some technical skill, the gameplay was ponderous and slow, with defensive lines sitting very deep, meaning little jeopardy when the ball was turned over as there was no space for attackers to get behind. Hosts Envigado took a surprise 1–0 lead early on with a smart finish, a low strike ricocheting in off the post. The reception was somewhat muted, though. While there were Envigado fans in attendance wearing orange shirts, there appeared to be little of the fan culture I saw elsewhere in Colombia. Their only chant, which I heard once or twice, was the word 'Envigado', and there were none of the banners depicting barrios, or tributes to fallen ultras, that I saw at Independiente Medellín.

Before half-time, Millonarios equalised through a smart passing move and the away end went wild as well as about half of the 'mixed' stand, but there was no trouble between fans. A second away goal in the second half was disallowed for offside after an intervention by the video assistant referee (VAR), a level of technology that seemed incongruous at the tiny Estadio Polideportivo Sur. It is perhaps understandable that the quality on show was low. Bright prospects generally leave the Colombian Premier League at the first opportunity, for better wages and opportunities elsewhere. But I had travelled all this way not to see a great game of football, but to find out more about a football shirt that helps tell the story of Colombia's violent past.

It took until the end of the game before I saw the specific shirt I came to this tiny stadium to write about, so I spent lots of time evaluating whether there were any stories in others worn by those around me. In typical South American style, these shirts tended to have many sponsors. European teams generally have one front-of-shirt sponsor and perhaps a second company on the sleeves, but South American teams often have five or six logos crammed onto the shirt. On Envigado's 2023–24 shirt the main logo is Pool, a drinks company, while smaller sponsors include: Aguardiente Antioqueño, the fiery aniseed-flavoured spirit that is the local drink of choice; Wplay, a gambling website; and Colanta, a local dairy producer. Some fans, however, were wearing an orange Envigado shirt, with no sponsor whatsoever. This itself tells an interesting story.

June 2014 was a big month in Colombian football. The national team began its first World Cup campaign since the Carlos Valderrama era sixteen years earlier and things began surprisingly well, the team beating Greece and Ivory Coast in their first two group games. Colombia beat Japan 4–1 to top their group and advance to the knock out stages. The football-mad country was delirious as Colombia beat Uruguay 2–0 to progress to the quarter-finals, a match featuring a spectacular volley by James Rodríguez instantly recognised as one of the all-time great World Cup goals. Excitement in the country reached fever pitch. Although Colombia were narrowly beaten by hosts Brazil in the quarter-final, this was the country's best-ever World Cup performance, capped off by Rodríguez winning the Golden Boot award for most goals in the tournament. This made him an international superstar and earned him a move from AS Monaco to Real Madrid.

Right in the middle of all this, a bombshell dropped in Envigado. On 26 June, the US Treasury added a new organisation to its Specially Designated Nationals and Blocked Persons, known as the 'Clinton List' after the US president who first brought in the sanctions scheme. It prohibits US citizens from doing business with those named, as well as freezing any of their US assets. Oficina de Envigado, a drug cartel and criminal group originally founded as the enforcement wing of Pablo Escobar's Medellín Cartel, was put on the list. In the middle of the World Cup the US government put out a statement saying the group had a 'significant role in international narcotics trafficking', spelling out the group's origins in Escobar's organisation in the 1980s and 1990s. 'In addition to its direct involvement in narcotics trafficking, La Oficina de Envigado is complicit in a variety of illicit activities, including money laundering, extortion, and murder for hire,' said US official Adam Szubin. 'These "secondary" activities further the operations of international trafficking groups.'[18]

A few months later came a dramatic twist. The name of another company deemed to be working with the cartel was added to the list: Envigado FC. The former club of World Cup hero James Rodríguez was sanctioned by the US along with majority owner Juan Pablo Upegui Gallego. US officials described him as 'a key associate within La Oficina' who has 'used his position as the team's owner to put its finances at the service of La Oficina for many years'.[19] In a hastily arranged press conference, Upegui said he was 'very surprised' by the news, denied any wrongdoing and offered the authorities the chance to inspect the club's books.[20] Upegui was the son of Gustavo Upegui, La Oficina's original leader who was tortured and killed in 2006. As the match was ending, and I was beginning to head out of the stadium and into the sticky early afternoon, I finally spotted what I was looking for: a man wearing a shirt with a little silhouette below the rear collar. The man depicted was Gustavo Upegui, the long-time leader of the Oficina de Envigado. Back in 2012, such were the links between the club and the cartel that the club literally had his face on their shirt.

Envigado FC would not be the last football club to be added to the US sanctions list. Akhmat Grozny, a Russian Premier League side owned by Chechen warlord Ramzan Kadyrov, met the same fate in 2020, with the US government saying the club was in the control of a man 'responsible for extrajudicial killing, torture, or other gross violations of internationally recognized human rights'. Envigado getting sanctioned was a big deal and the club therefore lost sponsors. This is why the club's shirt from 2014 to 2018 went sponsor-free, as I spotted on some of the replica-clad supporters around me in the stadium. While Barcelona's sponsorless shirts were a symbol of virtue, in Envigado it was quite the opposite. The sanctions were lifted in 2018 after the team was sold, and so newer replica shirts in the crowd around me featured sponsors. From the shirt with the gangster's face, to the shirts with no sponsor because of sanctions, to the newer more conventional shirts, Envigado's shirts tell the story of Colombian football's proximity to violence and crime.

Crime and football are intertwined all over the world. There are three main reasons: money laundering, gambling and prestige. First, money laundering, the 'washing' of cash stained by association with organised crime to make it appear legitimate to the authorities. This has long been a staple of any criminal enterprise. At a low level, this can mean street drug dealers running barber shops or convenience stores, turning banknotes and coins into electronic money. Businesses can inflate their profits, and provide a receipt if the tax man asks how a criminal bought a new house or expensive new car. 'Drug dealers are the only people who want to pay their taxes,' a Colombian football insider told me. At a higher level, it means more complex financial arrangements. The Medellín Cartel liked to use banks in the US and the Caribbean island of Curaçao to launder their billions. In 1981, Hernan Botero Moreno, owner of Atlético Nacional, was charged with laundering $57 million through a Florida bank, the profits from exporting vast quantities of cocaine.[21] He became the first cartel figure to be extradited to the US. When this happened, the Colombian football league was suspended, not to investigate wrongdoing but to mourn Botero's absence. Botero remained in jail in the US until 2002 before returning to Colombia, where he died in 2016. Owning a football club has long been an excellent way to launder money. At a lower level, a football match sees lots of cash change hands, on the gate and at the bars and snack booths. This is easy to inflate to the taxman, especially in places where cash is king and official attendances are unreliable. Cash obtained through illicit means can be easily 'washed' through the tills. Football also creates opportunities to wash dirty cash on a bigger scale. With the growth in the number of international transfers, and the skyrocketing sums of television and sponsorship money sloshing around the industry, more and more people are involved in a transfer – managers, families, owners, agents, sponsors and even companies owning players. Criminal activity can be concealed in this complexity, particularly as cash often flows between countries, making it harder for authorities to track. In 2013, the Italian tax authorities raided forty clubs while investigating potential money laundering and tax evasion in the sale of players.[22]

Second, criminals are attracted to football because of the opportunity to make money through gambling, most obviously in the form of match-fixing. The most dramatic recent example of this was the Calciopoli scandal in the mid-2000s in which senior Italian football figures were revealed to be pressuring referees. Juventus, the country's most decorated club, were stripped of multiple titles and relegated to Serie B.

The third reason criminals are attracted to football is prestige. A 1990 *LA Times* special report investigated the links between drug cartels and football in Colombia: 'It has been suggested that the cartels became active in soccer to launder money. But, considering the relatively small sums of dollars involved in the sport, it is more likely that they did it for sporting – and betting – reasons. It is one way for the cartels to compete for superiority without turning Uzis against each other.'[23] Criminals around the world enjoy owning football clubs to boost their profile and make themselves popular. In some cases this can be seen as a form of security – when considering whether to wipe out a rival, it may give room for pause if that person is famous in the sporting world rather than just another anonymous businessman. '(Pablo Escobar) doesn't just wash his money through Atlético Nacional,' writes David Arrowsmith in *Narcoball*. 'He invests in the club. This is his city, and his team. These are his people. Like a Roman Emperor, proclaiming bread and circuses, he will bring them glory, and they will love him for it.'

This book spends a lot of time looking at how the riches stemming from a valuable natural resource can upend the world of sport, be it gas in Qatar, oil in Newcastle, or cocaine at Atlético Nacional. For Italian club Parma, it was milk. Milk and fraud. In 1961, Calisto Tanzi, a businessman in the northern Italian city, inherited his family company which sold the famous Parma ham the region is renowned for. It grew after specialising in dairy, exploding in the 1980s while selling produce around the world. Just after the millennium, Parmalat had more than 36,000 employees globally and controlled more than half of the dairy market in Italy. In 1991, Tanzi, now rich beyond his wildest dreams, bought his local club AC Parma who had just been promoted to Serie A for the first time. The club won the Coppa Italia the following year.

Parma's rise coincided with a golden era for Italian football as the club became one of the vaunted 'seven sisters' alongside Juventus, AC Milan, Internazionale, AS Roma, Lazio and Fiorentina. From the mid-1990s onwards, Italy was where the best players in the world wanted to play and was an early example of a club football competition attracting global interest. I am slightly too young to remember *Football Italia*, which appeared on the UK's Channel 4 between 1992 and 2002, but to a generation of English football fans it was their weekly glimpse of the game beyond domestic shores. Its host James Richardson, now of the *Totally Football Show* podcast, still holds cult-like status.

Football writer David Goldblatt says two years are often given as the birth of modern football. One is 1992, when the Premier League was born. The other is 1995, when the 'Bosman ruling' enabled players to move freely between clubs in Europe when their contracts ended, making players more powerful and the game ever less bound by national borders. 'Both dates have their virtues, and rightly make globalisation and economics a marker of the modern game,' says Goldblatt. 'But in so doing, they obscure the enduring and pervasive importance of politics, populism and television in the transformation of European football, and in this field there is only one person, one place and one date to start with: Silvio Berlusconi, Italy, 1986.'[24] That was the year the wealthy media mogul, who would later become Italy's prime minister, bought AC Milan, announcing the takeover by landing a helicopter at the club's training ground while a speaker system blared out Wagner's 'Ride of the Valkyries'. 'In this he demonstrated his fidelity to the core truth of the modern game, and perhaps his only unwavering belief other than in his own magnificence: that football is a televised spectacle.'

Serie A in the 1990s was glamorous, commercial and looked great on TV compared to other leagues. Parma was at the heart of all this. The club's home shirt is traditionally white with a black cross. However, when shirt sponsors were introduced in the 1990s, Parma switched to *gialloblu*, yellow-and-blue, the colours of the city of Parma, for home shirts because it was tricky to incorporate a sponsor into the black cross design given the technology available at the time. These days technology is not an issue and Parma play in white-and-black at home, but the yellow and blue of the club's glory era is most likely what immediately comes to mind when people think of Parma, helped by this colour combination being unusual in European football. That *gialloblu* shirt is an iconic symbol of the era, alongside its sponsor, Parmalat, with its accompanying flower logo. A quick glance at Parma's all-time honours list makes clear that their own golden age coincided with that of Serie A. The club won the Coppa Italia three times between 1992 and 2002, and in the same period won the UEFA Cup as well as a Supercoppa Italiana, European Cup Winners' Cup and a European Super Cup. Parma had not won anything of note before nor have they since those glory days. The team was packed with players who would go on to become household names in Italy and beyond, including local star Gianluigi Buffon, one of the greatest goalkeepers of all time who would finish his career with a couple of seasons at Parma before retiring in 2023. He and another ex-Parma man, Fabio Cannavaro, would be the two key reasons for Italy's 2006 World Cup triumph. Peak Parma also had Gianfranco Zola, who would go on to star in the Premier League for Chelsea, Argentinian superstars Hernán Crespo and Juan Sebastián Verón, as well as Frenchman Lilian Thuram who would win the World Cup and European Championships while a Parma player.

The Dark Heart of Italy, a book by British author Tobias Jones, is full of acute observations. For example, Jones argues that British and Italian society, and British and Italian football, mirror each other in a curious way. Italians are known for their explosive tempers and noisy arguments, but the game they call *calcio* has the opposite character. The stereotypical Italian match is a battle of intricate tactics and well-organised defences. It is a far cry from the physical blood and thunder of the English game, an unlikely fit for a people known for being reserved and polite to the point of awkwardness.[25]

Jones lives in Parma and has long been a fan of the team whose 1990s glory was propelled by the dairy company still spotted on retro shirts in Parma and beyond. 'The fact that the sponsor contained the name of the city and the team made it seem not like an extraneous money-provider but as part of the squad,' he told me, rattling off a list of brilliant players who wore the shirt, with Tomas Brolin, Faustino Asprilla and Enrico Chiesa joining those named above. 'It was also a phase in the city's development that was called the years of "Parma da bere", literally "drinkable Parma". The city was rich, slick, stylish, there were international companies, but also an earthiness about the place, as you would expect from an economy largely built on pigs and cheese – Parma ham and Parmesan cheese. The nightlife was glitzy. It was an amazing time to be in the city.'

But it did not last. Corporate bankruptcies can seem a complex topic with a bewildering array of jargon, but the essence of the Parmalat fraud is not too hard to grasp. Bosses lied about how much money the company was making. When the company's financial performance started slipping in 1990, management tried to cover up the problems rather than fix them, embarking on a course of elaborate skullduggery such as boosting reported revenue through fake transactions, using these fake transactions as collateral to borrow more money, and hiding the debt from investors.[26] A warning sign came in March 2003 when Parmalat produced a forged verification letter from Bank of America, submitting it to an auditor as proof for €4 billion in cash that did not exist after faking the signature of a bank employee.[27] In December of that year, the scam began to unravel when Parmalat missed a payment, sending the share price close to zero. American regulators then went after the company, which was driven to bankruptcy.

Parmalat's origins are as a humble family-run company but its name is now synonymous with fraud on an epic scale. The overall size of the financial black hole was estimated at €14 billion.[28] Parmalat remains Europe's biggest ever bankruptcy, the continent's version of Enron, the US oil company that imploded in the 1990s. In some ways, it proved a precursor to the late-2000s financial crisis in the way that complex financial products concealed a deep flaw in the underlying business model.

Parma wasn't the only club sponsored by Parmalat. In the eighties and nineties the company had sponsorship deals with Real Madrid, Benfica and Marseille, as well as several South American clubs including Boca Juniors – the twilight of Diego Maradona's career was spent sporting the Parmalat logo. Perhaps most significant was Parmalat's deal with Palmeiras in Brazil, which helped turn the club into Brazil's richest, winning multiple titles with superstars like Roberto Carlos and Rivaldo.

Back on the pitch, Parma went into administration in 2003, but found a loophole which meant they could continue playing in Serie A with a slight name change. AC Parma became FC Parma and remarkably reached the UEFA Cup semi-final in this era of chaos.[29] The club was sold to a local businessman in 2007, which did not go well as the club were relegated soon after. Parma had some success in the years after that, finishing sixth in Serie A in

2014, but the following year finally went bankrupt amid mounting debts and unpaid salaries. Administrators ended up putting the trophies from the club's golden era up for sale, but the club were allowed to keep them after a deal was reached. After liquidation, Parma were refounded in Italy's fourth tier and secured three straight promotions to return to the top flight in 2018. The club has been yo-yoing between Serie A and Serie B ever since.

Post-Parmalat, the club's death and rebirth has seen it cycle through a range of local sponsors which generally nod to northern Italy's status as a consumer goods powerhouse. These have included coffee brand Gimoka, vacuum cleaner manufacturer Folletto and sailing wear company Navigare, the club's first sponsor after the 2015 rebirth. Later logos have included Cetilar, a cream for sore joints, and Prometeon who makes tyres, tapping into a proud Italian football tradition – one of the longest-running sponsorship deals in football history is Inter Milan's with Pirelli tyres, running from 1995 to 2021. (This doesn't come close to the longest-running in history, an honour going to Chilean third division side Rangers de Talca who have partnered with local food company PF since 1977.) The bankruptcy is becoming a distant memory for Parma fans. But remarkably, elsewhere in the world there is still a club sponsored by Parmalat.

Atletico Lusaka are a club based in the Zambian capital. Scrolling through their Facebook page reveals an unlikely visitor. FIFA president Gianni Infantino is pictured visiting the club's training ground in June 2024, the day before he was in Munich for the opening game of Euro 2024 to watch hosts Germany beat Scotland 4–1.[30] Infantino is a man on the move. In the days prior to this, he visited Malawi and South Sudan. FIFA's 'one member one vote' system means there is plenty to be gained from schmoozing footballing minnows, who get as much say in the vote for the

FIFA president as Brazil or Argentina, England or Germany. For its proponents, this system is democratic and helps grow the game without established powers dominating. To others it gives too much power to those who run the game in small countries, people like Jack Warner, the 'king of football' in his native Trinidad and Tobago, who rose through FIFA's ranks before being indicted for 'wire fraud, racketeering and money laundering' by the US government.[31] There is no suggestion there was anything untoward about Infantino's trip to the Zambian capital, though it was an unusual place for him to be visiting in such a big month for world football.

Scrolling through Atletico Lusaka's social media throws up another unexpected sight – the Parmalat logo. Bizarrely, although it is associated with Europe's biggest-ever corporate bankruptcy and Parma's rise and fall, the brand name lived on. It turns out the company is no longer run from Italy but is now a subsidiary of the French dairy giant Lactalis and has a global presence, with Zambia viewed as a growth market for its dairy products. I typed out some of this book from a hotel room in Cape Town in South Africa. As I was writing, I noticed that next to the kettle on my desk, alongside Nescafé sachets, teabags and packs of sugar, were little cardboard containers of milk. These carried the logos of Parmalat, with the same flower that appeared on those Parma shirts in the 1990s. The small print of the side said the milk was made by Parmalat South Africa in the nearby town of Stellenbosch. In Africa, Parmalat lives on in the footballing present, not just as nostalgia for a footballing past. That nostalgia is very strong, as I discovered when I thought I might buy a Parma shirt to celebrate finishing this chapter, but found out those authentic 1990s Parma shirts cost £150 or more. Maybe not.

The shirt is instantly recognisable among men of a certain age and is perhaps the ultimate 1990s nostalgia shirt in that it celebrates a team whose success is almost entirely concentrated in that decade. But the shirt also represents high-level corporate crime, a fraud that remains inseparable from the city and club that bore the Parmalat logo for so long. Like the Colombian club shirt with its little picture of a gangster's face, you don't have to scratch hard at football's surface to find links to criminality. The world's most popular sport often provides a way for offenders to launder money, or cover themselves in sporting glory, to distract from the seriousness of their crimes.

3

THE GLOBAL GAMBLE

FC Goa & Nottingham Forest

'Seventy-four per cent said they tend to lose money on traditional gambling. Two per cent said they tended to lose money with Football Index.'
  Customer survey posted on the Football Index website[1]

I had always wanted to visit India and got the opportunity in March 2023 when I pitched to *The Athletic* that I should cover the final of the Indian Super League (ISL), the country's pre-eminent football tournament, as part of a series on the world's most popular sport in the world's most populated country, with India having recently overtaken China. Football has long taken a back seat in the country compared to cricket, virtually a national religion, making India relatively unusual as a large country where football is far from being the dominant sport – the USA is another.

European football, especially the Premier League, is booming in popularity in India, as I discovered when I spent an evening with the Mumbai supporters' clubs of Arsenal and Manchester United. But I was mainly here for the ISL, not to be confused with the Indian Premier League or IPL, the short-form cricket league that runs for six weeks every spring and that's now one of the most valuable sports leagues in the world, alongside the Premier League and the NFL. The ISL is a comparatively low-key affair and has an unusual format. The league season culminates in a mini tournament where the top six compete to reach the ISL final. The team that comfortably won the league, Mumbai City, will play no part in the final because they were surprisingly beaten in the play-offs by Bengaluru FC, who will play ATK Mohun Bagan in the final. ISL aficionados say that the ISL Shield, the prize for winning the league, is a bigger accolade. But it doesn't have the razzmatazz of the final, which is taking place in Goa in India's tropical south.

Goa is unusual in a country that is 80 per cent Hindu with the remainder mostly Muslim. This particular region has a large Christian population, owing to its Portuguese colonial history. Little wooden churches and shrines to Jesus Christ and the Virgin Mary can be seen all along the crowded streets around the Pandit Jawaharlal Nehru Stadium as mopeds whizz past, many riders wearing the shirts of teams like Real Madrid, Manchester City and Liverpool. (Liverpool's red shirts tell quite a story, too. For many years, they had a little '96' on their collars to commemorate the 96 fans killed at the Hillsborough Stadium disaster in 1989. In 2021, Andrew Devine died of the injuries he suffered that day, so the following season, 96 became 97 on the shirts.) On the morning before the final in Goa, I visited some of the sports shops surrounding the stadium and thumbed through the replica shirts and tracksuits available for about a tenth of the price they cost in the UK. I bought a fetching yellow-and-black Borussia Dortmund shirt for $10, which had convincing Puma tags. The shirt retails for around twelve times that online from the UK, but when I got home, I realised the scratchy material suggests it is a counterfeit. After a few washes the logo of the sponsor, German telecoms firm 1+1, started peeling off.

After some fish thalis and an early night, it was matchday.

Ahead of big games in Europe, stadiums are under a strictly policed lockdown, but in Goa I could freely wander in. The stadium was originally built to host cricket, not ideal because a circular cricket field is roughly twice the size of a rectangular football pitch, meaning huge spaces between the touchlines and the crowd, not conducive to a good atmosphere. Before the game, I spent some time chatting to fans of Bengaluru FC, based in India's tech capital. Their star player is Sunil Chhetri, a veteran Indian striker who has scored more international goals than any active player at the time aside from Lionel Messi and Cristiano Ronaldo. Their manager is English stalwart Simon Grayson, who masterminded a ten-game winning streak to reach the final. 'He has turned this season around for us,' says Srinivas Jayaram, who flew into Goa with a group of fellow Bengaluru supporters that morning. 'We were bottom at the turn of the year.' I noticed that lots of Indian football supporters, many of them fans of the Premier League as well as local Indian sides, peppered their speech with the sort of Anglicisms I am used to hearing in post-match press conferences in England: '[Grayson] has done a great job with the lads,' said one.[2]

One of the group had a plastic bag filled with bottles of beer and whisky for drinking after the final whistle, whatever the outcome. Before the game, excitement was building around the stadium with rival supporters happily mingling as European pop music blasted out over huge speakers in the fan zone beside the stadium. There was a handful of foreign tourists, but the vast majority of fans were Indian. Some were local Goans, while others had travelled from Bengaluru, rubbing shoulders with fans of ATK Mohun Bagan, a team who come from India's football hotbed of Kolkata, where an Indian side famously beat a British Army team in 1911. The match was a key moment on India's journey to independence as it proved that Indians were no less capable than their colonial rulers.

I took my seat in Goa's stadium in the rudimentary press section. I was the only foreign journalist. All around me, fans held banners and sung songs referencing specific players, with dhol drums giving things a more rhythmic quality than I was used to hearing in England. However, only half the seats were filled and the cricket pitch dimensions meant noise from the opposite stand faded away before it reached the pitch. The big talking point at kick-off was the team's star player Sunil Chhetri, now in the twilight of his career, who would begin the game on the Bengaluru bench. He was called upon sooner than expected after an injury to young forward Sivasakthi Narayanan in the fourth minute. His side quickly went behind, but he scored a penalty to tie the game just before half-time. After ninety minutes, the score was 2–2, with Australian forward Dimitri Petratos – something of an anomaly as a foreigner in the Indian Super League – scoring both of ATK Mohun Bagan's goals. The game ended up going to penalties, and the Kolkata team won 4–3. Fireworks and ticker tape lit up the darkening sky as the team in green celebrated their victory.

I have been to many football matches but can safely say I have never seen a club rename themselves after the full-time whistle. But that was what happened, as ATK Mohun Bagan's owner, Sanjiv Goenka, announced on the pitch following the trophy ceremony that the club would ditch the 'ATK' from their name and henceforth be known as Mohun Bagan Super Giant. Fans had been campaigning to have ATK removed ever since a controversial merger in 2020. 'It's like winning two trophies in a single match,' a Mohun Bagan fan called Dave told me on the humid streets of Goa after the match as he waits to applaud his heroes leaving the stadium by coach. 'ATK is no more. It is Mohun Bagan. Mohun Bagan was there, Mohun Bagan is here, and Mohun Bagan will be there forever,' yelled Dave, poetically.

As for Bengaluru, thousands of blue-clad fans stayed late after the final whistle to applaud their team for reaching the final, many singing Simon Grayson's name. In the press conference after the game, I spoke to Grayson. 'Losing the final was frustrating, obviously it was, but I'm really proud of what we did.' In a later interview he told me that going from England's lower leagues to the Indian Super League had been quite a culture shock, with the scale of the traffic and the humid temperatures taking a while to get used to, but he was bullish on the future of football in this rare part of the world where the game still has plenty of room to grow.[3] Many fans streaming away into the night were locals, who snapped up their tickets for as little as £2, and some wore the bright-orange shirts of their team FC Goa. They came seventh in the eleven-team league and missed out on the playoffs. Lots were branded with a sponsor logo that is both familiar and unfamiliar to me: Parimatch News.

In my investigations into Premier League sponsors, the name Parimatch came up a fair bit. The company has had deals with Chelsea, Newcastle United and Leicester City. While most Premier League gambling sponsors can be traced back to East Asia, Parimatch is different, having Ukrainian origins while being headquartered in Cyprus. Parimatch 'News' was a mystery to me, though.

All became clearer when I googled the name after getting back to my hotel room. This led to a 'sports news' website with lots of generic content, mainly about cricket and football. It did not look like a regular news site. Many of the stories on the homepage were months out of date and a closer look at the text of some of the clunkily written articles made it clear something odd was going on. A bit of extra research, while battling to keep my eyes open through the jet lag, revealed that many of the articles were shoddily rewritten versions of other articles from legitimate news websites like ESPN, the *Sun* and the *Daily Mail*. The site did not appear to carry advertising nor have a paywall encouraging people to subscribe, so it was unclear how it made any money. The 'About Us' page said the site carries 'the most up-to-date news from the world of sports'. A staff list showed a dozen or so Indian writers who supposedly specialise in various sports. The editor of the site was listed as Pavel Rabtsevich. His short biography contained spelling mistakes like 'newspappers' and 'Editor-in-Cheif', not reassuring for someone whose job is to edit.[4] A look at Rabtsevich's LinkedIn page makes no mention of any journalistic experience at all, stating that the graduate of Belarusian State University is a product manager at Parimatch with 'extensive expertise spanning over six years in the rapidly evolving crypto and blockchain landscape'.

The site does not in fact mention gambling at all, despite being branded identically to the gambling company paying huge sums to advertise in English football. India – unlike the UK and most other European countries – has strict laws on gambling advertising. Simply put, it is banned, like gambling more broadly across the country. Nevertheless, gambling in India is hugely popular, it is just carried out via websites based in other countries. 'Parimatch News' is a way to advertise the gambling company Parimatch, while having the plausible deniability that the advert carried on FC Goa's shirts is for a news website not a gambling company, despite that being completely implausible after five minutes of online research.

Anirudh Thakur is an economist based in Mumbai and an expert in India's booming gambling industry. He told me that the country is sometimes called a 'grey market', which means that while formal gambling-related activities are generally banned and major gambling sites are not based in the country, in many areas there is little regulation at all, so online gambling is effectively legal for users. One example is in fantasy cricket games, somewhat like football's Fantasy Premier League but with the opportunity to buy 'tokens' for real cash, making it closer to gambling. An Indian court ruled these games can't be defined as gambling because they are primarily about skill rather than luck – the reverse being the core definition of gambling. Any fantasy game, and indeed betting on sport in general, combines the two.

India has long been a low-income country where adverts sell for far less than in places like the UK and USA. This is all changing quickly, though. Economist Thakur explains that the popularity of fantasy games is a key part of the rise of the IPL cricket league, with fans discussing which players have accumulated points and who they should substitute in and out of their team. Users say that fantasy games make them engaged in matches they wouldn't ordinarily follow closely. This can be true for conventional sports gambling too. Sky Bet, the sponsor of the three divisions below the Premier League known as the English Football League, controversially once used the slogan: 'It matters more when there's money on it.' This was condemned as irresponsible and is no longer used, but for many the slogan rings true.

Thakur says gambling in India had 'very bad' connotations until recently. 'People usually thought that bookmakers and people who bet on sports were people who had links to the underworld and gangs and mafia and things like that,' he said. 'I think because of the popularity of the IPL, it has more approval. It's more official-looking and safe. My sense is that the acceptability in terms of the general public is increasing.' His research specialises in so-called 'dark patterns' through which gambling platforms allegedly manipulate consumers into spending money. 'It's designed to be addictive ... There are very few regulations ... Because of the lack of government intervention in this area, I think there is a lot going on that we don't even know about.' In other parts of the world, gambling is increasingly being viewed through the lens of public health.

Indian gambling laws differ greatly by state but it is straightforwardly illegal for a foreign gambling firm to set up shop physically in India and advertise to locals directly. Yet it is not illegal for Parimatch, a gambling firm based in Cyprus, to pay an Indian football club to advertise a 'news' website, which provides a very basic form of news without any viable revenue stream and appears to exist simply to promote a betting website of the same name. A similar example is 'DafaNews', a main sponsor of the Pakistan Premier League, a cricket league in a Muslim country where betting firms are strictly banned. However, indirect advertising for the offshore bookmaker Dafabet via DafaNews, using exactly the same colour scheme and logo, is a big cash driver for the league.

Regulating online gambling is tricky because a national government only has the jurisdiction to set and enforce laws within its own borders. In the dizzyingly complex and internationalised world of gambling, firms and users span borders to serve and provide huge global demand, including in countries where gambling is banned. Many countries are now in the process of formalising and regulating their gambling industries, making the calculation that gambling is always going to happen, so it's better to keep a watchful eye and bank the tax revenue rather than let it go on behind closed doors. Brazil, for example, has explored the legalisation of gambling, with furious lobbying from the world's biggest gambling companies who want a foothold in this potentially huge market, but there are concerns too many people are getting into debt.[5]

The UK has the richest and most glamorous football league in the world, and has also been Patient Zero when it comes to online gambling liberalisation. The Gambling Act came into force in 2007, just months before the iPhone was released and changed the world – and the world of gambling – forever. Rob Davies is a journalist at the *Guardian* who specialises in gambling. He has written an excellent book called *Jackpot* (you can listen to the two of us discussing it on an episode of *Intelligence Squared* podcast released in 2022). Davies explains how the debates over the Gambling Act barely mentioned the internet or the smartphone:

> In the space of a few short years, a business rooted in the time-honoured traditions of the turf-scented racetrack and the cinematic glitz of the casino table had metamorphosed into something much larger and more pervasive. It had become a relentless automaton programmed to separate punters from their money by any means, at any cost.[6]

The new law fired the starting pistol on a fiercely competitive race as firms battled for a slice of a growing pie. Football was key to this. In the 2005–06 Premier League season just one shirt – Middlesbrough's – was sponsored by a gambling company. By 2019–20, half of the league's twenty clubs carried a gambling sponsor and seventeen out of twenty-four in the Championship, the division below. Football helped bring gambling into mainstream society, rather than it being an activity pursued at the casino or racetrack. Now people could gamble in the pub, in the stadium or sitting at home on the sofa.

These days in the UK, gambling is less associated with James Bond-type high rollers and has somewhat grubby and unglamorous connotations, associated with run-down high-street shops and screenshots of smartphone apps sent in WhatsApp groups. That is not to say gambling is all bad. I have enjoyed the odd accumulator bet in my time, and the industry supports jobs and pays substantial amounts of tax. But in the UK, the language is now all about safety, responsibility and public health, as there is growing public awareness of how gambling can be associated with poverty, mental illness and even suicide. Adverts carry messages like 'Time to think' and 'When the fun stops, stop'. UK politicians have long been trying to write new gambling laws that will be more restrictive than what came before, although there is endless wrangling and lobbying over the details.

In other parts of the world, though, the trend is moving in the opposite direction. In 2024, I was in New York for work – covering November's presidential election – and watched quite a bit of US sports TV. ESPN's *Daily Wager* programme features glamorous hosts discussing what bets are available for the upcoming games and speculating on what they themselves might bet on. Sports betting is booming in the US after a 2018 Supreme Court decision which struck down an effective ban. In the UK gambling ads pervade everything in football, despite some modest concessions such as the 'whistle-to-whistle' ban in which there are no adverts for gambling firms shown on TV between kick-off and full-time. Research by academics Rebecca Cassidy and Niko Ovenden has found that, while concern about advertising of gambling in football has focused on commercial TV channels, public broadcast of football highlights, which appear on domestic TV and YouTube and do not include advertising breaks, 'are almost saturated with gambling and other risky product advertising'.[7] Even if you do not see them in the formal advertising breaks on TV, you will see them in the billboards around the ground, and on the players' shirts.

FC Goa and their bright-orange shirt with Parimatch News

on the front of it shows the extent to which online gambling is internationalised, even reaching countries where the product is formally restricted. Another shirt that helps us explain the world of gambling is that of Nottingham Forest. The 'Garibaldi red' shirt of the East Midlands club, who were back-to-back champions of Europe under Brian Clough in 1979 and 1980, explains how the UK, the country which embraced online gambling laws earlier than practically any other, is now tightening its grip on gambling while much of the rest of the world is moving in the other direction. Perhaps it's cheating to use multiple shirts from the same club as one of my twenty-two shirts that explain the world but, taken as a collective, Nottingham Forest shirts between 2017 and 2024 tell us a lot.

As an Aston Villa fan with many friends who support Liverpool, my team's 7–2 win over theirs in October 2020 should be one of my all-time favourite football memories. But it somehow doesn't quite feel like it really happened as the match took place in an empty Villa Park, when Covid restrictions meant games were played behind closed doors, with fans watching from their homes rather than the stadium or the pub. In the highlights of that masterclass from Jack Grealish and Ollie Watkins, the stands were empty, and the stadium echoed with the isolated shouts of coaching staff rather than the roar of the home crowd.

During that strange period in 2020 and 2021, with little else going on, lots of football to watch but no one to discuss it with in person, I began paying closer attention to the billboards around the grounds and to the shirts worn by players. I became intrigued by the fact that not only were lots of gambling companies being advertised, but also that these firms were rarely ones I was familiar with in the UK. Instead, Premier League sponsors were often companies I had never heard of outside football, with many adverts written in Chinese Mandarin. If these companies weren't advertising to UK gamblers, I wondered, why were they paying millions of pounds to advertise on Premier League shirts and billboards? I spent months trying to answer this question, a quest which culminated in two major investigations which would go on to be cited in Parliament and nominated for a handful of awards.

An unusual friendly match in July 2019, when Wolverhampton Wanderers beat Newcastle United 4–0 in the Chinese city of Nanjing, provides a window into this sometimes bewildering topic. Premier League clubs often travel to far-flung places during pre-season to try to build their international fanbases. Both clubs' usual shirts featured advertising for Asian gambling companies, with writing in Chinese Mandarin. But awkwardly, gambling is illegal in China despite the practice having a rich history and being embedded in Chinese culture, with nearby countries like Cambodia and Myanmar hosting resorts which cater to Chinese gamblers in person and online. But domestically, as Article 303 of the country's Criminal Law makes clear, 'Whoever, for the purpose of profit, assembles a crowd to engage in gambling, establishes a place for gambling or makes gambling his profession shall be sentenced to fixed-term imprisonment of not more than three years.'[8] A 2005 Supreme Court interpretation declared that the 'purpose of reaping profits' is what defines whether gambling activity is subject to criminal law, rather than, for example, private bets between individuals over a card game. The interpretation also makes clear that people who set up online gambling websites will be regarded as 'opening gambling houses' and sentenced to prison. It couldn't be clearer – running gambling firms is illegal in China.

Because of all this, both Wolves and Newcastle wore unique, specially branded shirts. Newcastle replaced Fun88, a gambling website that had sponsored them for many years, with Chinese characters simply saying 'National Sports App'. It was never made clear what this app was. Wolves replaced their gambling sponsor ManBetX with an advert for Fosun, the Chinese industrial conglomerate that owns the Midlands club and that has nothing to do with betting.[9]

While running a gambling firm *in* China is illegal, there are no barriers to stop people running a gambling firm elsewhere, often the Philippines or Vietnam. These websites can then be marketed to Chinese people watching on TV, via Premier League football shirts, or on billboards in English stadiums. The advertisers cannot reach Chinese consumers in ways that would interact with the Chinese legal system, such as on Chinese TV channels or in newspapers and magazines published there, but they can do it via English football clubs, through a web of companies spanning international borders. 'What a lot of football fans won't understand is how little interest most of these firms have in the UK market and in UK bettors,' Alun Bowden, head of European markets at US research firm Eilers & Krejcik Gaming, told me back in 2021. 'It's just about trying to get brand exposure in Asian markets, where gambling advertising is banned or heavily restricted. It's a game within a game, and you're not playing.'[10]

Helping to facilitate this strange situation is a system known as 'white-labelling'. The UK Gambling Commission, which regulates the country's betting industry, describes this as the practice of setting up a website designed to 'look and feel like a company or brand, but the contents and services provided on the website are operated and managed by a licensed gambling company ... this is typically a commercial arrangement where both parties share any profit from the website.' By this method, companies based in light-touch jurisdictions, such as the Isle of Man and Malta, help Asia-based gambling websites gain legal access to the UK market, and they appear on Premier League shirts. Effectively this means there are two websites under the same name. There is the 'white-label' version of Fun88, a rudimentary operation run from an office in the Isle of Man. Then there is the actual version in Asia being advertised to consumers watching on TV, which UK fans will never see.

What this means is that when a UK-based football fan looks up a company like Fun88 out of curiosity, a website will appear which functions as a gambling website, and users can sign up and make bets which will pay out if they win. However, looking at the small print at the bottom makes clear this is all a mirage: 'Fun88 is powered by TGP Europe Ltd of 22A Castle Street, Douglas, Isle of Man, IM1 2EZ. TGP Europe Limited is licensed and regulated in Great Britain by the Gambling Commission under account number 38898.' This says the website is not run by Fun88 at all, it is run by a separate company which is on the Isle of Man, a 'crown dependency' of the United Kingdom which has its own legal system, making it far harder to scrutinise.

The company Fun88, which has also sponsored billboards inside the Tottenham Hotspur Stadium, is paying a separate company called TGP Europe, which is based in a tiny office on the Isle of Man, to run its website. The website is virtually identical to that of Yabo Sports, which has had deals with Manchester United and Leicester City, as well as countless other gambling sites. It is not made clear where the *actual* gambling companies, the ones on the billboards, are based or who runs them. I have asked the clubs and contacted the email address given on these placeholder websites (often the same email address for a handful of intermediary companies like TGP Europe) countless times. No response ever comes. The Gambling Commission has admitted to 'concern' that some white-label websites may not have effective anti-money-laundering controls or carry out 'sufficient due diligence' on websites to ensure there are no 'links to criminal activity'.[11] Simply put, nobody has any idea who is running these companies. In one case, a club official insisted that their sponsor was based on the Isle of Man and run by a local, despite being presented with clear evidence that the reality lay further to the east. The issue seemed to be ignorance rather than intentional deceit – the official clearly had no idea who was paying millions of pounds to sponsor his club.

One investigation led me down a particularly weird rabbit hole which showed me how sponsors use fake social media profiles to get sponsorship deals. In 2021, a website called Leyu Sports signed a deal with Chelsea who had recently been crowned champions of Europe. This deal was accompanied by a series of slick videos enthusiastically welcoming the club's new 'regional partner in Asia', which featured Chelsea players including César Azpilicueta, captain at the time, attempting to speak a few words of Chinese. The company's logo soon appeared on the billboards at Chelsea's Stamford Bridge stadium, accompanied by Chinese writing.[12] On LinkedIn a user called 'Anna MIC' wrote a post celebrating this deal, claiming it was brokered by her firm 'MIC Branding & Advertising' and tagging several members of Chelsea's commercial team in her message. Five Chelsea employees liked the post, indicating a direct link. Anna's profile picture showed an East Asian woman in her late twenties or early thirties.

A simple reverse image search, though, showed the picture was from a stock image library. On LinkedIn, 'Anna' frequently interacted with a colleague called 'Aaron Chan' who was also tagged in Chelsea's post. His profile picture was a picture of the Korean-American actor Daniel Henney, who has appeared in an *X-Men* film among other Hollywood hits. His representatives had previously warned of imposters using his photo for fraudulent purposes. I began asking questions by messaging the profiles, and 'Aaron Chan' was swiftly deleted, along with 'Anthony Shangkuan', a third 'employee' whose profile picture could be found in a stock image library beside the caption 'smiling Asian man using tablet computer'. This photo had also been used by an Indonesian dermatologist and a Filipino bank.

Even more bizarrely, the company all these employees claimed to work for – MIC Branding & Advertising in Dubai – did not appear in the United Arab Emirates register of businesses. Indeed, it had no online footprint whatsoever beyond these LinkedIn profiles. Weirdly, an official at another top European club told me their club had engaged with these people and noticed nothing untoward. And Chelsea employees were directly interacting with these people. But I was sure they did not exist. What seemed to be going on here was that a group of people from East Asia representing Leyu had approached Chelsea and had spoken to employees of the club over video calls. Their profile pictures looked similar enough that nobody from the clubs noticed anything unusual, but they were actually taken from public image depositories on the internet.

'There is a long history of pseudonyms and so on in grey- and black-market online gambling,' a knowledgeable insider told me. 'This helps those working in the area to evade Chinese clampdowns and avoid stringent checks on their sources of funding by gambling regulators.'[13] There have been multiple examples of Premier League clubs announcing gambling deals with people who appear not to exist, such as 'Kai Webb' of OB Sports, who signed a deal with Aston Villa, and 'Darren Wang' at i8.BET, who partnered with Everton.

Most baffling of all was 'Daniel Knox' of former Southampton sponsor LD Sports. He had an elaborate online biography as a

Chinese-American businessman who moved to the UK as a child and worked as a coach for Millwall FC, but none of these biographical details stood up to scrutiny – it appeared that Daniel Knox did not exist. It was all a charade to muddy the waters, a veneer of respectability on something that seemed very shady, and all part of the bigger game of enabling offshore website companies to advertise to Chinese gamblers by paying English football clubs, their logos appearing on Chinese TV screens despite the country's strict gambling ban.

You may be wondering what the harm is in all this. The UK has introduced relatively permissive gambling arrangements through successive elected governments. Is it really the job of the Premier League to enforce China's repressive laws? The problems lie not in the rights and wrongs of individuals choosing to gamble but in the story of who ultimately runs these websites. This is a question to which we often simply do not know the answer. The UK's embrace of the murky world of white-labelling enables companies to sponsor English football clubs without anybody knowing where the money comes from, raising serious concerns about organised crime and money laundering, something the UK Gambling Commission has admitted. Like so many others, Leyu Sports is also 'powered by' TGP Europe at that same address in Douglas on the Isle of Man. A look at this address on Google Street View shows a somewhat shabby-looking betting shop, part of the Joe Jennings chain on a modest high street. This is supposedly where multiple companies sponsoring clubs around Europe to the tune of hundreds of millions of pounds in total have all set up shop. Companies like TGP Europe and others take bets, pay out winners and interact with customers, despite the fact seemingly few people use this service. This is because the substantive business being advertised is based in Asia and means the Asian business can stay completely concealed from curious UK football fans who might happen to look up their club's new sponsor on Google.

The Gambling Commission says it carries out checks on white-labels, including the suitability of the company and its shareholders. But crucially this relates to the white-label operator – a couple of men on the Isle of Man – rather than the actual company being advertised far away in Asia. Nobody seems to know much about them at all. This includes the Premier League clubs that take their money, often dealing with intermediary brokers like SportQuake, a London-based agency who swiftly hung up the phone when I got through to a key person after they ignored lots of my emails. One senior figure at a Premier League team told me that clubs are 'between a rock and a hard place' because these deals ultimately do not break UK laws and provide desperately needed cash at a time when Premier League teams are in an arms race to spend more on players and wages without breaking increasingly strict Financial Fair Play (FFP) rules.[14] Raising money in other ways, such as raising ticket prices, faces a lot more backlash. Furthermore, using fake internet profiles on social media to discuss brands, while potentially unethical and deceptive to the public, is widespread and does not mean either the club or the white-label businesses have broken any UK domestic laws. 'White-labelling' in general is certainly not a breach of UK laws – on the contrary, laws actively facilitate the practice.

Dr James Noyes is a senior fellow of the Social Market Foundation think tank and one of Britain's leading experts on the gambling industry. 'Far too often, we have no real sense of the true ownership, source of wealth or consumer base of these so-called "white-label" gambling operators,' he told me, 'yet we see them everywhere on squad shirts and the sides of pitches.' Noyes wants white-label firms banned as the UK updates its gambling regulation. 'It is totally unacceptable that years after this problem was raised at the highest level with both the government and the regulator, we are still seeing serious concerns about the relationship between offshore gambling operators and English football clubs.'[15]

There have always been strong links between gambling and organised crime. Dutch academic Professor Toine Spapens explains why.[16] First, in countries where gambling activity is illegal, like China, crime groups spring up to meet the demand from consumers. Second, even where it is legal, organised crime groups often attempt to penetrate the industry because it provides opportunities to launder money and use the proceeds to fund other illegal activities. Think of the Italian-American Mafia in Atlantic City and Las Vegas. Third, criminals can make 'improper use' of legal forms of gambling, such as fixing sports matches, or otherwise conning legal gambling operators out of cash. Fourth, there is a link between gambling addiction and crime. Addicted gamblers may steal to fund their debts. Where gambling is legalised, such as in the UK, there is a degree of transparency around all this – there is no need to break the law to place a bet, and those facing gambling addiction can seek (arguably insufficient) medical and psychological help. But in China, the place where Premier League clubs are promoting betting websites via shirts and billboards, none of this is true, meaning the ultimate consequences are opaque. Doubtless, Premier League clubs are advertising to people who may get into trouble with the authorities as a consequence, and will receive no help at all if they are struggling mentally and financially. This is also the case in sub-Saharan Africa where online gambling is booming, as Rob Davies explains:

The use of smartphones is much more widespread than many people might expect of a continent that also suffers from so much poverty. In the absence of good national and international analogue communications infrastructure, mobile payments became normal even in rural, impoverished areas long before they caught on in so-called developed countries. This has made internet gambling easily accessible to hundreds of millions of potential new punters living in fast-growing economies where demographics skew towards younger cohorts with an appetite for risk.[17]

In 2020, Premier League club Everton ditched its deal with Kenyan gambling website Sportpesa amid worries about the effects of gambling in the country. Earlier that year, a delegation of African politicians had visited the UK Parliament to raise concerns about whether Premier League clubs were helping to drive gambling in Africa, with far less in place to help people than in the country where the clubs profiting from the advertising are based.[18]

Some excellent work in this area has been done by the investigative football news website Josimar, which in November 2023 published a deep dive into Kaiyun Sports, the company Nottingham Forest had signed up as a shirt sponsor a couple of months earlier.[19] Kaiyun had also had deals with some of the biggest clubs in Europe including Real Madrid, Chelsea and AC Milan, as well as with retired players, such as Wayne Rooney, Alessandro Del Piero and Filippo Inzaghi. Josimar revealed that Kaiyun was falsely claiming to be regulated by the Malta Gaming Authority and the government of the British Virgin Islands, as well as carrying the stamp of the UK's Remote Gambling Association, an organisation disbanded three years before Kaiyun was founded (so it says) in 2022. The Forest deal, announced at the start of the 2023–24

Premier League season, was accompanied by another one of those non-existent people – 'Byrne Howard' – who was also named in a Real Madrid announcement. This man has no online trace. When Premier League club Crystal Palace announced a deal with Kaiyun earlier the same year, they called him 'Brian Howard'. Like Byrne, Brian has no online trace either.

Kaiyun burst onto the scene in 2022, but Josimar's research makes clear the company is simply a rebranding of Yabo Sports, a similar Asian betting sponsor, which sponsored the likes of Manchester United, Leicester City and Bayern Munich, but suddenly disappeared when a group of 'high-school students from well-off families' reported to police in the Chinese province of Sichuan that they had lost money on the website, prompting investigators across the country to look into it.[20] Chinese law enforcement agents said they had found a 'large gambling group' operating on the mainland 'thanks to a network of 80,000 domestic agents who promoted the brand', taking bets from an estimated 5.6 million customers and generating a profit of $15.7 billion. Not turnover, but *profit*. There were hundreds of arrests, and a fall guy called Zhou was jailed for publishing football betting tips on the WeChat app. Kaiyun also ran a channel on a social media messaging app which featured pictures of naked women holding handwritten signs promoting the brand. 'The signs are not superimposed, meaning that women have been paid – or forced – to hold the signs,' Josimar wrote. The ethics of pornography, assuming everybody is a consenting adult, is a matter of opinion, but it is surely not a puritan's view that any link between this stuff and football is grubby.

There are also reported links between online gambling in East Asia and even more serious offences. Speaking generally rather than about any of the offshore websites named above, this may include money laundering, but also prostitution and human trafficking. Researchers from Play the Game, an initiative run by the Danish Institute for Sports Studies, have claimed there are links between Premier League sponsors and human trafficking in South East Asia. There have always been close ties between sex and gambling. While overtly sexualised advertising is banned in the UK, it is very common in many Asian countries. Gambling websites are frequently accompanied by sexualised photos of women, many of whom look very young, though there is no way of verifying their ages. This phenomenon hit the world of English football in 2021 when Norwich City, owned by TV chef Delia Smith and with a reputation as a clean-cut family club, signed a deal with gambling website BK8. Norwich fans quickly discovered the company was using seedy content to promote its services in Asia, including women in various states of undress, and a bizarre YouTube video in which women were performing mock sexual acts on hot dog sausages. It was all very embarrassing and the club swiftly ditched the deal.[21] BK8 subsequently said it had cleaned up its act and it signed up for the 2023–24 season on the even higher-profile shirt of Aston Villa (I didn't buy that one, even though it was the club's best season in decades). Clubs which have gambling sponsors tend to sell two different replica shirts: one with the sponsor for adults, and without it for children.

Another direct link between Premier League sponsors and illegal activity concerns a man called Alvin Chau. He was chief executive of the Suncity Group, one of the biggest gambling companies in East Asia, who made his money in Macau. The gambling hotspot off the coast of China turns over far more cash than Las Vegas by hosting junkets: trips organised for high rollers from mainland China to casinos in a territory where gambling is legal.[22] His group has deep commercial ties to many of the betting websites that sponsor Premier League teams, and it owned TGP Europe's parent company, TGP Holdings Ltd, thus enabling many offshore bookmakers to reach Premier League shirts via that Isle of Man company above a betting shop. In January 2023, he was sentenced to eighteen years in jail for more than 100 charges including 'organised crime and illegal gambling'.[23] Prosecutors accused him of creating and leading a criminal syndicate and said the government lost billions as a result. In 2022–23 almost half of Premier League shirt sponsors were 'powered by' TGP Europe, a company ultimately run by Chau.[24] The All-Party Parliamentary Group (APPG) for Gambling Harm declared that 'the reputational harm to the Premier League is considerable' and called for an inquiry.

It feels almost unfair to single out Nottingham Forest, because dubious gambling sponsors in the Premier League are so common, but the shirts of this most traditional of English clubs neatly tell the story of both gambling's relationship with football, and gambling's relationship with the world. Forest have two stars on their shirt because they are in the tiny elite group of clubs to have won more than one European Cup, but recent times have been tough. Following relegation in 1999, Forest spent twenty-three years outside the Premier League before promotion in 2022.

Going further back, just after their double European win in 1979 and 1980, Forest shirts were sponsored by local brewery Shipstones between 1984 and 1997, followed by Canadian beer firm Labatt's. After this, it was a decade of finance sponsors, mirroring Britain's liberalisation of the financial sector before the crash of 2008. First the logos of insurance company Pinnacle, then Capital One, a credit card company which briefly also sponsored England's League Cup. The first bookmaker sponsor in 2009 was Victor Chandler, one of the first bookmakers to realise the potential of online gambling.

Later, Forest were owned by the controversial Kuwaiti businessman Fawaz Al-Hasawi between 2012 and 2017 and for two of those seasons his surname appeared on the shirts as 'Fawaz Refrigeration & Air-Conditioning'. Then the gambling companies came back. First was 888, the company which had appeared on Middlesbrough's shirt in the mid-2000s when it was the only club in the top flight with a gambling sponsor. BetBright partnered with Forest for the 2018–19 season in a deal said to be the most 'significant front-of-shirt agreement in the club's history'.[25] The Irish company was sold to 888 in March 2019 in a move that sparked controversy because it said all outstanding bets would be voided, including season-long bets on the Premier League.

But that drama was a mere ripple compared to the Nottingham Forest gambling sponsor that would come next, one strikingly different to many others. In March 2021, I was meeting a friend on a Saturday afternoon in a London park during that bleak period in which the UK, like many other countries around the world, had severe restrictions on socialising because of Covid. Every time I checked my phone, I had another message. They all said the same thing: have you seen the news about Football Index?

Six months into my job at *The Athletic*, I was starting to carve out a niche reporting on the gambling industry and its ties to English football, having recently broken the story of how top-flight clubs facilitate illegal gambling in China. At the time, I was dimly aware of a website called Football Index through its prominence in football. The logo was a common sight on the side of London taxis and on public transport, as well as being relentlessly promoted on sports radio, particularly talkSPORT. It was also advertised on the shirts of Nottingham Forest and Queens Park Rangers, two clubs in England's second tier. I would soon be learning an awful lot more, as news was breaking that the company was imploding in real time, taking people's savings with it.

As a journalist, I never particularly enjoy publicly asking for help. It's always preferable to work quietly behind the scenes before dropping a story unannounced. But in this case, I had little choice. It was hard to figure out what exactly this website was or how it worked. I needed to speak to people affected. So, at 7.42 p.m. on that Saturday evening, I tweeted: 'Journalist looking into #footballindex. Keen to talk to anyone affected.' I have never experienced anything like it. Hundreds of replies and messages appeared within hours, with people perhaps more glued to social media than they might otherwise have been on a Saturday evening given the pandemic restrictions in place.

The messages were overwhelming, but I started to triage them, making note of the ones that seemed most interesting, or where the sender was willing to chat on the record. Some were shocking. One man, who I went on to speak to multiple times over the course of several months, had lost more than £200,000. Others had lost smaller sums but with more devastating consequences, such as a young man in Wales who had saved a few thousand pounds working his first-ever job after leaving school the previous autumn. Then, suddenly, it was all gone. 'It just completely tipped me over the edge,' he told me over the phone. 'So many emotions just built up, I finally admitted to myself that I needed help. I saw a helpline number and I rang it.' He was dreading telling his family and confided in me that he felt close to the brink in those dark hours and days. A key part of this story was shame. People found it hard to tell their loved ones that they had lost huge sums of money on a football gambling website. I wrote up some of these stories, while digging into what had gone on behind the scenes, and the response was massive, sparking several more investigations.[26]

When I first started looking into Football Index, it was tricky to determine exactly what it was. Was it a straightforward gambling website? Was it a game like Fantasy Premier League? Was it an investment product? It seemed like all these things and none of them. A popular radio advertisement for Football Index described it as 'a hugely popular stock market for football players ... customers can buy shares in players that rise and fall in value based on their performance on the pitch, and demand on the index'. The idea was essentially that just as shares in companies rise and fall in value based on their performance, the same could be true for footballers. Just as people who owned early shares in Facebook or Apple could later sell them at a huge profit, the same could be possible for those with a sharp footballing eye who could pluck out an unpolished youngster who would go on to conquer the world. The key idea was that if you bought a player share low and sold it high, you could make real money. Shares in players would also pay out regular cash 'dividends', just like real companies do, but based on metrics like how many goals they scored or the number of games they played, rather than based on how well a company is doing financially.

The flaw in the plan, obvious in hindsight but not at the time to the tens of thousands who put big sums into the platform, is that the whole idea was built on sand. A company's share price is a tangible thing, a piece of an actual entity which has revenues and costs, employees and profits. It is a piece of something that exists and is worth real money. But a Football Index share in a footballer is not. A share in Erling Haaland has no connection to the tangible, very valuable human being that is Erling Haaland. It is quite unlike shares in, say, Tesla or Google, which are simply little portions of those huge companies, which might go up or down in price, but nobody could dispute the fact they hold real value. As well as prices in virtual footballer shares dictated by how well players were performing in real life, the value was ultimately subject to the wider whims of the market. For example, a 'share' in Manchester United's Portuguese midfielder Bruno Fernandes plunged from £7.23 on that fateful Saturday morning in March 2021 to around £1 a few days later. This was not because Bruno Fernandes had a terrible injury or had fallen out of favour with his manager, but because the bottom fell out of the Football Index market. Players who held thousands of Bruno Fernandes 'shares' in their online portfolios effectively lost huge amounts of cash.

In my subsequent conversations with people who lost money on the site, many described how they were enticed by the idea, relentlessly pushed to them through misleading advertising, that they could make money based purely on their football knowledge, just like savvy financial investors can make money buying shares in companies that will rise in value. Football Index employees were invited on radio programmes to discuss the 'share price' and 'dividends' of real-life footballers, encouraging fans to use their knowledge of the game to make real cash.

All investments go up and down but for a long time Football Index shares seemed to only rise in value. The results of a customer survey posted to the Football Index user website, leaked to me in my off-the-record interviews with former employees in the weeks after the collapse, said just 2 per cent of users lost money on the platform, compared to 74 per cent for traditional gambling.[27] This was a figure familiar to former employees I spoke to who were tasked with promoting the product, as well as customers like Lewis Perry, who discovered the site in summer 2018. He told me he doubled his money in four months, so poured in more and more of his savings. It all turned to dust.

The 2 per cent figure does not make any sense. Whatever the

rights and wrongs of conventional gambling, the business model is straightforward. Many losers finance a smaller number of winners, and the difference between the two is the revenue the company uses to pay its employees, pay its taxes and bank any profits. The idea of only 2 per cent of users losing money was baffling and has led some critics to accuse Football Index of being a 'Ponzi scheme', named after the 1920s American conman who used money invested with him to pay early investors. His scheme collapsed when he couldn't attract enough new money to pay those who wanted to pull their cash out. It was clear in the days after the collapse that Football Index shared elements of this, the firm telling customers that while it 'had substantial cash reserves', it had sustained 'consistent and substantial losses due to very low deposit levels which depleted their reserves'.

That link between new deposits funding existing obligations is a classic sign of a Ponzi scheme, a description that a spokesperson for Football Index passionately denied to me back when it had a spokesperson, and before everyone involved vanished off the face of the earth including co-founders Mike Bohan and Adam Cole. A document presented by a group of industry experts to the Gambling Commission in January 2020 said the firm was a 'pyramid scheme' vulnerable to collapse, at a time when the company was booming, occupying two floors of expensive offices in Paddington in central London.[28]

The problems first arose when confidence in the platform was hit by the Covid pandemic when regular football matches, the events that drove interest in the platform and income to users through cash dividends based on players' real-world performances, were paused for several weeks. Amid this chaos, the company announced cash dividend payments would be slashed 'in order to ensure the long-term sustainability of the platform'. The footballer shares, with no inherent value whatsoever, duly plummeted as people attempted to pull their money out. The company was also accused of signalling that things were buoyant a few weeks earlier by 'minting' new shares at high prices, effectively sucking in more of users' cash before the looming crash.

While Football Index was ostensibly a gambling platform and was regulated by the UK Gambling Commission, many users saw it as something very different – a vehicle for financial investment. For example, I spoke to Daragh Corrigan, an Irishman who deposited £25,000 into Football Index and topped this up with a further £5,000 after his initial investment did well. His portfolio had crashed to a fraction of this when I spoke to him, one of the few to have lost money who was comfortable sharing his real name.[29] The vast majority of those who lost out preferred to stay anonymous, often because they were ashamed and embarrassed about telling their loved ones.

The dream of permanent profits might seem ludicrous to outsiders, especially now plenty of time has passed since Football Index collapsed and the site has become synonymous with regulatory failure and human misery. However, users I spoke to cite two main reasons for keeping the faith despite some warning signs. First, the company kept giving users assurances about its health. In June 2020, just as football was restarting in some parts of Europe, co-founder Adam Cole replied to a customer on Twitter that he expected the platform to be 'ten times bigger' in two years based on its current trajectory, while a job advert posted that January said 'we have a strong product attracting hundreds of thousands of users in the UK, now looking to expand internationally'.[30] It was well known that the company was planning to expand into Germany, and a document from six months later that was leaked to me revealed that the company spent £15 million of customers' money on plans to expand into India and the USA, at a time when the business was collapsing around their ears.[31]

Remarkably, three years after the collapse, Cole re-emerged in association with a strikingly similar new product. I revealed in an investigation for *The Times* that he was an investor in and adviser to a footballer trading platform called KiX, which was using Football Index as a 'proof of concept'. The new site offered users the opportunity to 'hold the hottest players, earn rewards when they perform, sell your footballer tokens . . . putting that hard-earned football knowledge to work'. This was all strikingly similar language, and internal documents leaked to me revealed Cole's involvement alongside Abdullah Suleyman, who was head of trading at Football Index. David Hammel, a campaigner for those who lost out, described the news as a 'real kick in the teeth'.[32] In response to questions, a spokesman for KiX confirmed that Cole was an investor and adviser to KiX, but said he did not have 'executive input at operational or board level' and noted that he has 'at no time faced any criminal proceedings or investigations nor any disqualifications as a company director'. The spokesman acknowledged 'similarities' between the two projects but claimed KiX was 'a completely new platform operating to an entirely different model and structure'.

The original sin of Football Index was that it was regulated as a gambling product when it had important differences. 'We are a completely unique product,' said Adam Cole on a podcast in June 2020. 'To be honest, the Gambling Commission doesn't fully understand all the ins and outs of our business model.' This was borne out by conversations with other employees in the company, speaking after the crash, who said that the regulator was asking them to explain how the company worked, and got little in the way of answers. The company relentlessly used the language of 'investing' and the 'stock market', rather than making clear it was gambling. As well as the sins of the company and its founders, the UK gambling regulator also bears plenty of responsibility when it comes to the Football Index disaster, in which about £100 million vanished from the portfolios of customers – who thought they were investing rather than playing a speculative game – while adverts for Football Index were still being trotted out on the radio, on the side of taxis and on football shirts at Loftus Road in West London and at the City Ground, the home of Nottingham Forest.

Immediately after the Football Index debacle, Forest became one of the more wholesome clubs when it came to shirt sponsorship. During their promotion season of 2021–22, when French goalkeeper Brice Samba became a hero for saving crucial penalties in a play-off semi-final against Sheffield United, the club was sponsored by BOXT, a boiler company based in West Yorkshire. This was an example of a firm selling a tangible, everyday product in a season where most Championship clubs were sponsored by gambling companies, many with peculiar paper trails.

Things got even more heartwarming when Forest arrived back in the Premier League for the first time in twenty-three years. For some time the club had no sponsor at all. Unlike pre-2006 Barcelona, though, this was not for principled reasons, but because Forest's bombastic owner, Greek Evangelos Marinakis, had set the price too high and failed to sell the club's prime advertising real estate. After a few months playing with a blank red shirt, the club announced a front-of-shirt deal with the United Nations Refugee Agency, which did not pay for the privilege of sharing a good cause with millions of Premier League viewers. As Financial Fair Play rules started to bite, though, with Forest splashing the cash trying to cling on to their Premier League status, the club needed money urgently. One way was selling star forward and local lad Brennan Johnson to Tottenham for £50 million. Another was selling the front of the Garibaldi red shirt to the highest bidder – Kaiyun Sports.

Premier League clubs agreed to a voluntary ban on gambling companies on the front of shirts from 2026–27, and many were trying to cash in as much as possible in advance of this. It may seem a noble gesture but gambling ads will still be everywhere else in football – on billboards, on shirt sleeves, on TV and on social media apps. There is also an element of mutually beneficial disarmament. If nobody is advertising on the front of their shirts, there is no competitive disadvantage to not doing so, so gambling websites can save cash without losing out. While the boom in gambling may be slowing down in the UK as regulation and public opinion is beginning to turn against it, the reverse is true in the rest of the world, as demonstrated in the shirts of FC Goa in India and countless others. The sudden growth of a thrilling but addictive industry, which fundamentally changed in character when it moved from the casino to the smartphone, could be one of the most consequential yet unremarked upon trends of our time. Football shirts do not just help us understand this story, they are a critical part of it.

4

WORLD ON THE MOVE

Changing Lives FC & France National Football Team

'I learned that the ball never comes when you expect it to. That helped me a lot in life, especially in large cities where people don't tend to be what they claim.'
Albert Camus, philosopher and former goalkeeper for Racing Universitaire d'Alger

One chilly Saturday lunchtime in November 2023 I took the train from my home in London to the town of Billericay, an hour away to the east in the county of Essex. I was travelling to meet the UK's only refugee football team. I had heard about Changing Lives FC and was expecting to watch a low-key game of football before hearing some stories about how the sport can be a positive force. But things didn't quite turn out that way.

This was my first time in Billericay, a name familiar to me for a couple of reasons. First, it's the hometown of Gavin from *Gavin & Stacey*, one of the best British TV shows of the twenty-first century which tells the story of an Essex man and a Welsh woman who speak to each other over work phone calls, then meet and fall in love. The second reason is that Billericay is the hometown of the former Premier League referee Andy D'Urso. Back in the 1990s, when I was first getting into football, match reports always carried the name of the referee's hometown in brackets: A. D'Urso (Billericay). (An aside: this practice thrust the Hertfordshire town of Tring into unlikely prominence as it is home to not one, but two men named Graham who have refereed an FA Cup final – Graham Barber and Graham Poll.)

Andy D'Urso is famous for a photo where he is surrounded by a furious mob of Manchester United players, with captain Roy Keane screaming in his face, after having the temerity to award a penalty against United at Old Trafford back when the team were in their pomp in 2000 under the management of Sir Alex Ferguson and seemed to get a lot of very fortunate refereeing decisions.

D'Urso was of course of particular interest to me because we had the same surname. As a child, people would often ask if he was a relative. Occasionally, I have written or tweeted something defending referees from some of the mad conspiracy theories which circulate after a controversial decision, and have received a reply along the lines of 'Well, you would say that wouldn't you, D'Urso?' As for whether we are related, the answer is no and yes. No, in that I have never met him and cannot tell you of any concrete connection. Yes, in that D'Urso is an uncommon surname deriving from one tiny place, the village of Minori on the Amalfi Coast, an hour south of Naples in southern Italy, so everyone with that name does seem to be somehow related. One of the megastars of Italian TV is Barbara D'Urso who, like the referee, I've never met but is probably a relative. In the 1930s, when southern Italy was desperately poor, many people emigrated to cities like New York and London. After setting up modest businesses and becoming slightly better off, the London southern Italians moved out of crowded inner-city areas as is the typical cycle of migration. In the case of my grandfather, it was to the central area of Clerkenwell, then Finchley in north London, and then to Surrey just south of the capital, where my own father was born before he moved north to Birmingham before I came into the world. Other Italians moved out to places like Billericay. For the refugee team Changing Lives FC, this Billericay game is an away fixture. The team play in all red, their badge featuring a heart and a globe as a sign that the team is made up mostly of refugees. The shirt, alongside the all-blue shirt of the French national team, give a window into the far bigger story of global migration. These are not shirts where it is the sponsor that tells the story, but the symbolism of the shirt more broadly.

The team is based in Harlow, twenty-five miles to the north-west but still in Essex. The club had said I was welcome to come and watch a game and speak to some of the players afterwards. Kick-off was at 1.30 p.m., but I had trouble with my trains so arrived in Billericay an hour or so late, just as the second half was getting under way. I assumed this wouldn't be too much of a problem as my focus was more on speaking to players than catching every minute of the match, which I would still see plenty of. Or so I thought.

When I arrived at the recreation ground, at a time that should have been well into the second half, there was no game being played at all. What I saw instead shocked me. Beside the pitch there was an actual physical confrontation going on, with a group of players wearing the kit of Changing Lives FC – all red with maroon sleeves and sponsored by sportswear site kitunlocker.com – squaring up against a group of opposition players wearing purple kit. (The opposition were from the lower reaches of Essex football, and have no connection to the comparatively high-flying Billericay Town FC.) Voices were raised and players were holding back their teammates. Even from a distance, it was hard not to notice that everybody on the red team was a person of colour while the purple team was entirely made up of white players. Eventually, things settled down without any punches being thrown and players drifted away from each other, and the pitches on foot or towards their cars, long before the game was supposed to finish, as the match was abandoned.

To find out what on earth had just happened, I spoke to the coach, Sanchit Singh, who I had been in contact with to arrange the visit. Singh, from India, had come to the UK to study at the University of Essex and was in the process of training to be a football coach. Before I spoke to him, he was pacing around while on the phone for a long time, standing on the deserted pitch, looking stressed. He explained that he had instructed his players to leave the pitch early in the second half after what he described as a series of terrible refereeing decisions which saw the opposing side unpunished despite being physically aggressive, followed by his team conceding a penalty for an innocuous challenge by one of his players. Being on the wrong side of dubious refereeing decisions is a normal part of grassroots sports and Singh says it is important for his players to understand that things will not always go your way, but this felt different, he says. There is an important factor at play which everyone is reluctant to say explicitly. This team, entirely made up of refugees, feels it is often treated harshly by referees and opponents because of who they are and how they look. The team recently made a formal complaint to the Football Association after a rival player asked a Changing Lives player 'Where is your passport?' Other players have heard 'Go back to where you came from'.

In elite-level football stadiums in England, overtly racist incidents are far rarer than they used to be in the recent past, though there is still a long way to go. It's therefore jarring to hear players say they were on the receiving end of racist and discriminatory treatment at a football match ultimately overseen by the Football Association. A year or so before this, the Changing Lives FC minibus, which clearly describes the charity's work, was stolen and later found torched. Lots of equipment had been left, leading to concerns the motivation was not theft and that the bus had been specifically targeted.[1]

Despite this shadow hanging over things, softly spoken coach Singh, wearing his Changing Lives-branded gilet underneath his coat, told me he enjoys working with the team. 'All of them are really talented,' he observes, helped by the fact that many played street football as a child in their home countries, which demands closer control of the ball than when the game is played on big grass pitches. Communication is an issue because many players speak limited English, although a couple of players are British. Singh speaks Spanish, which helps when talking to players from Latin America, as well as Urdu, similar to the language spoken by some of the Afghans in the team. His job as a performance analyst and coach goes far beyond picking the team and choosing the tactics. It includes coming up with ways to communicate, such as establishing English phrases that will be mutually understood. He advises the players on diet and fitness, and carries out video analysis, recording matches and training sessions before showing the footage to players to help them refine their game. He says working with refugee players can be intensely rewarding but also bring its own challenges. 'They've often seen a lot of violence,' he explains. 'We try to teach them psychological methods to calm them down.' While in the past his players have been at fault for overreacting to something on the pitch, he claims this was not the case today and is furious about the way he has been treated by the opposition and the referee. His players feel the same.

I spoke to one of them, a twenty-three-year-old Sudanese man. He was reluctant to give me his name or go into too much detail about the circumstances in which he left his home country. This was understandable. Many refugees and asylum seekers have experienced horrific events and are locked in complex bureaucratic situations which make them wary of a stranger with a notepad. But his eyes lit up when I asked about Changing Lives. He had been in the UK for four years and spoke excellent English, unlike many of his teammates. Holding formal refugee status, he has the right to work and is busy as a delivery driver when not playing football. He was allocated a place to live in Harlow by the government and quickly found the club. 'I feel like I'm more connected with the other players here than other teams,' he explained. 'It is good for entertainment, but you see the dark side of football.' He has been on the receiving end of racism, he said quietly, from overt slurs to what he sees as overly harsh refereeing and rough treatment from opposing players.

One of his team mates is Alan, a centre-back from Veracruz in Mexico who also speaks excellent English. He is an asylum seeker, which means he does not have formal refugee status nor the right to work. Like his Sudanese teammate, he was reluctant to be drawn on the specifics of his life story and the status of his asylum application, but said his home region is dangerous, with violence related to drug cartels and trafficking. His life is tough but he sees football as a way to leave these stresses behind. 'I feel welcome in the team,' he grinned, seeing it as his place of happiness when things are otherwise tough. He too has had offensive comments from the opposition, referencing shouts about passports and being told to 'go home' he said, adding that opponents might treat him and his teammates better had they been through comparable hardship.

The team was initially set up by David Simmons, who helped link up the team with Changing Lives Community Services, a charity in Chelmsford. 'The talent in the team is unreal,' he told me. 'Some of them could go further up the league'. He reeled off a list of the countries his players come from – Sudan, Eritrea, Botswana, Egypt, Afghanistan, Iraq, Albania. His next project is setting up a women's team and he was excited that the club had recently received some kit sponsorship and that a TV documentary company was interested in working with the team. 'It makes [the players] feel part of the community. It makes them feel wanted and feel connected. It's a very special team.'

It's common to read about how we are living in an 'age of migration' or a 'migration crisis', with people on the move more than ever before, driven by conflict and climate change. The overall numbers have gone up, but the proportion of the world's population living outside their home country has remained remarkably constant at around 3 per cent over the past century or two. Even when it comes to refugees, the share of the world's population seeking safety outside their home country has stayed relatively the same since the huge spike that followed the Second World War, with numbers briefly spiking in response to events like the Syrian Civil War, which led to large numbers coming to Europe in 2015, and Russia's invasion of Ukraine seven years later, before trending back down, then rising again. In 2025, the highest number of refugees globally came from Afghanistan, Syria and Venezuela. When it comes to migration in general, what has changed dramatically is the direction in which people have flowed. Migration was high between 100 and 200 years ago, but these flows were primarily from Western Europe to places like North America, South America and Australia. Now people generally move in the opposite direction.

The most fundamental change, according to Dutch academic Hein de Haas, has been 'the transformation of western Europe from the world's main source of colonists and immigrants to an important destination for migrants.'[2] Even then, the picture is more nuanced than an exodus from south to north, with the Gulf states an increasingly important destination for migrants from Africa and Asia, which sports journalists discovered when poring over the details of the shoddy treatment of the migrant workers who built stadiums for the 2022 Qatar World Cup. Countries like Brazil and South Africa have also become major destinations for regional migrants, while most migrants around the world never leave their own country. 'We are here because you were there,' declared the writer Ambalavaner Sivanandan, who migrated to the UK from Sri Lanka, then called Ceylon, in 1953. After the Second World War, Britain shifted from being a colonial superpower to a post-imperial nation in the shadow of the USA. There was plenty of ethnic and religious diversity in the form of the Irish, some Jews, and my ancestors the Italians, but there were very few people with dark skin. This changed rapidly, starting with the ship *Empire Windrush* which came from the Caribbean to the UK in 1948, creating several waves of migration from former British colonies in the Caribbean and sub-Saharan Africa, as well as India and Pakistan. That same year, a law created the new status of an 'imperial subject', meaning people from those countries had just as much right to live and work in the UK as someone born in London. 'After 1948, a non-white person born in colonial Kenya or Jamaica had enjoyed citizenship, on equal terms, to Winston Churchill,' explains writer Ian Sanjay Patel.[3] This was intended as a last-ditch attempt to shore up the fraying bonds of empire, rather than the first step in turning Britain into a multi-ethnic society as proved to be the case. Huge numbers arrived from the slowly crumbling British Empire in the years before citizenship laws were tightened in the 1960s.

Britain's shift from an almost mono-ethnic society to a diverse one happened quickly. According to 2021 census data, around

18 per cent of the population of England and Wales belong to a black, Asian, mixed or other ethnic group. This is likely to be significantly higher by the next census in 2031 because of high immigration and the fast-growing number of children with mixed ethnic backgrounds. These changes have not all been plain sailing. Discrimination and prejudice are still commonplace, be it in the form of overt hatred, or more subtle discrimination, such as immigrants and their children often have worse job prospects or health outcomes. There has been notable racial tension in urban areas, such as the Brixton and Toxteth riots in the 1980s, while the Brexit vote of 2016 was in part motivated by a rejection of the immigration policies pursued by successive governments over a long period of time. Politicians repeatedly pledged to lower immigration, which had clear public support, but numbers nevertheless kept rising. However, gloomier predictions have not come to pass, such as the infamous speech given by Conservative MP Enoch Powell in 1968. 'In this country in fifteen or twenty years' time, the black man will have the whip hand over the white man,' he fulminated, predicting that 'rivers of blood' would run through the streets if migration continued.[4]

That speech was given in my hometown of Birmingham, which recently became one of the UK's first 'majority-minority' cities where white British people make up less than half the population. It would be naive to pretend there haven't been problems along the way, but this radical demographic shift has not been accompanied by 'rivers of blood'. It is now not only inner-cities which are diverse, but black or Asian people are a common sight in smaller towns around Britain, many of them third- or fourth-generation immigrants, Brits with mixed ethnic backgrounds who are no more Indian or Jamaican than I am Italian.

Football has been perhaps the most visible way in which the

descendants of immigrants from Britain's former colonies have come to play a prominent role in public life. Viv Anderson, born in Nottingham to Jamaican parents, became the first black player to represent the senior England team, in 1978, going on to earn thirty caps. The most famous of England's early black footballers was John Barnes, who was born in Jamaica before moving to London aged twelve. He played for his country seventy-nine times between 1983 and 1995 and became familiar to younger England fans through his rap on 1990 football anthem 'World in Motion'.

In recent years, countless more players have followed in the footsteps of Anderson and Barnes. These days, an England line-up will unfailingly contain multiple players with a mixed ethnic background. It is so commonplace that it rarely gets a mention. (There have been very few professional British footballers from a South Asian background, though, despite that group being a somewhat larger portion of the UK population.) England's relatively successful era under Gareth Southgate is associated with names like Bukayo Saka, the child of Nigerian immigrants to London, and Marcus Rashford, whose family came to Manchester from the Caribbean. Others are of mixed heritage, such as Jude Bellingham, who has a white British father and a black mother who has the distinctive accent of the Black Country near Birmingham where she was raised. His family are relatively private, and it is not clear where exactly in the world her ancestors moved to the Midlands from. It is simply not a particular talking point when compared to the focus on Bellingham's performances in an England shirt and his big money move to Real Madrid. Three-quarters of a century has now passed since the first large-scale immigration to the UK from Africa and the Caribbean, and these England players are no longer defined by their ethnicity or links to faraway places they may have never visited.

Viv Anderson and John Barnes were trailblazers, but the next generation are not. 'The ineradicable presence of black and mixed-heritage players in the team made the equivalence of England and whiteness harder and harder to sustain,' argues David Goldblatt.[5] This is true in the club game too. According to the Black Footballers Partnership, during the 2022–23 season, 43 per cent of Premier League players and 34 per cent of players in the English Football League were black, many times higher than the percentage within the general population.[6] (The figure for coaches is far lower.) This includes black British players as well as foreigners coming to play from all over the world, from Africa and the Caribbean, and countries closer to home. Thierry Henry, the best ever Premier League player for some, is a Parisian with parents from France's colonial outposts in the Caribbean.

It is rare these days for English professional teams not to field a single black player. This is true not just in the international glamour of the Premier League, but also far lower down the English pyramid, including teams like Grimsby, Shrewsbury and Morecambe, places where the local black population is very low. Football has played a huge role in not just familiarising white people with racial diversity, but in creating a situation in which white people, who might not know a single black person in real life end up actively celebrating their achievements. It is harder to rationalise abusing an opposing black player when your own team has one or many. There are still examples of racist abuse at football matches and many more subtle prejudices still exist – such as stereotyping black players as overly physical, or disproportionately getting on their back when they make a mistake – but things have got better.

Apparent progress on the issue of racism in English football was sullied after the final of the European Championships in 2021 which saw England lose on penalties to Italy in London's Wembley Stadium. I was there. My Italian heritage meant I was cheering on Fabio Grosso's winning penalty-kick when Italy beat France in the World Cup final back in 2006, but there is no doubt where my loyalties lie when it comes to England vs Italy. I was gutted to see England lose that final. Crowd trouble had put a downer on things before kick-off, with security overrun by fans, many high on cocaine, trying to force their way into Wembley. An official report said it was a miracle that nobody was seriously hurt.[7] I am always keen to defend football fans from the outdated and snobbish stereotypes which say the game is loutish – a 'game for gentlemen played by thugs', unlike rugby which is a 'game for thugs played by gentlemen'. This sort of thing is not only tedious, but untrue these days. Football had a justifiably dark reputation in the 1980s and 1990s when 'the English disease' of hooliganism was rife, and the terraces of clubs like Chelsea, Millwall and West Ham became recruiting grounds for the far-right National Front. These days, a million or so people attend matches each weekend across the UK with very little in the way of genuine trouble. But it is impossible to defend or minimise the dire scenes at Wembley that day. Being there was scary and unpleasant and in the hours after the final, another bleak storyline played out. The three players who missed the crucial spot-kicks for England – Bukayo Saka, Marcus Rashford and Jadon Sancho, another England player of mixed heritage – were all hit by a torrent of racist abuse on social media, although much of it seemed to originate from outside the UK. It was a sign that the links between English football and racism have not entirely gone away.

Unlike in Europe, hooliganism in the UK has rarely had close links to politics on the left or the right, although a friendly between England and Ireland in Dublin in 1995 was abandoned after a riot by English fans, some of whom were later identified as belonging to neo-Nazi group Combat 18. Things have improved since and matches between the sides in both Dublin and London in 2024 passed off without incident. Geoff Pearson is an expert on football disorder based at the University of Manchester. 'From the late 1980s through to the mid-1990s, we got on top of the problem domestically,' he told me. 'We do still have people that attend matches looking to fight fans of rival teams, but the numbers of people that do that are very low.'[8] The clear decline in overt racism from the stands has many causes, such as the shift to all-seater stadiums in the early 1990s, and the commercialisation of the Premier League making the game more accommodating to women and children. Also, CCTV and camera phones mean bigots and agitators are more likely to be caught. On social media, however, none of these factors make a difference, and modern technology provides a new means of dishing out vile abuse.

The next shirt to explore the issue of race and immigration in football is familiar to football fans as one of the defining images of the sport in the twenty-first century: the all-blue of the French national team. Since the World Cup began in 1930 the teams to feature in the final most times are Argentina, Brazil, Italy and Germany. Over the last three decades, France has been more successful than any other. In the seven World Cups from 1998 to 2022, a period that happens to encompass the entire history of international football that I can remember, France have reached four finals. No other country has reached more than two in that time. They won the World Cup on home soil in 1998 and then again in Russia in 2018, also losing the final to Italy in Germany in 2006. The World Cup final in Qatar in 2022, one of the greatest football matches of all time, saw Kylian Mbappé score a hat-trick but end up on the losing side as Lionel Messi finally capped arguably the greatest career of all time by winning the World Cup with Argentina on penalties. France also won the European Championships in 2000 and lost the final in 2016.

It was not always this way. France had never reached a World Cup final before 1998, though did win the 1984 European Championships, albeit when the competition had only eight teams. Before 1998, France was very much in the second tier of footballing nations, with little outside interest in their domestic league and few French players known internationally. (Dazzling 1980s midfielder Michel Platini, later a UEFA executive banned from the sport for eight years for ethics violations, is an exception.) Things changed after the 1998 World Cup win supercharged interest in the game. Paris has become the most productive talent factory in world football, while the success of Qatari-owned Paris Saint-Germain has made the French club globally famous with superstars like Neymar, Messi and Parisian star boy Mbappé helping to secure French football's place at the top table in terms of money and glamour, even if the ultimate prize of the Champions League proved elusive.

Living in the French city of Lyon for three months in 2016 was great fun, and the timing was excellent because the end of my stay coincided with Euro 2016. I went to games in Lyon, Nice and Saint-Étienne, as well as seeing England draw 1–1 with Russia in the port town of Marseille, a game marred by violence instigated by Russian fans, which I luckily managed to avoid. France is a brilliant country to travel around watching football, with a good train network and plenty of nice cities in which to eat and drink in the sun. France is an excellent host, but football is not as ingrained in the culture as it is in England, Germany, Italy and Spain. While sitting in Saint-Étienne's Stade Geoffroy-Guichard to watch Croatia's fiery

2–2 draw with Czech Republic, it struck me that in the 'neutrals' section, the part of the stadium not taken up by the two official supporters' groups, there were huge numbers of English fans and surprisingly few were French. When the same tournament took place in Germany eight years later, it was far harder to get tickets. Some of this can be put down to football becoming more popular around the world and more countries competing, but there is no question that watching live football is far more deeply rooted in German and British culture than French. Wales fans were also well represented in a tournament where they surprisingly reached the semi-finals, propelled by the talismanic Gareth Bale of Real Madrid. England bombed out after embarrassingly losing to Iceland 2–1 in the round of 16, a low-point for the national team before a gradual revival under Gareth Southgate.

Many years after I spent my months in Lyon, when I was a journalist with *The Athletic*, I would occasionally be sent on reporting trips to France, enjoying the chance to keep up my language skills. On one of these visits, I met up for a beer with Christophe Larcher, a journalist with *France Football*. We discussed his countrymen's relative lack of fanaticism, despite the recent successes of the national team and the global marketing phenomenon that is Paris Saint-Germain. 'In England, football is the culture,' he told me. 'If you go to Newcastle or Sheffield, everyone wants to talk about football. But if you go to Rennes or Angers, it is not like that. Our culture is food, it is art. Football, not so much.'[9] It is not that the French are all apathetic – teams like PSG and Marseille have long had big and vibrant ultras groups – but football does not penetrate mainstream culture in the same way as other parts of Europe.

I was in Paris to pay a visit to Bondy, a place that has almost become a pilgrimage for football journalists. As the signs in the suburb to the east of Paris say, '1998 was an excellent year for

French football' – not because of the World Cup win, but because 'Kylian was born'. Bondy is just 10 kilometres from the picturesque sights of central Paris, but looks very different, all concrete apartment blocks and graffitied flyovers, although the stereotype that everywhere outside central Paris is a hellscape can be overegged a little. Bondy is not the Paris of *Amélie*, the 2001 film which shows a young woman finding love and adventure on the charming streets of Montmartre. But nor is it the Paris of *La Haine*, an influential and grittily dystopian film depicting life in Paris's grim suburbs, released six years earlier.

Mbappé grew up in a relatively comfortable household in Bondy, with his father a footballer and his mother a handball player. His parents come from two former French colonies, Cameroon and Algeria. Overlooking a highway on the way to Bondy is a huge mural depicting the town's most famous son, paid for by his sponsor Nike, depicting the young Kylian dreaming of becoming a world-conquering superstar, dreams realised in the Moscow rain in 2018 when Mbappé dazzled the world before lifting the World Cup while still a teenager.

A short walk across Bondy from the Mbappé mural, the sound of footballs crashing against metal cages mixes with the cheers and jeers of teenage spectators. An under-16 side in all-green are playing a pre-season friendly against a team in yellow. The green team is AS Bondy, the club at which Mbappé began his career before transferring to the INF Clairefontaine, France's national academy, at the age of eleven. The game is of a very high quality, the teenagers displaying excellent technical ability as well as pace and power. Dozens of local youngsters have come along to watch the game. Some wear Paris Saint-Germain gear, and there are also plenty clad in the colours of Barcelona, Real Madrid and Manchester United, but no other French teams.

Paris Saint-Germain were founded in 1970. Remarkably, after the Second World War, no team from the nation's capital and economic powerhouse won Ligue 1 until PSG bagged their first title in 1986. It was followed by a second in 1994, but the club still lagged far behind the big names of French football like Lyon, Marseille, Bordeaux and Nantes. Everything has changed now, though. PSG won ten out of twelve league titles between 2012 and 2024. This success has been funded by the Qatari government who bought the club in 2011 and placed it at the core of their soft-power mission to turn a tiny desert state into a sporting superpower, with the 2022 World Cup as the centrepiece. I visited Paris at the time Mbappé was having to deal with the arrival at PSG of Lionel Messi, perhaps the only footballer in the world, along with Cristiano Ronaldo, who could overshadow France's superstar. Two years later, Messi moved on to Inter Miami as the undisputed poster boy of Major League Soccer, after a short but lucrative period in Paris in which Messi won domestic trophies but the attacking trio of Messi, Neymar, and Mbappé failed to make it past the first knockout phase of the Champions League in two attempts. Neymar would end up in Saudi Arabia, before returning to Brazil, and Mbappé at Real Madrid, which had long been his dream.

Qatar and Paris Saint-Germain have always seemed an odd combination, the ultimate New World regime choosing the ultimate Old World city as its centrepiece. PSG has had some of the best, and certainly best-paid, players in the world, while the city itself is arguably the most beautiful, historic and culturally interesting city in the world. But it is hard to escape the feeling that the combination doesn't quite fit. To some it is all a bit gauche and the PSG project has often felt somewhat joyless, as superstars dominate their domestic league at a canter before struggling in the Champions League, with players getting little practice in genuinely competitive games before they meet the likes of Manchester City, Liverpool and Real Madrid. Nobody ever seems particularly happy at PSG. Mbappé finally joined Madrid in 2024 after years of rumours and wrangling, and PSG is now trying to embrace its Parisian and French identity, rather than just importing the sport's biggest names. (Though a local, Mbappé was signed for a huge fee from AS Monaco.) PSG want to better exploit the club's proximity to talent like precocious midfielder Warren Zaïre-Emery, from Montreuil near Bondy, who became a PSG regular at the age of just 16. Time will tell how that goes.

Before the joke about 1998 being a great year for French football because Kylian was born, in 1994 Nike ran an advert that riffed on the year England won the World Cup: '1966 was a great year for English football. Eric was born.' The poster showed the charismatic French forward Eric Cantona with his popped collar, posing in front of the St George's Cross. He was one of the Premier League's most exciting players, briefly at Leeds United before Manchester United where he dazzled with his trickery and larger-than-life personality at a time when foreigners were a rarity in the English top flight. He was once convicted of assault after aiming a kung-fu kick at a Crystal Palace fan who abused him. In the aftermath he gave a press conference in which, slowly and deliberately, he made an enigmatic statement: 'When the seagulls follow the trawler, it is because they think sardines will be thrown into the sea.' He then walked off. Journalists and football fans have spent three decades trying to decipher what he meant by that.

Since retiring, Cantona has become an entertaining political voice on sensitive topics, often going against the prevailing winds, whether that be encouraging customers to withdraw their money from banks in protest at the global financial crisis or raging against the Qatar World Cup because of the 'horrible' treatment of migrant workers. In a documentary about the 1998 World Cup, which he retired shortly before, he referenced how the triumphant team were named 'black-blanc-beur', or 'black-white-Arab'. 'A France team that wins is black-blanc-beur, and a France team that loses is scum from "les banlieues",' he surmised, referring to urban France's hardscrabble suburbs.[10]

The phrase 'black-blanc-beur' was coined as a nod to the racial harmony apparently embodied by the national team's triumph in 1998 which saw a French-Algerian, Zinedine Zidane, score two of the three goals in the final. A white man, Didier Deschamps, lifted the trophy as captain and would later do so as manager in 2018. And several black players, like Lilian Thuram and Marcel Desailly, were instrumental members of the 1998 team. Two days after the victory was Bastille Day, the French national holiday celebrated on 14 July. President Jacques Chirac congratulated 'this simultaneously tricolour and multi coloured team', a reference to the French flag and the team's racial diversity. Historian Benjamin Stora argued the victory closed a chapter in French history by proving a Frenchman could identify with both metropolitan France and a former colony.[11] Zidane, born to Algerian parents in Marseille, became an icon of integration. (Another Franco-Algerian footballer was philosopher Albert Camus, who played in goal for Racing Universitaire d'Alger.) As the academic Christopher Thompson argues, the World Cup win was seen as a triumph for the 'inclusive civic nationalism of French republicanism' rather than the 'exclusionary ethnic nationalism of the xenophobic National Front', a party whose leader, Jean-Marie Le Pen, had in 1996 criticised footballers who 'come from elsewhere' and fail to sing the national anthem. His claim that non-white players lacked an authentic bond to their country was met by a backlash from mainstream politicians. As part of the debate, goalkeeper Bernard Lama, from French Guiana, said: 'I did not ask to have my ancestors deported in slavery', addressing the uncomfortable truth that recent immigration trends and colonial history can be viewed as two sides of the same coin – we are here because you were there.[12]

The national anthem, or the failure to sing it, is a topic that comes up a great deal relating to footballers with immigrant backgrounds, such as Mesut Özil, a Turkish-origin German who played for Real Madrid and Arsenal, and who was criticised in Germany for not singing the national anthem. He would eventually fall out with the German football authorities over what he saw as discriminatory treatment, and fought with his club Arsenal after being disciplined for tweeting 'political' statements about the treatment of the Uighur Muslims in China.[13]

After the 1998 final, the good vibes continued as France won the European Championships two years later. The man of the match was Thierry Henry, while the goals were scored by Sylvain Wiltord, born in Paris to parents from Martinique, and David Trezeguet, of mixed-ethnic heritage with an Argentinian mother. However, the following year, cracks began to appear in the new relaxed relationship between race, football and broader French society. A 2001 match between France and Algeria is remembered for all the wrong reasons. Although the game in Paris was only a friendly it was charged with emotion as the first-ever fixture between France and a country that had been more than a colony. It was part of territorial France, to the same extent as Lyon and Marseille, until 1962. In 2001, Algeria was a relatively young independent country with a huge diaspora in France, who outnumbered those in the stadium supporting the reigning World Cup and European champions. The French anthem was jeered, an indication of the bitterness many young people of Algerian descent felt towards the country in which they grew up, where racism was common and Arabs' prospects often poor. During the second half, with Algeria trailing 4–1, fans invaded the pitch and the match was abandoned. Riot police were deployed as debris rained down on security.[14]

The year 2002 was bad for French football, and racial integration in France more broadly. The national team crashed out in the group stage of the World Cup in South Korea and Japan, sensationally losing the first game of the tournament to their former colonial outpost Senegal, the pre-tournament favourites not improving after that, the camp riven by infighting. A couple of months earlier the country had been shaken by the result of the presidential election. In French presidential elections voters choose from a large pool of candidates who are narrowed down to two, who compete in a final run-off vote. Typically, this is between the centre-left Socialist Party and a candidate from the centre-right, but in 2002, far-right Jean-Marie Le Pen beat the socialist candidate into third place, therefore reaching a run-off against centre-right incumbent Jacques Chirac. World Cup-winning defender Marcel Desailly, born in Ghana, was among those who publicly implored the country to back Chirac, saying that it was 'imperative to do everything possible to block [Le Pen's] path to power'.[15] Millions of voters ended up 'holding their nose' and choosing Chirac as the lesser of two evils. He won the run-off by a huge margin, but the episode shocked the French political elite. In 2017 and 2022, Le Pen's estranged daughter Marine, who ascribes to a somewhat sanitised version of the same politics as her father, would twice reach the run-off stage, beaten comfortably on both occasions by Emmanuel Macron, but gaining far more votes than Jean-Marie.

Following the 2002 election the idea of football as a force for positive change and racial harmony suddenly felt distant. 'Happy memories had, only four years later, lost much of their symbolic resonance,' says academic Christopher Thompson.[16] In 2005, racial tensions bubbled over as riots gripped the country, the year after another disappointing early exit from the European Championships in Portugal. While the multi-ethnic national team had so recently been a cause for celebration, it later became a stick used to beat them, with influential philosopher Alain Finkielkraut saying 'these days the team is black-black-black, which makes it the laughing stock of Europe'.[17]

Throughout all this, three-time FIFA World Player of the Year Zinedine Zidane remained one of the most popular people in France, transcending racial divides as the symbol of that magical Paris night in 1998 when France won the World Cup for the first time. Three years later, Real Madrid broke the world transfer record when signing him from Juventus. At Madrid he was one of the 'Galácticos' alongside the likes of Luís Figo and Roberto Carlos, and memorably scoring a sensational volley to win the 2002 Champions League final. His last game was the 2006 World Cup final in which France played Italy in the Olympic Stadium in Berlin. (On holiday in the German city in October 2023 I toured that stadium which famously hosted the 1936 Olympic Games, at which African American sprinter Jesse Owens won four gold medals in a blow to the host Adolf Hitler's ideology of Aryan supremacy.) Zidane somewhat tarnished his legacy by sensationally headbutting Italian defender Marco Materazzi, who had allegedly insulted the Frenchman's sister, with ten minutes of extra time remaining. France went on to lose the penalty shoot-out. In some quarters, this uncontrolled act of violence appeared to confirm the French public image of the aggressive and volatile Arab male. Still, Zidane's legacy remains, as one of the greatest Frenchmen in modern history.

France arrived at the 2010 World Cup in South Africa as one of the favourites after reaching the final in two of the three previous tournaments. Things panned out more like 2002 than 1998 or 2006, though, with more vicious infighting and another embarrassing early exit. The row centred on a dramatic falling-out involving striker Nicolas Anelka, who launched a profane rant at manager Raymond Domenech during half-time of the opening game against Mexico which France lost 2–0. Anelka was sent home. Details were leaked to the press and captain Patrice Evra called the mole a 'traitor' as things descended into farce, with players boycotting training in protest at Anelka's dismissal.[18] President Nicolas Sarkozy condemned the scenes as embarrassing for France. The team got one point and no goals before crashing out. 'We now have proof that the France team is not a team at all, but a gang of hooligans that knows only the morals of the mafia,' said that man Alain Finkielkraut again, suggesting that 'gentlemen' be found to replace the team's 'arrogant thugs'.[19] 'The unprecedented revolt appeared to confirm the widespread perception in France that the players personified the individualistic, money-obsessed values of the crime-ridden banlieue housing projects where many top French players grow up,' says Christopher Thompson. 'This image was fuelled in part by television coverage of players not singing the *Marseillaise* or waving to the camera during the playing of the anthem.'[20] Things would get even uglier a year later.

In 2011, an explosive story appeared in the magazine *Mediapart* revealing 'French football chiefs' secret plan to whiten *Les Bleus*'.[21] The report said national team manager Laurent Blanc, a star of the 1998 World Cup as a player, had played a role in secretly approving a quota system to reduce the number of players in the youth set-up of the French Football Federation from black and

Arab backgrounds. 'We are facing a situation which is unique in Europe because almost 45 per cent of our young players have a double nationality and, among them, about 20 per cent decide to play for a country other than France after we trained them,' technical director François Blaquart was reported as saying. 'Is it really the federation's role to develop players for other countries?' Blanc was reported to have told a meeting that it was necessary to 'limit' players who 'leave to play in North African or African teams'. According to *Mediapart*'s sources, the issue was not discussed merely in terms of nationality but also of racial quotas of 'blacks' and 'beurs'. The discussions also concerned players who were too young to have selected a national side.

'These kids are being denied access to training and I call this discrimination,' announced Patrick Lozès, president of the Representative Council of Black Associations in France. 'The lack of diversity in the French Football Federation structures paves the way for institutional racism'.[22] Blanc was also reported as describing 'the blacks' as 'large, strong, powerful', a common stereotype in a sport which often views black players through their physical attributes rather than their intelligence or skill. Blanc was eventually cleared of breaking discrimination law by sports minister Chantal Jouanno, who nevertheless called the comments 'borderline racist'.[23]

The issue of racial quotas was particularly explosive in a country that prides itself on colour-blind treatment of its citizens in the French republican tradition. Unusually, the state does not collect ethnicity data on its own citizens, a practice which has been criticised for making it difficult to resolve racial injustices when it is not known exactly what they are. A spokesperson for French president Nicolas Sarkozy told the press that quotas in the national team would mean 'the end of the republic'.[24] The sports minister opened an investigation while prominent black figures in French football, such as Lilian Thuram and Patrick Vieira, condemned their former teammate Blanc. 'France has, at its heart, a problem where it has been unable or unwilling to accommodate the sons and daughters of its former colonies, even though France benefited and enriched itself greatly from the relationship,' declared defender Benoît Assou-Ekotto, who was born and raised in France but represented Cameroon, the country of his father.[25] Striker Nicolas Anelka, in the French team that won Euro 2000, traces his roots to the island of Martinique. 'When the France team fails to win,' he said a year earlier, 'people start talking straight away about the players' skin colours and religious beliefs.'[26] Striker Karim Benzema, who won the Ballon d'Or in 2022 for his goalscoring exploits for Real Madrid, once said 'if I score, I'm French. If I don't, I'm an Arab.'

More recently there have been signs that France may be becoming more relaxed about race and its colonial legacy in a footballing context, or perhaps success just makes everything easier. Ahead of the 2018 World Cup in Russia, Didier Deschamps assembled a squad that was majority-black with its stars including Paul Pogba, whose parents emigrated from Guinea, and N'Golo Kanté, a midfielder with Malian roots. Academic Laurent Dubois later wrote in the *New York Times*:

> As the 2018 World Cup approached, the far right didn't publicly attack the team. Doing so seemed like a potential political liability. That may be because for many French people, particularly those in younger generations, the multiculturalism long demonised by the right is now simply reality. The family stories of many of these players are increasingly part of the fabric of French life.[27]

In 2018, Kylian Mbappé announced himself to the world with four goals in the tournament as his team beat Argentina, Uruguay and Belgium before rolling over Croatia 4–2 in the final. Emmanuel Macron joined Vladimir Putin, four years before he became an international pariah following the invasion of Ukraine, on the pitch in Moscow as the rain poured down. A couple of days later Kanté took his mother to a ceremony for the winning team at the presidential palace. She wears an Islamic face veil, a garment often the subject of deep controversy in France, a country uncomfortable with overt displays of religion due to the tradition of republican *laïcité,* or secularism. This time nobody cared. The Kantés greeted fellow Muslim Paul Pogba with the traditional Islamic greeting of '*salam alaikum*'. 'This moment was striking because of how natural it seemed,' said Laurent Dubois. 'The players broadcast a sense of ease about being African, French and Muslim all at once.'

Then there was Mbappé. Rather than coming from one clearly identifiable foreign country, he is of mixed heritage. The striker is deeply French, yet also a living embodiment of his Cameroonian father and Algerian mother, and holds iconic national status in tiny French villages as much as the banlieues of Paris. After his sensational World Cup performances, he became the symbol of modern France as Paris Saint-Germain's star player. Writer Vincent Duluc has described Mbappé as 'black-blanc-beur rolled into one'.[28] He did gain a bit of a reputation as a diva at Paris Saint-Germain, where he wielded enormous power before his move to Real Madrid. 'There's a certain whiplash,' Duluc told *The Times*, 'which happens when you go from that breakthrough moment where the whole world thinks you're amazing, to being part of the furniture, when people begin to see your faults.'[29]

A low point for Mbappé was the quarter-final of the European Championships against Switzerland in 2021, which France were expected to win comfortably. It went to a penalty shoot-out and he uncharacteristically missed his spot-kick, which contributed to France's surprise early exit. There were reports of tensions with teammates and, like the English players who missed penalties in the same tournament, the young superstar was racially abused on social media.[30] Compared to Zidane, the previous hero of a multicultural France, Mbappé is more inclined to stick his head above the parapet. 'I cannot play for people who think I'm a monkey,' he told the president of the national federation, Noël Le Graët.[31] Le Graët had been criticised two years earlier for downplaying racism, saying that 'when a black player scores a goal, the whole stadium is on its feet . . . this phenomenon of racism in sport, and in football in particular, does not exist at all or barely exists.'[32] Mbappé has since proved that the 2018 World Cup was no fluke, racking up absurd scoring numbers for Paris Saint-Germain and France, and starting his Real Madrid career with lots of goals, including a spectacular hat-trick against Manchester City in the Champions League in February 2025. Alongside Norwegian striker Erling Haaland, he is the clear candidate as the world's greatest player of football's new era, the heirs to Lionel Messi and Cristiano Ronaldo.

One of the best ways to understand how immigration works in the modern world is through football. TV footage of faraway places, or of boats full of refugees arriving on the shores of Europe, are invariably accompanied by examples of people wearing one of the world's few truly universal symbols: the replica football shirt. The all-red of Changing Lives FC in the English county of Essex shows how football can be a tool to drive integration, which is not always an easy process. The relationship between Europe and Africa was, once one of colonialism and is now one of immigration. The all-blue kit of France, represents the sometimes uneasy relationship between some of the French public and the increasingly diverse national team. It can symbolise social discord but also the country's two modern World Cup wins. Football is one of the most visible symbols of racial diversity, and is a rare walk of life where poorer citizens from immigrant backgrounds can become world superstars. The perception of what an Englishman or a Frenchman looks like have been altered by football, and immigration has changed the meaning of these two national shirts, as well as many others.

5

AMERICAN EXCEPTIONALISM

Houston Dash & Inter Miami

'Born under another sky, placed in the middle of an always-moving scene, himself driven by the irresistible torrent which sweeps along everything that surrounds him, the American has no time to tie himself to anything. He grows accustomed to naught but change and concludes by viewing it as the natural state of man.'[1]

Alexis de Tocqueville, 1831

In all the football matches I've been to in my life I presume I've been banned from bringing along a handgun, although I'm not sure it's ever been explicitly stated. This is Texas, though, and things are different here. When I went to a game at the Shell Energy Stadium in downtown Houston in March 2024, there were signs making clear that, pursuant to penal code 30.06, I may not 'enter the premises with a concealed handgun', making the stadium an exception to the state's 'open carry' firearm laws. The orange shirt of Houston Dash, the women's team which plays in this stadium and carries the logo of a local hospital as a sponsor, as well as the pink shirt of Inter Miami which signed Lionel Messi as its star player in 2023, help tell the story of football in the USA, a country where the sport has long been a sideshow, but things are quickly changing.

I came to Texas to learn more about football in the country that dominates the world in almost everything except football. Americans, of course, call it 'soccer', a word which European football fans are allergic to but in fact originated in England as an abbreviation of 'association football'. The game takes on other linguistic quirks when it crosses the Atlantic. Americans refer to sports teams as singular rather than plural – a Brit would say Arsenal *are* good, but an American would say Arsenal *is* good. This could be viewed as a reflection on how European teams largely grew out of factories and workplaces as community organisations, while American teams are more straightforwardly corporate entities.

Another linguistic quirk is that Americans tend to say 'I like sports' rather than the singular 'I like sport' in British English. The US is perhaps also the only country in the world where it is common to support four or even five different club sides in various sports. Throughout most of the world, only one sport – football – has a serious following at club rather than international level but in the US, the game has traditionally lagged the 'big four' of American football, baseball, basketball and ice hockey. In the US these teams often complement rather than rival each other for fans' attention. It is normal, for instance, for someone to support 'all the Boston teams'. If a soccer side is added to that list, it would be natural to support them too. As with so many things, the US does it differently.

'American exceptionalism' is a phrase first coined by the French writer Alexis de Tocqueville, who visited the new country across the Atlantic two centuries ago. He used the phrase to refer to the USA being the first start-up nation, springing from what he saw as the unique character of the American Revolution. As well as noble ideas of liberty and democracy, the USA was, of course, built upon the massacre of Native Americans and the enslavement of African

Americans. These days, the phrase 'American exceptionalism' is often used derisively, shorthand for a jingoistic arrogance that has led the US to blunder through foreign wars while neglecting domestic problems. President Ronald Reagan once said there was 'some divine plan that placed this great continent between two oceans, to be sought out by those who were possessed of an abiding love of freedom and a special kind of courage'.[2] It all sounds a bit absurd to an outsider, although as one who has visited the US many times and sees its flaws alongside its wonders, I think the country *is* exceptional – not in the sense of being more virtuous than anywhere else, but in being unique among nations in so many ways. As de Tocqueville observed, it was founded in the name of the abstract idea of freedom, which pervades its politics and culture to this day. It is the world's dominant country by many measures. It is comfortably the largest economy in the world. Its companies and celebrities are known everywhere. And for all its political turmoil in recent years, US economic growth has been strong. Americans are significantly richer than Europeans on average. Its military is miles bigger than any other, allowing it to project power across the Atlantic and Pacific. The world's exceptional country's relationship with the world's exceptional game, though, is a fascinating one because this is a field where the US does not dominate at all. 'Football in the USA,' writes David Goldblatt, 'gathers a coalition who see a version of the nation that is normal, not exceptional; playing others rather than dominating them.'[3]

In the 1980s, FIFA saw the commercial potential in bringing the game to the world's richest country and the US was awarded the 1994 World Cup. Organisers feared apathy but there was plenty of excitement, and commercially it was a huge success. Afterwards, FIFA had long wanted to take the World Cup back to the US, and the 2026 tournament, the first with forty-eight rather than thirty-two teams, was awarded to the USA in partnership with Canada and Mexico. These days World Cups are increasingly shared between countries, there being more aspiring hosts than there are tournaments to go round and the number of games with a 48-team tournament is 104, up from 64, making hosting a huge logistical task even for a country the size of the US. The 2026 World Cup is really a second American tournament in all but name. Canada and Mexico were awarded thirteen games, the US seventy-eight including all from the quarter-finals onwards. The biggest event in sport, the World Cup final, was awarded to the Giants Stadium in East Rutherford, New Jersey, across the Hudson River from Manhattan. It just pipped the vast AT&T Stadium in Arlington, Texas, home to the Dallas Cowboys NFL team, host of a semi-final and several other games. One interesting subplot to the tournament is that Donald Trump's son-in-law, Jared Kushner, played a key role in securing the World Cup during Trump's first term, scheduled to take place eighteen months after Trump's second election victory in November 2024.

It was Arlington that I visited on a trip to Texas a little more than two years before the 2026 World Cup kicks off. I had visited the US's cosmopolitan coastal cities, places like New York, Boston and San Francisco, on several occasions. In these places football is insignificant compared to its European and South American heartlands but it has long had some presence thanks to high immigrant populations and lots of foreigners passing through. In the thousands of miles in between the coast, sometimes dismissed as 'flyover country', football has often been seen as a game for women and children rather than men. I was eager to explore the country's Republican-voting interior, places that voted for Donald Trump three times, the land of barbecue, guns and high-school football, to see if things were changing or if the US remained exceptional as one of a handful of countries in the world where football holds little interest. But before visiting the AT&T, I went to another Texas stadium, this one far smaller and purpose-built for football, where bringing in handguns is expressly forbidden.

I am used to English stadiums which are designed to keep out rain. Texas has a different problem: heat. This is particularly pressing as, while most football leagues around the world run roughly from August to May, Major League Soccer (MLS) is a calendar-year sport played through the peak of summer. This means many games are played in extreme heat. The Shell Energy Stadium in Houston was completed in 2012, the naming rights bought by one of the biggest names in the city's leading industry: oil. The stadium is home to Houston Dynamo of the MLS and Houston Dash of the National Women's Soccer League (NWSL) and is designed to minimise the impact of the sun in a city where the mercury can top 115ºF (46ºC). (In March when I visit this is not a major issue.) Rather than hard plastic, the stadium's seats are made of mesh which stops spectators' backs becoming unpleasantly sweaty during a match.

It is the country's first purpose-built soccer stadium in a downtown area, one not located in distant suburbs like many others in the US. Many US soccer teams play in venues designed for other sports, which often doesn't work well. For instance, New York City FC spent many years alternating between two baseball stadiums, Yankee Stadium and Citi Field, which means awkward gaps between spectators and the pitch, though NYCFC later constructed a bespoke stadium built for football. Houston's stadium is small but perfectly formed, with spectators close to the pitch, and somewhat reminds me of Premier League club Brentford's home in west London. Both stadiums make use of an innovation I'm surprised is not more common – multi coloured seats dotted around in no pattern. To the untrained eye, this makes a half-full stand look full, as it is hard to distinguish between the seats and the actual people sitting in them.

Around the perimeter of the pitch, premium, comfier seats are perched ostentatiously in isolation, giving a closer view. In basketball, the best seats are low down and 'courtside', a term that MLS teams sometimes use in their marketing for these seats, but is an alien concept to a European football fan. After all, it's harder to get a good view of what's going on from lower down near the pitch. The grass quality is excellent, despite the challenges of maintaining perfect green in a place where it gets very hot and rarely rains. I am here to see the Dash, the women's team, who are playing Racing Louisville from Kentucky. The Dash and the men's side Dynamo have different names and badges, again different to Europe where women's teams tend to have the same name, badge and kit as their male counterparts.

The Dynamo were founded first in very American circumstances. Back in 2005, less than a decade into the MLS's life, the San Jose Earthquakes were having an excellent season. The California side won the Supporters' Shield, the award for winning the most games in the 'regular season', a trophy not to be confused with the MLS Cup, which is awarded to the winner of a mini tournament at the end of the season. The Earthquakes' owner, entertainment company AEG, were struggling to find a suitable stadium in San Jose so simply moved the team to Houston, which was seen as a big and potentially lucrative 'media market' lacking a soccer team, especially given the large local Hispanic population. In Europe, such an act would be sacrilege. In 2003, Wimbledon, lovable underdogs based in south London, relocated to the city of Milton Keynes sixty miles away after an ongoing struggle to find somewhere to play. The move sparked outcry and the new club, MK

Dons, are still reviled by many fans of all colours. A new phoenix club, AFC Wimbledon, was founded shortly after and have since risen through the leagues, playing against MK Dons many times in England's third and fourth tiers in recent years, contesting one of the game's most bitter rivalries.

In the US, it is common for clubs to relocate across far greater distances in search of a bigger 'media market'. In 1946, the Cleveland Rams NFL side moved thousands of miles west from Ohio to Los Angeles, where they played until 1994. They then moved back east to St Louis, winning the Super Bowl in 1999. In 2015, the team was moved by Stan Kroenke, who also owns Arsenal, back to LA. America's second-biggest city had no NFL team for two decades but now has two, the Rams and the Chargers, who moved from San Diego in 2017.

As well as moving teams around in pursuit of profit, another American phenomenon involves corporate officials sitting down to come up with a team name and team colours. This is unlike Europe where badges, colours and names have emerged organically over decades, often with quirky backstories. Hollywood actor Tom Hanks supports Aston Villa because of the unique name. 'The very first time I came to London, the football scores were on in the morning, and it was all these cities I didn't quite understand. Where is Stoke? Where is Blacksworth [sic]? Where is Slough? I didn't know. And then along came the score . . . "Aston Villa". I said, "Aston Villa – what a beautiful sounding vacation paradise. I'll lay in the sun, bring me a piña colada. I'll spend two weeks in Aston Villa."'[4]

The north of Birmingham isn't a typical holiday destination, but Hanks stuck with the team and has even attended a few games. The club's name comes from an actual villa which once stood in the area. Tottenham Hotspur are named after Sir Henry Percy, better known as Sir Harry Hotspur, an English nobleman whose descendants owned land in the area.⁵ The Swiss top division features both Grasshopper Club Zürich and Young Boys of Bern, while African club football has some particularly excellent names, like Miscellaneous Sporting Club from Botswana, Invincible Eleven from Liberia and Cape Coast Mysterious Ebusua Dwarfs from Ghana. US teams tend to sound like they have been decided by a marketing committee, which is often the case.

The story of Houston Dynamo's name also features another American theme – offensive sports team names. Club officials were inspired by German teams which have their year of foundation in their name, like Schalke 04 and Hannover 96 (for 1904 and 1896 respectively). With the club's founding year of 2006 not sounding very impressive, Houston's management chose the city's founding year of 1836. This backfired. The *New York Times* reported that many Hispanics in the city greeted the new name 'with a shudder' due to its association with a year that 'a group of English-speaking interlopers waged a war of secession that resulted in Mexico's loss of Texas, ushering in more than a century of violence and discrimination against Mexicans in the state'.⁶ This was a particular problem given that the new team was hoping to tap into the city's football-mad Mexican community, the city of Houston already having attracted big crowds for soccer games featuring Mexican club sides, a reason cited for the move from San Jose. The name was swiftly changed to Houston Dynamo, reflecting the city's role at the heart of the space industry. In recent years the Washington Redskins NFL team have changed their name to the Commanders, and the Cleveland Indians to the Guardians, both ditching names justifiably deemed offensive by many Native Americans.

As for the colour of Houston Dynamo's kit, former club president Chris Canetti explains that 'there was a lot of red and a lot of blue in the league when we came into it. We wanted something to distinguish ourselves and wanted to be in a situation where if you saw an orange jersey in the United States, you knew with certainty that it was a Dynamo jersey.'[7] The women's team took the same colours when it was founded in 2013 as an 'expansion team' in the National Women's Soccer League. The new team took the name 'Dash', referring to the speed of a horse, a very Texan animal.

While trying to decide which MLS or NWSL team to feature in this book, I had two criteria. First, I wanted a team far from those cosmopolitan coastal cities. I wanted to go somewhere where the sport is relatively alien. Houston fits the bill nicely. Second, I wanted a shirt that spoke to that notion of American exceptionalism, the idea that the US is fundamentally different and unique. The shirts worn by the Dynamo and the Dash – in the same colour and with the same sponsor, albeit with a different badge – struck me as fascinating too. Both have been sponsored for a while now by the MD Anderson Cancer Center, with the word 'cancer' struck out to represent efforts to eliminate the disease. This seemed odd from my European perspective. Why is a hospital sponsoring a football team? The centre, based nearby at the University of Texas, is at the global cutting edge of treatment and research, and the arrangement seems in many respects a wholesome one as far as football sponsorships go. Not only does it celebrate a world-leading local employer, but the partnership also involves promoting several cancer-prevention initiatives, no bad thing in a part of the world where obesity is a huge problem. These initiatives include free sunscreen for fans, a tobacco-free stadium, blood donation drives and on-pitch celebrations of cancer survivors.[8,9] I initially thought this might be a purely charitable arrangement like Barcelona's with UNICEF where the logo is carried for no fee to promote a good cause, but that isn't the case. The MD Anderson Cancer Center paid a healthy sum, several million dollars a year, to sponsor the two teams combined. The idea of a big local hospital spending money on football advertising, rather than on doctors and machines, seemed like a mad one to me. But in the US, healthcare is big business. The system is privatised, run on an insurance basis rather than being centrally funded by the government, although government subsidies for the poor and the elderly exist. The US spends far more per person on healthcare than equivalently wealthy countries, but doesn't necessarily get more for it. Life expectancy in the US is far worse than in European countries that spend comparable amounts on healthcare, although this gap is heavily driven by a higher death rate among young people killed by drug overdoses, gun violence and dangerous driving. For those who do have access to good health insurance, though, provision is probably better than in 'socialised' European systems. The US has better cancer survival rates than European countries, though this is partly explained by more Europeans reaching old age, where cancer is far more prevalent. Another reason is that more Europeans smoke. Whichever side of the argument you fall on, when it comes to healthcare, the USA and Europe are extremely different. The hospital name on the shirts of the Houston Dash and Dynamo is partly a marketing device to drum up donations, and also a straightforward advertisement to encourage consumers – seriously ill people – to consider the services of their hospital rather than others. I did slightly reconsider how exceptional this was when accompanying a friend who supports York City, a club in the fifth tier of English football, on a disappointing 3–1 defeat away at Barnet in north London in February 2025. The billboards at Barnet's stadium carried signs for Hendon hospital, a local private healthcare facility. A difference is that in the UK hospitals like this generally deal with non-emergency conditions, and that cancer treatment is still available for free – if flawed and sometimes with long waiting lists – to anyone who needs it. York themselves were sponsored for several seasons in the 2010s by Benenden Health, a private healthcare provider, while the Vitality Stadium, home of longstanding Premier League side Bournemouth, is also named after a health insurance company. So, this stuff is not completely limited to the US.

Before the game in Houston began, I took a lap of the stadium and was struck by the presence of lots of big groups of schoolchildren. The club encourages them to get more bums on seats – the stadium was nowhere near full, but a gate of a few thousand fans is respectable in a part of the world where club football is a new phenomenon. Suddenly, about half an hour before kick-off, I heard the distant din of drums. Lots of drums. Walking towards the source of the noise, I encountered twenty or so drummers. Charmingly, some were encouraging young children to hit a drum with their hands before other drummers gathered around the child, engulfing them in a wall of sound, making them feel like they were part of the band. This might seem cringeworthy to the hardened European football fan, but felt like an example of taking a universal game and injecting it with local culture – the American tradition of big bands. 'We have about twenty or thirty band members and we practise before the game in the parking lot,' group leader Cameron told me, a safe distance away from his noisy bandmates. 'Kids come and bang drums, we surround them and make them feel part of it.' He supports all Houston teams: the Texans in the NFL, the Astros who won baseball's World Series in 2017 and 2022, and the Rockets in the NBA. But the two soccer teams are his favourites. This is a refreshing element of football in the US. It is completely normal to support men's and women's teams, both at the club and international level as different branches of the same entity. Although some Europeans think like this, it is rare, simply because men's teams have far deeper histories and traditions. In Texas it is all new.

Cameron also notes the appeal of following Houston Dash when the cheapest tickets are $12 in a country where sport is ruthlessly commercialised. American sports teams often charge simply as much as the market will bear, meaning hundreds or even thousands of pounds for big NBA and NFL games, with none of the social taboos on expensive tickets that exist in Europe. Visitors to England are sometimes baffled that it is simply not possible to get tickets for a sold-out Premier League match through official channels, even with the willingness to pay way over the odds. The stadium in Houston is far from full for this early-season league game but there have been sell-outs for play-off matches. Unlike the Dynamo, the Dash attract genuine stars. For instance, English striker Rachel Daly played in Houston for six years after coming through the US college system before moving to the Women's Super League (WSL) where she won player of the season in 2022–23 after her goal-heavy, record-equalling season for Aston Villa. Another former Houston Dash star is Carli Lloyd, one of the most famous US soccer players of all time and a genuine US celebrity.

In the concourse just before kick-off, after sampling some excellent Mexican food, I saw a 'make your own sign' station where young children were drawing pictures and writing words of encouragement to hold up during the game. Again, my European footballing brain cringed at this, but maybe it shouldn't have. I also saw adverts for a 'British Night', which turned out to be a promotional gimmick for the following week's men's team game against the San Jose Earthquakes. 'Join us for a night of football (the original kind), and pre-match festivities including display cars, English food and drink and games,' the poster said, showing

London landmarks as well as a traditional policeman's hat and a Triumph Spitfire sports car. Standing beneath the poster were a middle-aged Mexican couple, Carlos and Diana, both wearing the shirts of Mexican club Tigres. They were primarily here to see the Mexicans in the Houston team including star player María Sánchez, a right-winger.

Before kick-off came that classic American sporting sight – a glamorous woman singing the national anthem in an impressive but somewhat over-the-top manner, her voice warbling as the camera zoomed in on her before cutting away to a fluttering American flag. All around me people stood to attention, many placing their right hand above their heart. The game kicked off, and this itself was noticeable, as kick-off was eight minutes later than advertised, for unclear reasons. For all the chaos of European football, games never kick off late apart from in exceptional circumstances, such as policing or traffic problems – otherwise it would create a knock-on effect to broadcasting schedules and gambling markets among other things. Once the game did get under way and the Dash started passing it around, the biggest cheer was reserved for María Sánchez, a stalwart of the Mexican national team in her fourth season with the Dash. The previous December, she signed the largest contract in NWSL history – $1.5 million over three years. Three weeks after my visit, though, she confirmed on social media that she had 'requested an immediate trade', as is possible in the MLS system where players have more control over their own destiny than in Europe.[10] She left for the San Diego Wave shortly after.

The opening minutes were not good from a home perspective. The Houston back line was repeatedly sliced through by Louisville, who scored a goal ruled out for a close offside, and then somehow missed an excellent chance shortly after. Glancing around me to take in the scene as Houston survived the opening barrages of attack, I took in the advertising boards, as I always like to do when watching a match in a new stadium. They were mostly for local businesses, like the Houston branch of Take 5 Oil Change, for motor repairs. As well as its hospital shirt sponsor, Houston Dash has an 'official fertility sponsor', something I have never seen before, despite all sorts of weirdly niche deals in European football. Manchester United has a 'global mattress and pillow partner', MLILY, based in Jiangsu in China, a company which the club website says is 'proud to lay claim to having the biggest foam production base in Asia, producing over 4,000m^3 of foam blocks of different densities on a daily basis'.

The game was not a classic and, by the end of the first half, the crowd were doing Mexican waves, never an endorsement of the entertainment on offer. María Sánchez was the brightest player on the pitch, the US-born Mexican repeatedly causing problems for the left side of the Louisville defence before cutting balls back into the box, but these opportunities were squandered. Selfishness in front of goal was an issue for both sides who seemed to be in the habit of taking pot shots straight at the goalkeeper rather than working the ball into more dangerous positions. A standout player was Houston goalkeeper Jane Campbell who saved the home team on a couple of occasions. Midway through the first half, she raced out of her goal to bravely put her body between the goal and an oncoming Louisville striker. A few minutes later, she made a brilliant point-blank save when an opponent got on the end of a looping free kick.

Louisville looked a bright side too, with quick passing through the midfield and good control on the ball, but no end product, with the Dash defending valiantly. In the dying moments, Louisville striker Kayla Fischer finally beat goalkeeper Campbell, but a Houston defender sprinted back and athletically scooped the ball off the line. After fourteen minutes of injury time it ended goalless.

Watching the highlights back on YouTube later, I was struck at how professional the whole thing looked with an excellent stadium and multiple camera angles. Sometimes women's football can look a little amateurish on TV, not through any fault of the players but because of facilities and broadcasters not investing as much money into it as the men's game. That is not the case in the NWSL.

A few days earlier, four hours to the north of Houston, on the edge of Texas's second city of Dallas, I paid a visit to the Sixth Floor Museum at Dealey Plaza. This is the site where President John F. Kennedy was assassinated in 1963. I was in town to watch the US men's national team and began my trip to the AT&T Stadium with an experience familiar from previous trips to the US – scrambling along a grass verge while giant vehicles roar past. I like walking. Americans, in general, do not. When I asked my hotel receptionist in Arlington how best to walk to a stadium which Google Maps told me was slightly more than a mile away, she gave a quizzical look and told me it simply wasn't possible. 'You can't.' I put this down to cultural differences and cracked on, before realising she was right, it was literally not possible. I could see the stadium from my hotel car park a short distance across a road bridge. But when I got to the bridge it was clear there was no safe way to cross it on foot. After starting to attempt the walk along the hard shoulder, I quickly changed my mind and headed back to the safety of a fast-food restaurant where I called a taxi for the four-minute journey.

The AT&T Stadium is named after one of the country's biggest telecoms firms and sits in a vast sporting district which includes not one baseball stadium but two. The Texas Rangers, once part-owned by Texas governor George W. Bush before he was elected president, won baseball's World Series in 2023.[11] They played at Globe Life Park from 1994 until 2019. Its grand brick exterior is still standing, but now houses office space. There was nothing particularly wrong with the stadium, but Texas is being hit hard by climate change and it is impossible to air condition an outdoor venue. This problem will only get worse – by the 2060s, Dallas is projected to record fifty-five days a year of temperatures in excess of 100°F, compared to an average of fifteen days in the 1990s and 2000s.[12] Baseball is the US's summer sport and Globe Life Park was comfortably the hottest stadium in Major League Baseball when the owner said the lack of air-conditioning 'made it difficult to play games during inclement weather and prevented the stadium from attracting concerts, special events and the jewel of professional baseball, the All-Star game'.[13] On the March day I visited, though, the conditions were rather British – grey and drizzly. Globe Life Park's replacement right next door is a new climate-controlled stadium with a retractable roof, the similarly named Globe Life Field. I peered through the blacked-out windows into the vast dome as visitors in Texas Rangers caps posed for pictures with statues of famous former players outside. Further along, past the two baseball stadiums, was Texas Live!, a complex of bars, restaurants and shops. A water fountain was out of service and had a sign next to it outlining 'water feature rules': 'changing diapers within six feet of fountain' was prohibited, as was 'use of the fountain when ill with diarrhoea'. Fair enough.

   I kept walking towards the biggest venue in this complex of big venues, the vast AT&T Stadium, which looks like a spaceship has landed in the suburb of Arlington. This venue is home to the Dallas Cowboys, often named 'America's Team' due to their massive national fanbase, despite not reaching a Super Bowl since back-to-back wins in 1995 and 1996. It is nicknamed Jerry World after Jerry Jones, the Cowboys' larger-than-life owner who has turned the team into the most valuable organisation in sport, valued at $9 billion in 2023 according to *Forbes*.[14] The top of that list is dominated by American sports teams, with Real Madrid down in eleventh place at $6 billion the highest-ranked soccer team, and Manchester United narrowly behind them. Like United, the Cowboys have maintained commercial dominance despite mediocre results on the pitch. A key factor in the huge valuations of American sport teams, and comparably low ones for European football clubs despite their bigger global stature - alongside the simple fact that America has far more consumers than any European country and those people are on average significantly richer and buy more stuff - is that American leagues do not have relegation. This is very different to football where even the biggest clubs have the risk that a bad season could mean dropping out of the top league entirely, meaning a sudden and disastrous drop in revenue. This makes it far harder to produce reliable long-term financial plans compared to US sports. Although it is unlikely any of Europe's biggest football teams will be relegated any time soon, Manchester United have failed to qualify for the Champions League several times since the departure of Sir Alex Ferguson in 2013. Plans for a European Super League, floated in 2021 then quickly abandoned after huge fan backlash, were about changing all this so that the biggest teams would play each other more often, with places allocated by money and status rather than sporting merit. Fans hated it and the plan died.

The US men's national team are often referred to by the not very catchy acronym 'USMNT' to distinguish them from the more successful 'USWNT'. I was in town for the semi-final of the CONCACAF Nations League, CONCACAF being the football confederation made up of countries from North America, Central America and the Caribbean. CONCACAF, alongside other continental confederations including UEFA, introduced the Nations

League as a sort of glorified version of international friendly matches. The USMNT won the first two tournaments in 2021 and 2023. The games in Arlington had a curious format. The semi-finals were organised as two games for the price of one, back-to-back matches on a Thursday evening, before the final on Sunday. The first semi was USA vs Jamaica and the second Panama vs Mexico. The tournament is sponsored by some Middle Eastern names – Qatar Airways and Aramco – that we will come onto later.

Walking towards the AT&T Stadium, I could see the roof was closed, though because of rain, not heat. This would be my first experience watching professional football indoors. To get there, I had to walk through the massive parking lot. As a casual follower of American sports, I have heard about 'tailgating', the tradition of consuming food and drink from the boot of someone's car before a game. This doesn't translate to European football culture because our cars are too small. We also prefer to drink in bars or pubs, and fewer people drive to matches. If you take a look at Google Maps' satellite view and compare the AT&T Stadium in Arlington with Wembley Stadium in London, the Santiago Bernabéu Stadium in Madrid or the Stade de France in Paris, you will see that all four are comparable in size, but while the European stadiums are surrounded by urban buildings, the Texas stadium is in a sea of grey asphalt. People drive everywhere in Texas.

There was plenty of space for tailgating, but it was hard to find evidence of it happening, not helped by the fact it was a weekday afternoon and the weather was unusually bad. But I did meet a group who had made the journey from Panama City. They were handing out margaritas from the back of their SUV. Remarkably, one of the group was 'Pito' Rodríguez, who won fifty-nine caps for the Panama national team including appearances at the 2005 CONCACAF Gold Cup where the tiny Central American country reached the final before losing to the USA on penalties. Rodríguez didn't speak English, but some of those he was with did. 'Panama has money, but we have nothing for sport,' said his friend. 'It's not fair for our players.' CONCACAF consists of forty-one member associations, from Canada in the north to Panama in the south, plus the entire Caribbean. These Panamanians believed the confederation is biased towards the two countries – Mexico and the USA – that contain three-quarters of the body's population. They darkly suggest that if Jamaica were to somehow beat their hosts in the first game, the referee would find a way to ensure Mexico beat Panama later to ensure decent viewing figures for the final.

Waiting for the gates to open I met Aldo Cabrera, a young man carrying a flag split in half: on one side the stars and stripes of the USA, on the other the green, white and red of Mexico. 'I was born in Texas, but my parents come from Mexico,' he tells me. 'I grew up in the borderlands.' His allegiance has traditionally been with the nation of his parents, but things are changing. 'The last two years, the USA has got better, and Mexico has got worse. The US has more players in Europe now. In high school, you see kids playing soccer more than football and baseball.'

Once inside, I take a walk around this vast arena with its huge concourses and state-of-the-art technology. I've watched football in many places and the AT&T Stadium in Arlington has objectively the best facilities of any of them. It is huge. European stadiums are generally packed into an urban area where every square metre is at a premium. Here, eating and drinking is part of the experience as much as the actual sport itself; the range and quality exceeded anything I've seen in an English ground. The prices were steep, though. Still, I got my free meal – topped nachos – in the press box, which was also huge. There was a jumbotron with screens above the pitch, like the one I saw at Schalke's stadium in Germany, but far bigger. Everything is huge in this part of the world.

Ahead of kick-off I wandered the stadium's vast concourses to get a feel for the atmosphere. Any journalist will be wearily familiar with the 'vox pop', the practice of stopping passers-by to ask them questions. It is unscientific but sometimes helpful for getting a feel for a place. I have vox-popped countless times in the UK, and some other countries too, and it's generally a bit of a thankless task. People are usually wary and, if they do speak to you, their replies are somewhat mumbled. In the US, the experience is totally different. Perhaps it is the culture of high-school debating, or a deeper culture of optimism and confidence, but vox-popping in Texas was an absolute dream. Everybody I spoke to was delighted to chat and rattled off a series of well-articulated points as I scribbled on my notepad.

Chris, Ben and Julian were a group of USMNT fans who had travelled to Dallas all the way from Washington DC, a three-and-a-half-hour flight away. 'If you're a soccer fan in the US, the women's and men's national teams are really the teams you root for,' said Ben. 'They have history, and they play at a higher level than the club sides.' Only two players in that day's US squad were playing at the top of the European game. Weston McKennie at Juventus as well as star player Christian Pulisic, who at the time was doing well at AC Milan after a disappointing spell at Chelsea. He joined from Borussia Dortmund on the back of a £58 million transfer fee and lots of hype. A hot topic among those I spoke to was how national team players had been failed by their clubs in Europe, with English clubs coming in for a kicking. Chris argued that Weston McKennie was badly treated by Leeds United, while Pulisic, easily the biggest name in US men's soccer, was set up to fail at 'dysfunctional' Chelsea, he argued.

I also met Connor and Sheyna, a couple who had made the

three-hour drive to Dallas from Oklahoma City. Their local club OKC Energy, who played in the USA's second-tier USL Championship, recently ceased operations. With no professional team and far from the country's liberal coasts, Oklahoma City is one of the last places you might associate with football, but they both told me the sport was getting bigger and bigger where they lived. 'I'm a soccer coach,' said Connor. 'All the kids have Lionel Messi jerseys.'

'People follow the European leagues more because we don't have an MLS team,' Sheyna explained, adding that her favourite sport was 'misunderstood' by friends and relatives. 'People say it's not really physical.' She observed that soccer's relative lack of physicality may be to its benefit in the long run, given the gathering body of grim evidence linking American football, where huge men running into each other and colliding helmets is an intrinsic part of the game, to a brain disorder called chronic traumatic encephalopathy (CTE). 'People who don't watch (soccer) say "Who wants to see people kick a ball for ninety minutes and not score any goals?"' But she astutely noted that the low-scoring nature of football is exactly why it is a brilliant sport. Games can and frequently do change trajectory in the blink of an eye, and upsets are far more common than in high-scoring sports.

Newly built stadiums are often criticised for lacking in character, but I didn't feel that was the case there. The AT&T Stadium felt vast, shiny and distinctively *American*. Unfortunately, the game was a bit of a damp squib. The curious double-header arrangement meant the first semi-final kicked off at 6 p.m., early on a weekday when there was a lot of other sport going on including the climax of the NCAA college basketball tournament, a huge deal in Texas. The stadium was remarkably empty. I was surprised. I had come to cover football's next frontier, where everyone was telling me the game was booming. Sure, there were mitigating circumstances. As well as the 6 p.m. weekday kick-off being tricky, Texas is not a soccer hotbed compared to other parts of the US, Jamaica have little in the way of travelling support, and the Nations League had not caught the public imagination. Even so, there couldn't have been more than a couple of thousand people in the vast stadium. It did slowly fill up as time went on, but many of them curious Mexicans taking in the free game included with the one that they really cared about later.

There were also a hundred Outlaws, the hardcore group of fans who follow the USMNT around the world, bedecked in stereotypically all-American garb like cowboy hats and stars-and-stripes. They were making a fair bit of noise with drums, as well as singing 'U-S-A' and the tongue-in-cheek chant 'It's called soccer!' What noise came from the home fans was swiftly quietened when Jamaica took a shock lead after just thirty seconds through Greg Leigh of Oxford United in England's third tier. It was an amateurish goal to concede, a speculative throw-in splitting the US defence before a deflected cross bobbled into Leigh's path, his header weakly parried into the net by Nottingham Forest goalkeeper Matt Turner.

After the initial shock, the US struggled to assert their position as favourites, hogging possession but doing very little with it. The game was ponderous, the bizarre setting of a huge but almost empty stadium not helping the game's intensity levels. As full-time approached the stadium was around one-third full, the crowd mostly noisy Mexicans in early for their team's game, supporting Jamaica as easier prospective opponents in the final, and eager to get one over on their neighbours. Many of the billboards for the USA game were in Spanish, advertising brands like Panafoto, an electronics manufacturer in Panama City, alongside various Mexican companies. It was a curious inversion of the usual economic power dynamic between the US and Latin America.

In the 96th minute, USA goalkeeper Matt Turner came up for a corner-kick. The ball flew straight past him, past the US attacking players, and was headed in by Cory Burke, a Jamaican defender who was playing his club football in the US for the New York Red Bulls. The own goal, levelling the score at the death, appeared to stun the Jamaicans who found it difficult to pick themselves up in extra time. Haji Wright of Coventry City scored twice for the US during the added thirty minutes to put them through to the Nations League final.

That same evening, the stadium now almost full, Mexico easily swept aside Panama 3–0, although the scoreline didn't tell the full story as Panama had more shots and possession than their more fêted rivals. I had left for elsewhere in Texas by the time the final came around three days later but the competition was won 2–0 by the USA with goals from Tyler Adams of Bournemouth and Giovanni Reyna of Borussia Dortmund, the latter being the son of two national team players, Claudio and Danielle Reyna. This completed a 'three-peat', the US having won all three of the first CONCACAF Nations League competitions. My time in Texas showed me football in the USA has promise but there is an awful long way to go before it gets close to the popularity of the country's other big sports, especially in places like Dallas and Houston.

It is not fair to say football in the US began in 1994. The first-ever international fixture outside the UK saw the USA host Canada in New Jersey in 1885, and the American Football Association was the second professional US sports league to be formed after Major League Baseball.[15] In its early years, the club game was dominated by Clark ONT, a team with its origins in New Jersey's Clark Thread Company factory which had the tallest chimney in North

America. The ONT stood for Our New Thread, the team's name effectively an advert for a new fabric – the country's embrace of commercialism in sport has a long history. Other early US teams included St Louis Vesper Buick, named after its automotive sponsor, and Bethlehem Steel, named after the Pennsylvania steel company that was its chief benefactor. Football was relatively big in the US in the early twentieth century, especially in the industrial north-east, and the US came third in the first ever World Cup in Uruguay. But things fizzled out during the Great Depression of the 1930s which devastated many of the industries which had sponsored teams. Lacking the deep cultural and social roots which the game had in Europe and South America, the sport disappeared into obscurity, though the US did sensationally beat England 1–0 at the 1950 World Cup.

Attempts were made to revive the sport in the 1960s, but a foreign game with simple yet rigid rules was an odd fit for a confident superpower used to doing things its own way. The North American Soccer League was founded in 1968 with some changes – draws were abolished and replaced with a shoot-out in which players started 35 yards out and had five seconds to dribble and shoot. It was seen as sacrilegious by football's old guard but a version of it, the penalty shoot-out, would go on to become standard as a tie-breaker. In June 1975, American soccer made the news globally when the best player in the world, Brazilian striker Pelé, joined the New York Cosmos. The documentary film *Once in a Lifetime* immortalises the wild summer of 1977 in New York City, a place riven by bankruptcy, a serial killer and power blackouts.[16] The famous Studio 54 nightclub hosted football legends including Pelé as well as Franz Beckenbauer, Giorgio Chinaglia and Carlos Alberto, alongside showbiz icons like Elton John, Barbra Streisand and Grace Jones, who would ride around naked on a white horse.

The football itself was a bit of a culture shock. TV honcho and Cosmos investor Steve Ross witnessed German legend Beckenbauer assume his familiar role dictating play at the back, only to tell his coaching staff, 'Get the Kraut into midfield!'[17] After Pelé scored a bullet header to equalise in his first game at the Cosmos' home on Randall's Island, he informed Clive Toye, the club's British general manager, that he would be heading home to Brazil to seek treatment for a curious green fungus that had appeared on his foot. Pelé was told this was the green paint which was used to make dirt patches on the field look more like grass for the benefit of TV viewers.[18]

The Brazilian superstar certainly boosted the profile of the game in the US, with the Cosmos routinely packing out the Giants Stadium's 80,000 seats, before the team collapsed into a soap opera of warring egos. Pelé won the 1977 Soccer Bowl in his last game for the team, planting a seed that would flower many years later with the arrival of David Beckham and, some years later, Lionel Messi. Other stars to come to the US included English World Cup winners Geoff Hurst and Bobby Moore. Another was England striker Trevor Francis, who had been football's first £1 million-pound signing following his transfer from Birmingham City to Nottingham Forest in 1979. He was loaned to Detroit Express in the summer off-season in 1978 and 1979. 'Every time I get the ball, the commentator goes crazy and calls me "Trevor Francis Superstar",' he said. 'I was interviewed by a woman journalist soon after I got here and one of the first things she wanted to know was how long I'd been a superstar. I said "about three days".'[19]

As the 1980s ticked around, the league's financial problems were laid bare by recession. Teams were still shelling out huge sums on glamorous arrivals, but the league was barely making any money, and struggling to get heard in a country where it lagged behind four other sports as well as countless other entertainment options. In 1981, the Soccer Bowl was contested between the two best sides, the Chicago Sting and the New York Cosmos, but fans in neither city could see it live. It was 'tape delayed' in Chicago because the network chose to show a rerun of *The Love Boat*, a sitcom based on a cruise ship. Running out of money and interest, the NASL folded in 1985.

The league failed but there was still interest in the game. In 1984, Los Angeles had hosted the Olympic Games and 101,799 fans packed out Pasadena's Rose Bowl for the men's gold medal match in which France beat Brazil 2–0, showing that there was huge appetite for football in the US if it could be packaged up in the right way. (Ten years later, the same stadium would host the World Cup final, with Brazil beating Italy on penalties after a 0–0 draw, Roberto Baggio missing the crucial spot-kick.) Football was becoming more and more popular as a participation sport, particularly for women and children.

The men's team had long been poor, failing to qualify for the World Cup in the decades after that shock win against England in 1950 but things changed in 1990 when Paul Caligiuri scored a looping shot to help his side beat Trinidad and Tobago in a World Cup qualifier with what the American media dubbed 'the shot heard round the world'. It meant the USMNT would be at Italia 90, their first tournament in forty years, going some way to legitimising FIFA's decision to give the following tournament to the US.[20] 'That victory not only changed the course of US soccer forever, but it brought the largest sports market into the FIFA family forever, and that has a huge impact for global soccer,' Caligiuri said later. 'We're no longer considered a niche sport or a foreign sport. This is an American sport.'[21] (He went on to describe the win in the Caribbean as 'the greatest victory of any sport, ever', which is a bit of a stretch.) The US team bowed out of Italia 90 with three defeats, though this was a team largely made up of college-standard players on a shoestring budget, competing against monied professionals. They put in a surprisingly strong performance against the hosts in Rome, only losing 1–0, laying the groundwork for the summer four years later when football in the US would truly come of age.

With the benefit of hindsight, the 1994 World Cup in the US, the fourth won by Brazil, can be viewed as a critical turning point in the global game, when football's commercial potential and global economic reach was recognised for the first time.[22] Defying the country's reputation as a footballing backwater, stadiums were packed, attracting first- and second-generation immigrants from footballing hotspots and visiting tourists, as well as curious locals keen to find out more about the world's most popular sport. Remarkably, the tournament has the highest average attendance of any tournament ever with more than 69,000 per match, and the highest overall attendance of over 3.5 million, despite only twenty-four teams competing (the number of participants increasing to thirty-two for the following tournament in France in 1998).[23] The US has lots of huge stadiums – although almost every game was sold out in more obvious footballing hotspots like Germany in 2006 and Brazil in 2014, stadiums were smaller on average.

A 1994 news report by British broadcaster Channel 4 showed interviews with Chicago residents who barely knew what soccer was, let alone the finer details of the World Cup about to kick off in their city. Americans who do follow the game are forced to confront something this country is not used to: mediocrity. Los Angeles Dodgers coach Tommy Lasorda, clearly ignorant about the game, was also questioned by Channel 4. 'Don't ever come to me and tell me that America doesn't have a chance to win the

American soccer tournament. They have a chance, and I predict that America will win!'[24] They did not win. The USMNT did well to get out of a tough group but lost in the next round to eventual winners Brazil.

One of the biggest legacies of USA 1994 was the establishment of the MLS. When the US were awarded the tournament back in 1988, part of the deal was that the country's footballing authorities had to establish a top-flight soccer league following the collapse of the NASL three years earlier.[25] In the 1990s and 2000s it became much easier for Americans to follow the game outside major international tournaments, both domestically with the MLS and overseas where players like Landon Donovan, Clint Dempsey and DaMarcus Beasley were playing in Europe's top leagues. Football has some advantages compared to American sports for a TV audience. First, it is far shorter. With a whole game lasting less than two hours including half-time, it is an easier commitment to watch in full than American football or basketball, which are closer to the three- or even four-hour mark. (Faced with declining attendances, baseball has recently introduced far stricter timing rules which have sped up games without changing any of the core rules, and has been a huge success.)

Also, European football games generally take place during weekend mornings in the US, a time when most people are at home and there is little competition from other entertainment. Broadcaster NBC uses the hashtag #MyPLMorning to promote the game and it has been a big success. The league signed a six-year deal in 2022 worth $450 million per season, more than five times the first deal signed nine years earlier. The morning slot is a large part of how the league markets itself. Joshua Robinson and Jonathan Clegg, authors of *The Club*, the definitive history of the Premier League as a business, describe the appeal:

You could sleep in on a Saturday morning, watch a game at 10 a.m., and still have the rest of the day to live like a functional human. Or if you happened to be up at 7.30 a.m. with a bouncing five-year-old, you could at least have some live sports with your coffee before the cartoons took over. And if you wanted more, you could take in a whole double-header in the same time it takes to slog through a single college football game, with 80 per cent fewer adverts for pick-up trucks.[26]

The new MLS finally kicked off in 1996 with ten teams, divided into a Western Conference and an Eastern Conference. All professional US sports leagues have some sort of geographical division, in the early stages at least, because of the vast distances involved. The US kept up its reputation as football's laboratory, a place where innovations which might offend fans elsewhere could be tried out. One example was a variation on the traditional penalty shoot-out where an attacker runs from distance. While some Europeans may find it gauche, there is an argument that it's not only more entertaining but better rewarding of skill rather than luck. Nevertheless, it has been abandoned, alongside other ideas to increase interest like timeouts, kick-ins instead of throw-ins, and making the goals bigger. Attendances in the MLS in the 2000s were not great, although soccer's reputation got a boost from the 2002 World Cup in South Korea and Japan which saw the US's first ever World Cup knockout win, beating neighbours Mexico 2–0 before losing to eventual finalists Germany in the quarter-finals.

Then came the MLS's big moment when the most recognisable footballer in the world attempted to follow in Pelé's footsteps by breaking America. On 10 January 2007, David Beckham announced that he would finish his contract at Real Madrid that summer and join the little-known LA Galaxy. 'He's going to Hollywood to be half a film star,' scoffed Real Madrid club president Felipe Calderón. 'Our technical staff were right not to extend his contract, and that has been proved by the fact that no other technical staff in the world wanted him other than Los Angeles.'[27] Beckham had the last laugh by winning La Liga at the end of that season and leaving Madrid a hero. Arriving at a time when the MLS was in a bit of a rut, Beckham gave the league a huge injection of glamour. His arrival was met with 5,000 fans, 700 journalists, a news helicopter and cannons spurting out confetti. He was awarded not only a huge salary, but an unusual revenue-sharing deal allowing him a cut of TV revenue and shirt sales.[28] Beckham's initial success was limited and there was some resentment from his team mates including USMNT star Landon Donovan, who told the press the Englishman 'wasn't committed' to the team. Donovan would become the face of US Soccer following the national team's first big breakthrough cultural moment – an injury-time winner against Algeria in the 2010 World Cup in South Africa. This showed Americans the magic of football as a low-scoring game where everything can change in an instant.

At first, Beckham was unimpressive on the pitch but like so often in his career his ability shone through when it mattered. He won the MLS Cup in 2011 and 2012 before leaving the US – for a while – with his reputation enhanced. Beckham would return to the US a few years later in a very different role. A curious part of the lavish contract Beckham signed with LA Galaxy was the option to buy an MLS 'expansion team' for $25 million.[29] In January 2018, the MLS gave approval to a new team. Beckham would be part of the ownership group in the city of Miami, long seen as ripe for a football team because of the city's huge Hispanic population. It has been noted that soccer is the US's only truly racially diverse sport. The

NHL is mainly white, while the NBA and NFL are mainly black. Major League Baseball has many Hispanic players, but African American numbers are falling. Comparatively, the MLS features white, black and Hispanic Americans, as well as players from all over the world, and this is represented in the sport's fan base.[30]

This new club – named Internacional de Fútbol Miami, but universally known as Inter Miami – would embrace the city's bilingual character. After trying a few different colours, the team announced it would play in bright pink, a nod to Miami sunsets, flamingos and the city's art deco buildings. 'Drive around Miami and it's a very recurring colour,' Beckham later told *The Times* newspaper. 'At the time, a lot of people were saying "Don't go for pink". I was the one who said it must be the main colour. So that was me. I'm actually very proud of it.'[31] After years of wrangling over a stadium, Inter Miami played their first game in March 2020.

In 2023, after years of groundwork, Beckham secured the prize he had long dreamed of – signing Lionel Messi, who had just spent two underwhelming years alongside Neymar and Kylian Mbappé at Paris Saint-Germain. The announcement put noses out of joint in Saudi Arabia – the country's tourist board had a long-standing and hugely expensive contract with Messi as a paid ambassador. Many expected him to play in the Kingdom at the end of his career, a final act in the Messi vs Ronaldo saga. But Miami stole a march on the Saudis, offering the Argentinian the chance to secure his legacy by helping the global game to finally conquer the US, the timing neatly fitting with the 2026 World Cup.

Beckham offered Messi the chance to play alongside former Barcelona teammates Luis Suárez and Sergio Busquets, as well as being managed by Gerardo Martino, an Argentine from Messi's hometown of Rosario. Although the gulf in quality between Messi and some of his opponents is often stark, the move has been a success, and driven huge enthusiasm for the game including in unexpected places like Houston. Inter Miami visited Houston Dynamo at the Shell Energy Stadium in March 2025, but before the game the hosts put out a dramatic apology for an unforeseen development - Messi was injured and would not be playing. Not only did the Dynamo share the news in a grave tone, with text on a black background, they offered freebies as recompense: 'To show our appreciation, fans who attend tomorrow night's match can claim a complimentary ticket to a future Dynamo match this season. Additional details will be provided early next week.' The move was ridiculed by European football fans on social media, who used it as evidence that the MLS is not a proper league, as no true fan would be disappointed that their opponent's star player was out injured. But this is America, things are different here.

Messi's pink Inter Miami jersey is the symbol of a new era for American soccer. As the *New York Times* declared, 'the jersey has become, apparently overnight, the hottest piece of sports merchandise on the planet' because of 'a simple capitalist equation: the result of an irresistible combination of one of the most recognizable and beloved athletes of his generation, a distinctive exotic color, and the ruthless efficiency of textile factories in Southeast Asia'.[32] Adidas had to quickly make lots of fabric in a specific shade of pink – Pantone 1895C – which can now be seen in parks and stadiums everywhere in the world. In lesser numbers, the yellow of Al-Nassr, the Saudi Arabian club where Cristiano Ronaldo chose to end his career, can be seen too. The final acts of the two greatest careers of the modern age played out in the two last remaining money fountains football has managed to find: Saudi Arabia, as well as the USA, the country that is always the exception and never the rule.

6

BEYOND OIL AND GAS

FC Barcelona & Real Madrid

'Today I feel Qatari. Today I feel Arab. Today I feel African. Today I feel gay. Today I feel disabled. Today I feel a migrant worker [sic]. I feel like them because I know what it feels like to be discriminated, to be bullied as a foreigner in a country. At school I was bullied because I had red hair and freckles.'
FIFA president Gianni Infantino on the eve of the 2022 Qatar World Cup

In the aftermath of the Second World War, the Qatari capital of Doha was a run-down port of 15,000 people, where the tallest building was a two-storey fort built by the Ottomans in the nineteenth century. Qatar was then ruled as it is now by the Al Thani monarchy, but as a mere protectorate of the British Empire rather than an independent state. Hunger and malnutrition were widespread in one of the postwar world's most desolate backwaters.[1] Much has changed since then. These days, Qatar looks like something from the space-age future, a very modern place that, more than any other country in the world, is defined by football.

In July 2022, I visited the tiny desert nation a few months before it hosted a World Cup shrouded in controversy. The heat was relentless and the air was thick. In the middle of the day it felt unpleasant, even dangerous, to be outside for more than a few minutes. Yet somehow everywhere I went there was bright-green grass. It was along the Corniche road running around the bay beneath Doha's gleaming towers, it was in the grounds of the lavish hotel where I attended a pre-tournament FIFA conference, and it was in Al Bidda Park in the centre of Doha which was as verdant as an English garden in springtime. This was all possible because of a vast network of water pipes. Life in this region is all about pipes. Pipes filled with gas have helped turn Qatar into what is by some metrics the world's richest country per head of population. Pipes carry oil out of the ground in nearby Abu Dhabi and Saudi Arabia. Other pipes carry seawater, which is desalinated through intensive industrial processes and turned into the fresh water essential for bathing, drinking, and turning yellow desert into bright-green grass.

Qatar is home to almost three million people although just one in ten are Qatari citizens. The rest are migrant workers. My week-long fact-finding mission for *The Athletic* involved visiting all eight host stadiums in the tiny little Gulf country which in 2010, to the shock of the sporting world, won the right to host the 2022 World Cup after a process that has been dogged by controversy ever since. American investigators and FIFA itself have said executive committee members took bribes to vote for Qatar. Within a few years of the vote, almost every one of the twenty-two-person committee had been accused of, or charged with, corruption.[2] But the show went on, and Qatar will be forever remembered as where Lionel Messi finally won the World Cup after a final that is thought of as one of the most thrilling matches of all time. Qatar has been transformed in ways that go far beyond the stadiums. According to one estimate, the government spent around $250 billion – a mind-boggling sum – on development associated with the tournament. Doha was rebuilt almost entirely, the geography of the place carved up to accommodate matchday traffic with new hotels built for the masses to stay, new towers constantly rising from the desert. The final was played in Lusail, a city on the edge of Doha. It wasn't just the stadium that was built from scratch but the entire city of Lusail was too, its founding documents written in 2004 and the scale of those plans hugely expanded after the tournament was awarded to Qatar.

I visited in the oppressive summer heat, at a time when the eyes of the world were not yet on the country. I was there on the pretext of a pre-World Cup official meeting to which I got little access as a journalist, but it helped for gaining entry to the country. I was really there to explore. Qatar is essentially just the city of Doha and its outskirts. It is tiny. In the previous two tournaments, in Brazil then Russia, stadiums were hundreds or even thousands of miles apart. In Qatar just forty miles separated the two farthest-apart World Cup stadiums. I did most of the travelling under my own steam, by taxi and on the stunning new metro system, which seemed to have more cleaning staff than passengers. One stadium, though, Al Janoub, I went to on an official visit. Designed by famed Iraqi-British architect Zaha Hadid, the sweeping exterior looks like the traditional sailboats from which the early Qataris used to dive for pearls. The tour was carried out by stadium manager Abdulaziz Al Ishaq, who showed me and a group of other foreign journalists, mainly from Africa and Asia, around his pride and joy. We saw the spectacular facilities, including huge changing rooms with Jacuzzis, and separate entrances for not just VIPs but also VVIPs who would include world leaders and Gulf royals. The crowning glory was the technology that directly cooled the stadium's interior, ensuring elite sport could be played amid the sweltering desert heat. There was no roof but tiny air vents beside the pitch and embedded in spectators' seats blasted out cold air. Standing beside the pitch, the technology was barely noticeable. It simply felt like visiting a football stadium on a crisp English summer's day, pleasant but not hot, the ideal conditions for playing a cup final at Wembley, rather than the reality of summer in the Gulf where it is a constant technological challenge for humans to stay alive. I had the opportunity to interview 'Dr Cool', Sudan-born Dr Saud Abdulaziz Abdul Ghani, the scientist who came up with the technology. He suggested the technology could be useful beyond Qatar, such as for the stadiums in Mexico and the southern states of the US hosting World Cup games in 2026 at the height of summer.

After the tour, Al Ishaq opened the floor to questions. I was keen to pose the question that my editors back in London expected me to ask – and indeed would be disappointed if I returned having not done so, given senior Qatari officials were proving hard to pin down for an interview. I put my hand up and asked words to the effect of 'What about the workers who died building this place?'

This did not go down well.

'Whatever you say is not acceptable,' the stadium manager snapped at me. He looked not just annoyed but surprised, as though he had never been challenged on or criticised for any aspect of his work. 'I get a lot of appreciation for what is happening here,' he went on, being overtly spiky with me to the visible horror of his accompanying slick minders from FIFA. 'I want people to know that we are making a lot of effort.'[3] Over time, his anger faded to smiles as he remembered the party line, rattling off the list of changes that had been made with regards to workers' rights since Qatar was announced as a host.

While the build-up to the World Cup was dominated by controversies, by the time I arrived, everything was almost ready.

I discovered a country with a confident attitude. Qataris felt as though they were done apologising and self-flagellating and felt justifiably proud to be the first Arab and first Muslim country to host the tournament, a view shared throughout the region. The tournament was under intense criticism internationally over the issue of human rights. Homosexuality remains illegal in the country, there is no free press as we know it, and power is concentrated in the hands of the unelected royal family. But most of all the criticism concerned migrant workers, the people from Africa and Asia who built this country up from the desert sand to its position as a global power.

The International Trade Union Confederation, Amnesty International and Human Rights Watch have all been strongly critical of Qatar's treatment of migrant workers in which labourers were recruited by agents who saddle them with debt, before they gain admission to Qatar or other Gulf countries with similar systems. Workers are then subjected to the 'kafala' system which ties workers to their employer. This means the employer has a great deal of control over the worker, often forcing them to surrender their passport, paying them less than the workers thought they had agreed to, and housing them in worse conditions than they were promised before they uprooted their life to move to the Gulf from places like India, Bangladesh or the Philippines.[4] There are no trade unions or other routes for seeking legal redress. These workers built the stadiums in the sweltering desert heat where it is not just uncomfortable but unsafe to spend long periods outside. Heat kills. On my visit in 2022, I was looking to see if new rules prohibiting outdoor work between 10.30 a.m. and 3 p.m., which had been repeatedly strengthened due to international pressure rather than Qatari benevolence, were being followed. I saw no evidence to suggest otherwise, though of course only witnessed a tiny proportion of the most visible work under way at a time most of the major construction projects were finished.

I spoke to dozens of migrant workers when I was in Qatar, from hotel staff to taxi drivers, security guards to waiters. Most said they were broadly happy with their lot, enjoying the opportunity to earn far better money than was possible back home. It is tempting but wrong for Western visitors to conclude that all is well from encounters like this. In Qatar, criticising the government is not just taboo but literally illegal. Migrant workers on fragile visas are unlikely to speak their minds. It is fair to say, though, that things had doubtless improved between 2010, when Qatar was awarded the tournament, and the time I visited. Multiple investigations have shown that labour rights were particularly bad at the start, with hundreds of migrant workers thought to have died in the early stages of Qatar's long twelve years as presumptive host. Reforms between 2013 and 2016 introduced stricter rules for employers and since 2017 Qatar has been working with the International Labour Organization to abolish kafala and replace it with a state-run system. Amnesty International has called on Qatar and FIFA to go further by allocating money to compensate workers and their families for the deaths and injuries that took place. Few deny that by 2022 things had improved, but the original sins of the Qatar World Cup can never be wholly forgotten or forgiven.

In the Western media, the run-up to the tournament was a constant drumbeat of stories of human misery with little focus on football. Qataris admitted privately to me that they were excited for all this to be over. Some were frustrated that their country was getting so much flak over human rights when the situation was worse in neighbouring countries like the UAE and Saudi Arabia, which later won the rights to host the 2034 World Cup to comparatively little consternation. It is true that both were more repressive places than Qatar in 2022. The scrutiny of human rights in Qatar was relentless in the UK press in the run-up to the World Cup, but when some Premier League clubs held training camps in Dubai at the same time, likely built by people working in worse conditions and staffed by people with fewer rights than their equivalents in Qatar, this was barely discussed in the UK media. Qataris were infuriated by things like this, the perception being that their regional rivals were getting away with things they were not. Another argument I heard lots was that the UK and USA got rich while engaging in outright slavery, so it is hypocritical to criticise Qatar for lesser sins. I had little time for this – two wrongs don't make a right – but it is worth at least engaging with the fact that many in the Arab and Muslim world find Westerners disingenuous on the issue of human rights when Western military involvement in the region has killed so many.

It is hard to feel sorry for Qatar, though. The rulers of this immensely rich country made an active choice to invite the world, and make this tiny state synonymous with the biggest competition in world sport. It is a bit rich to then take issue when people report back on what is going on. Another common line is that there was not similar scrutiny on Russia, another repressive place, before it hosted the tournament in 2018. Firstly, this is not quite accurate. Many excellent articles were published in the UK and beyond in the run-up to 2018 raising concerns about how the tournament could be a propaganda coup for Vladimir Putin who, four years earlier, had sanctioned the invasion of Crimea. Secondly, if the criticism of Russia wasn't noisy enough, then it should have been – a lesson to go harder on Qatar, not to ease off. It is the job of journalists to be sceptical, even negative, rather than taking at face value the efforts of expensively assembled public relations teams, in many cases staffed by British ex-journalists who had no doubt received huge pay rises upon leaving the media industry. I am sceptical that improvements in Qatar would have happened without relentless media attention. Improving rights did not seem a priority in the years after the tournament was awarded in 2010, when there was little scrutiny. This was when labour regulations were at their shoddiest, and when many workers, mostly from the Indian subcontinent, faced appalling conditions, many dying without their families ever receiving adequate compensation.

Some years on it is an open question whether hosting the World Cup was good for Qatar. The tournament went off broadly without a hitch. The vast infrastructure investments changed the country beyond recognition and it is now the perfect place to host other events in the future, such as when it hosted the 2023 Asian Cup at short notice when China cancelled because of the country's onerous Covid-19 restrictions. Qatar's surprise win on home soil gave a boost to national pride after a poor showing at the World Cup. 'Qataris view the World Cup with immense pride and satisfaction,' says Mahfoud Amara, associate professor in sport management and social sciences at the University of Qatar. 'It has bolstered Qatar's confidence.' He told me he felt some 'relief' once the intense scrutiny fell away after the global media turned its attention elsewhere, not least Saudi Arabia given the country's massive investment in global sport. On the other hand, hosting the World Cup turned Qatar into a lightning rod for criticism, not helped by the unusually long twelve-year gap between announcement and tournament. For millions in the West who had little knowledge of Qatar before, the country is now forever associated with corruption allegations and claims of human rights abuses. A bizarre rant by FIFA president Gianni Infantino just before the tournament began – 'Today I feel Arab' – was intended to rebut much of the criticism but had the opposite effect.

Qatar is now synonymous with football, but the last decade-and-a-half has been expensive and exhausting. Kristian Ulrichsen is an author and fellow for the Middle East at the Baker Institute in Houston, Texas. He says it is hard to shake the feeling that a quarter of a trillion dollars could have been better spent. He told me he attended a conference in Lusail, a year after Messi lifted the World Cup trophy in the stadium next door, and the hotel was completely empty. The country has the ability to host the world, but only needed to once. Qatar is a sporting hub, and to a lesser extent a business one, but has little to offer tourists despite the relentless adverts for 'Visit Qatar' that are difficult to avoid if you follow sport or watch television. I would not recommend visiting Qatar unless you have a specific reason to. There is little in the way of natural beauty given its tiny size. It is a very different place to Dubai, a commercial powerhouse and hard-partying city which is relatively comfortable with Western cultural norms – if not Western political freedoms – in the conservative Middle East. The reasons Qatar hosted the World Cup go far beyond turning the country into a tourist attraction, though. Qatar's embrace of sport is a tool to protect itself against existential threats.

Sheikh Hamad bin Khalifa Al Thani was emir of Qatar from 1995 to 2013. He took the throne at a time when Qatar's population barely numbered half a million people, a figure that would increase five-fold in two decades. The emir had to grapple with two big strategic questions. First, what to do with the country's vast gas inheritance, the astonishing scale of which was not fully clear until the mid-1990s. Qatar has 0.03 per cent of the world's population and covers 0.008 per cent of the world's land area, but has

13 per cent of the planet's natural gas, critically important around the world for heating homes and generating electricity. Under Sheikh Hamad's rule, the country invested in gas extraction infrastructure. Production skyrocketed and the sleepy desert city of Doha was suddenly a goldmine. Sheikh Hamad's second big concern was how to get along with his neighbours. Qatar's only land border is with Saudi Arabia, a country that has never been entirely comfortable with Qatari independence, as demonstrated during the blockade of the country's airspace and sea routes that threatened to derail the 2022 World Cup a few years before it kicked off. Iran and Iraq to the north are constant sources of uncertainty and threat.

Because of all this, Sheikh Hamad set about making powerful friends, especially the USA. The $1 billion Al Udeid Air Base became the biggest US military installation in the region. This turned Qatar into a place that the US armed forces, representing 39 per cent of the world's military spending, is deeply invested in keeping secure. Qatar hosts the Pentagon Central Command and has been the base for the US's and UK's multiple military interventions in the Middle East. Under Sheikh Hamad, Qatar also invested in 'soft power', making huge investments in Western companies as well as donating to universities. One of the World Cup venues was at Education City, an area which includes satellite campuses of several Western educational institutions which have been criticised for setting up shop in a country where freedom of expression is limited to say the least. When I visited Education City as part of my Doha trip at the height of summer, shiny trams passed by at regular intervals, but there didn't seem to be anybody on them.

As part of its soft-power push, Qatar also set up the Al Jazeera TV channel in 1996, which has done some admirable journalism in a region not known for such things, although independent criticism of Qatar is nowhere to be seen. Even better known is Al Jazeera's subsidiary, beIN Sports, the biggest sports channel in the Middle East and North Africa. The channel became a political football in 2017 when Saudi Arabia, Bahrain, Egypt and the UAE suspended diplomatic relations with Qatar and cut off access via air, land and sea. Saudi Arabia blocked beIN and began broadcasting its own pirated version of the channel, beoutQ.[5] Ending this piracy was the key not just to peace in the Gulf, but to the British government agreeing to the Saudi Public Investment Fund's takeover of Newcastle United. beIN is now a huge global player in sports broadcasting. The Qatar World Cup, beIN Sports and Paris Saint-Germain, the French club the monarchy has owned since 2011, became a triumvirate of Qatari power projected through sport.

The Khalifa International Stadium, which hosted several World Cup games including Germany's shock 2–1 defeat to Japan, is part of a complex that also houses Qatar's sport museum. This highlights how Qatar's big idea – becoming a global sporting hub to guard its future existence – goes far deeper than hosting one tournament. The country also hosted the Asian Cup in 2011 and 2023. Outside football, the museum shows how Qatar's new global image began with the Asian Games in the 2000s. The country has held countless international tournaments in tennis, boxing, gymnastics, cycling and wrestling, and other sports. In many countries, hosting big sporting events is becoming a harder sell to local taxpayers, but democratic approval is not a problem in autocratic Qatar. The 300,000 or so citizens buy into the idea of spending vast sums of government cash generated by selling natural gas for the purpose of make their country a sporting Mecca to indirectly protect Qatar from its hostile neighbours.

When I tell people I am writing a book about football shirts and their sponsors the conversation generally turns to iconic examples. In England that often means those sponsorship deals that lasted a decade or more in the 1980s and 1990s, harking back to any fan's nostalgia for the great sides of their youth – JVC and Arsenal, Sharp and Manchester United, Crown Paints and Liverpool. Outside the UK the example that most often comes up is the red-and-blue shirt of Barcelona and its various sponsors, or lack of them. The shirt famously was unsullied by a sponsor until 2006. As a child I had a sponsor-free Barcelona shirt, which might be worth a fair bit if I still had it. The classic football shirt industry has boomed in recent years, with replica shirts from the 1990s often prized because fewer were bought and sold back then. The last game Barcelona played without a sponsor was the Champions League final in Paris in 2006, a 2–1 victory over Arsenal which secured the club's second-ever Champions League title. Shortly afterwards the club's board agreed to carry a logo for the first time, that of UNICEF, the United Nations' children's fund, who do essential work helping the world's most needy children. Barcelona's move was a charitable gesture rather than a business deal, with the club also donating €2 million to UNICEF.

The timing was good for the charity in terms of exposure – Barcelona's golden era was just beginning. Wearing the UNICEF shirt, the club beat Manchester United in both the 2009 and 2011 Champions League finals. The latter was a 3–1 victory in which Barcelona were utterly dominant over a fine United team that had just comfortably won the Premier League. The performance is widely viewed as the peak of one of the greatest teams of all time, not only in football but in any sport. It is tricky to compare football teams across the decades, but this iteration of Barcelona has surely been the best club side of the twenty-first century so far. Pep Guardiola, a Catalan local and a legendary player for the club, managed the side for just four seasons from 2008 to 2012 but won a remarkable fourteen trophies in that time. As well as being a winning machine, Guardiola's team pioneered a style of heavy-possession, close-passing football that would revolutionise how the game was played around the world, particularly how goalkeepers are now expected to be good with their feet rather than just being responsible for stopping the ball going in the net. That Barcelona squad featured many players from the Spanish national side including Xavi Hernández, Andrés Iniesta and Carles Puyol who won a World Cup and two European Championships between 2008 and 2012.

But most of all, this was the era of Messi. In the three seasons before he made his debut, Barcelona were also-rans, finishing fourth, fourth, then sixth in La Liga. In Messi's seventeen seasons at Barcelona, the club won the league ten times. The Argentinian played for Barcelona from 2004 to 2021, breaking every conceivable individual record along the way. Before his debut, Barcelona had won the European Cup, later renamed the Champions League, just once, in 1992. In the age of Messi, the club won club football's biggest prize four times, in 2006, 2009 and 2011, and once more in 2015 as a new iteration of Barcelona, led by the iconic forward trio known as 'MSN' (Messi, the Uruguayan Luis Suárez and Brazilian wonderkid Neymar), won a hatful more trophies under Spanish coach Luis Enrique.

Before Messi, Barcelona was a 'money-losing machine' that risked remaining a 'small local brand', more akin to Valencia than Real Madrid, the club's former chief executive Ferran Soriano wrote in *Goal: The Ball Doesn't Go in By Chance*.[6] These days, in large part due to Messi and Guardiola, Spain's two big clubs come as a package. Barcelona vs Real Madrid, Messi vs Ronaldo,

El Clásico. This is a phenomenally powerful global brand although it has waned in significance a little since the departures of Messi and Ronaldo. The league's two greatest players ever have moved on but El Clásico remains a mouthwatering prospect with Kylian Mbappé, Vinicius Junior and Jude Bellingham at Real Madrid competing against a Barcelona that, after many expensive mistakes in the transfer market, have returned to their roots as the world's greatest talent factory, with homegrown youngsters such as Gavi, Pedri and Lamine Yamal replacing Xavi, Andrés Iniesta and Sergio Busquets.

Spain's big two dominate TV revenue, at one point hoovering up 90 per cent of the total value of La Liga's TV rights. The era of peak Messi and Ronaldo has been described as La Liga's 'wasted decade' because the wider division saw little benefit from the pair's stardust.[7] An unequal revenue split meant the two giants were able to continue signing the world's best players, with the biggest stars more likely to end up in Madrid or Barcelona than Manchester or London, but at the expense of other Spanish clubs. Comparatively, England not only makes more money selling its TV rights, but distributes it more equitably, meaning historically small English clubs can outspend some of Europe's biggest names. 'AC Milan gets out-bid by Bournemouth, Leeds, Brighton and Brentford, rather than by Man City and Man United,' Milan CEO Giorgio Furlani told *The Athletic* in 2023. 'That's the reality, and that economic power is largely fuelled by broadcasting rights.'[8]

In March 2023, I saw the global power of El Clásico rivalry in full force, when I watched the fixture in Mumbai in the company of the city's Real Madrid supporters' club. Running late for kick-off, I jumped in a rickshaw from my hotel, the doorless vehicles quicker than a taxi in navigating the city's clogged roads. When I hopped out a couple of streets away from the bar, I was eye-level to a large cow, a common sight wandering the streets of urban India. Mumbai's Madridistas were gathering in the 3 Wise Monkeys bar in the Khar area of the city. The game kicked off at 1 a.m. on a Monday morning local time. Despite the working week beginning in a few hours' time, the venue was packed. Although most were non-Spanish speakers, all belted out the words to club anthem 'Hala Madrid y nada más' and spoke passionately about their love for Madrid and dislike for Barcelona. 'We support Real Madrid because they are European royalty, the best club in the world,' Jitesh Shahani, a key figure in the group, told me over a beer. 'Every year you've got to win at Real Madrid.'[9]

In the midst of Barcelona's golden era, with Messi and Guardiola at the height of their powers, a change to the shirt was announced during the 2010–11 season which would conclude with that 3–1 Champions League final win over Manchester United. This game would be the last time UNICEF featured on Barcelona's red-and-blue shirts. After this, a new name – the Qatar Foundation – would 'join' UNICEF as shirt sponsor after agreeing to pay the extraordinary sum of €150 million over five years, the biggest in the history of football at the time. 'Barcelona say they will seek a way to combine the two logos, but the Qatar Foundation would be the prevalent one if a solution cannot be found,' the Associated Press reported.[10] But when the 2011–12 kits were released, all prominently carried the logo of the Qatar Foundation, which unlike UNICEF was paying handsomely for the privilege, apart from a rarely worn third kit which retained the UNICEF's logo for one season before being wholly replaced. The Qatar Foundation's Barcelona deal was announced just eight days after the country was declared as host for the 2022 World Cup, almost lost in the noise, but another sign the tiny Gulf state was flexing its muscles on the global stage like never before.

This was a peculiar sponsorship deal. The Qatar Foundation was founded in 1995 by the emir to boost 'education, research and community development'. Much of this work is genuinely altruistic and benefits the lives of people in Qatar and beyond, and there are many good people working there on important causes. However, it is ultimately an arm of the government, and it is decidedly strange for a charitable cause to spend such a huge sum sponsoring a football club. It is not inherently untoward for charities to spend money on marketing and soliciting new donations, and indeed some hospitals in the USA sponsor football teams for this reason, like the MD Anderson Cancer Center which sponsors the Houston Dash. The Qatar Foundation was not sponsoring Barcelona for fundraising purposes, though. It was all about promoting the name of Qatar. Whatever the noble charitable endeavours of the foundation, the 2022 World Cup host was in fact trying to burnish its image by paying to have the country's name on the shirts of the best team in the world at the time. There is an analogy here with 'white-label' gambling websites – both are shirt sponsors which claim to be one thing but are in fact advertising something else entirely.

The deal was slammed as 'vulgar' by Dutchman Johan Cruyff, the Barcelona legend who revolutionised the club in the 1980s by instilling the fluid philosophy of 'Total Football'. (The Dutchman is responsible for a quirky football shirt story. At the 1974 World Cup, his national team struck a deal with Adidas to feature the famous three stripes on the orange jerseys. Cruyff had a sponsorship deal with Puma, so refused, and a separate deal was struck for him to play in a shirt with just two stripes.) Decades later he did not like the Qatar deal. 'We have sold this uniqueness for about six per cent of our budget,' Cruyff grumbled.[11] Joan Laporta, club president from 2003 to 2010 and again from 2021, had initiated the

UNICEF deal and was disgruntled at its replacement. 'Our team looks like the Qatar national team now,' he complained.[12] Laporta had previously summarised the club's 'Més Que Un Club' (More Than A Club) slogan with four examples – Cruyff, Catalonia, La Masia, UNICEF. Cruyff as the club's spiritual godfather, Catalonia the independently minded region of Spain where Barcelona is situated, La Masia the club's much-vaunted academy, and UNICEF as a symbol that this club did things differently to the corporate money grabbers who run the game elsewhere.[13]

Sandro Rosell succeeded Laporta in 2010 and took a different view. He inherited many of the debts racked up under his predecessor and argued that the deal with Qatar – a country which he had longstanding business links with – was a financial necessity. Barcelona's ownership structure is unusual. Unlike England's big clubs, where one or a handful of wealthy individuals are outright owners, Barcelona is effectively football's biggest democracy in which 150,000 members, called *socis*, elect the president. 'In the days before television rights,' explains Simon Kuper in his book *Barça*, 'it was their subscriptions that made Barça into one of Europe's richest clubs: more than 60 percent of the club's revenues in the late 1970s came from season tickets. By 2020, that proportion had fallen below 5 per cent. The *socis* don't care, they still consider themselves the club's "owners".'[14] But football's shifting sands meant the club needed external cash to keep up with their rivals.

Intriguingly, Barcelona executives did little to dispel the idea that Qatar's motivations were cynical. 'So far there is nobody who pays more,' said Rosell.[15] His vice president Javier Faus went further. 'It is true that Qatar does not treat its immigrants well, but it's not much different to what happens here. They are aware of it and are working on it.'[16]

Just a few months later, Qatar would make another dramatic

investment in football by buying Paris Saint-Germain. Under the Qataris, PSG not only recruited superstars like Messi, Neymar and hometown hero Kylian Mbappé, but also turned the club into a lifestyle brand. In 2018, Justin Timberlake stepped out on stage in Paris's Bercy Arena wearing a jacket featuring PSG's Eiffel Tower logo spliced with a silhouette of a jumping Michael Jordan, his famous 'Jumpman' logo. Rapper Travis Scott was seen wearing the logo shortly after, creating a buzz that the club was courting a new audience among fashion-conscious youth. PSG gear with Nike's Air Jordan logo can now be seen on street corners around the world, part of a huge branding deal that has elevated PSG from a football club to a global streetwear brand, prominent in the US, Europe and beyond. PSG has stores in New York, London and eight other countries around the world, as well as a huge store on the Champs-Élysées in Paris, outside which I hung around interviewing people in 2021 shortly after the club signed Messi. The Air Jordan deal has been a phenomenon and PSG rank top in the world for club football commercial income.[17]

At the same time as hosting the 2022 World Cup and buying PSG, the Qatari state has put vast energy into exerting influence and shaping policy around the world, donating to academia and think tanks, investing in media and industry, and developing connections with politicians. Qatar has donated billions to American universities. All this involves a precarious balancing act, with Qatar trying to enmesh itself deeper with the institutions of the West while avoiding offending members of the 2,000-strong Qatari royal family or becoming a target for Islamic extremists in the region. The country has been criticised for hosting leaders of the Taliban and Hamas, along with 'hate preachers' in mosques who have praised the likes of Bin Laden.[18]

When Barcelona signed up with the Qatar Foundation,

journalists pored over the organisation's back story. Spanish newspaper *El Mundo* noted the foundation had given money to the extremist cleric Yusuf al-Qaradawi who had advocated terrorism, wife-beating and antisemitism.[19] An Israeli newspaper subsequently linked the foundation to Hamas, the Palestinian group that has committed countless acts of terrorism including the 7 October 2023 attacks in Israel. The storm blew over, but the accusation of funding extremists has dogged Qatar ever since, alongside countless other issues, especially the treatment of migrant workers.

In 2013, two years after Barcelona took money from a shirt sponsor for the first time, one word on the shirt changed. Qatar Foundation was out, and Qatar Airways was in. A supposedly charitable arrangement was now a straightforwardly commercial relationship with the country's state-owned airline. This marked a definitive end to Barcelona's idealistic vision of rejecting the corporate idea of sponsorship. 'We share values, ambitions, courage and excellence with FC Barcelona,' announced Qatar Airways' executive director Akbar Al Baker.[20] Messi won his fourth Champions League in 2015 while wearing the airline's logo. Qatar Airways has sponsored many other top teams since including PSG, AS Roma in Italy, Boca Juniors in Argentina, Bayern Munich in Germany and Club Africain in Tunisia. It also sponsors multiple football confederations: the African, Asian and South American groupings carry its logo on the billboards of their tournaments. The biggest deal of all, though, was with FIFA itself. Qatar Airways was a major sponsor of the 2018 and 2022 World Cups, the airline's branding conspicuous in Russia and Qatar.

The Qatar Airways era at Barcelona ended in 2017 when the Japanese electronics firm Rakuten offered a huge amount of money to sponsor the Catalan side's shirts, staying there for five years before being replaced by music streaming service Spotify,

Above Raúl is one of the greatest Spanish players of all time. He played for German club Schalke at a time when they were bankrolled by Russian gas company Gazprom.

Left Luka Jović played for Red Star Belgrade before moving to Real Madrid later in his career. The Serbian side kept Gazprom on their shirts after Schalke and the UEFA Champions League ditched the company as a sponsor.

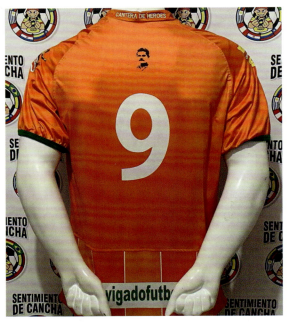

Left The 2012 shirt of Colombia's Envigado FC featured the face of Gustavo Upegui, who founded the club before he was murdered in 2006. His son, who succeeded him as owner, and the club were later sanctioned by the US government for alleged links to drug trafficking.

Left Hernán Crespo played for Italian side Parma in the 1990s when the club won several trophies. The club was bankrolled by Parmalat, a local dairy company later implicated in a huge fraud.

Below At the home stadium of Goa FC there are adverts for Parimatch News, a 'news' website which is used as a way of advertising the gambling firm Parimatch, in a country where doing this overtly is illegal.

Left Brennan Johnson wore a Nottingham Forest shirt sponsored by Football Index between 2019 and 2021, before the gambling company imploded spectacularly.

Above Changing Lives FC, based in the English county of Essex, is a football club made up entirely of migrants, asylum seekers and refugees.

Left Kylian Mbappé, born in Paris to a Cameroonian father and Algerian mother, won the 2018 World Cup with France as a teenager. The blue of the French shirt represents a team now mostly made up of migrants and their children.

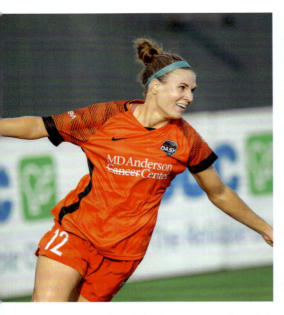 

Veronica Latsko of the Houston Dash in the National Women's Soccer League. The club has long been sponsored by a local hospital, the MD Anderson Cancer Center.

The Inter Miami shirt worn by Lionel Messi could be the visual symbol of the USA — long one of the last outposts of footballing apathy — finally embracing the world's most popular game.

Messi, seen here with Cesc Fàbregas, began his 17 years at Barcelona playing in a shirt with no sponsor, then came UNICEF and the Qatar Foundation. Next came Qatar Airways, a sign of Barcelona's 'more than a club' image falling to commercial pressures.

The peak years of Messi playing against Cristiano Ronaldo at Real Madrid involved both being billboards for Middle Eastern airlines, in Madrid's case Emirates in Dubai.

Newcastle United were bought by Saudi Arabia's Public Investment Fund in October 2021. Soon afterwards the club unveiled a shirt similar to the Saudi national team's green-and-white kit, worn here by Brazilian midfielder Joelinton.

The prisoners of Robben Island played in whatever shirts they could acquire from sports shops across the water. The pitch and goals remain today as a symbol of how the game was a tool in South Africa's democratic struggle.

In 2017, English midfielder Gareth Barry broke the all-time Premier League appearance record for West Bromwich Albion. His shirt was sporting the logo of Palm, the 'eco-town' company of club owner Guochuan Lai.

Chinese club Guangzhou Evergrande, which signed stars like Brazilian midfielder Paulinho in the mid-2010s, was deeply entwined with the Evergrande property company. China, and Chinese football, has since retreated from the world stage.

Mary Earps made headlines around the world when she criticised kit manufacturer Nike for not selling her England women's goalkeeper shirts. They later did, and Earps won the BBC Sports Personality of the Year award in 2023.

A purple kit worn by Brazilian club Corinthians represents the importance of female fans in the country's game.

Celtic's green-and-white represents the club's Irish links. CD Palestino in Chile, who represent the country's Arab community, have worn the same colours. These two clubs identify with each other's nationalist causes from afar.

An orange away kit worn by Rangers, worn here by Colombian striker Alfredo Morelos, symbolises the club's identity on the Protestant side of Scotland's sectarian divide.

English midfielder Dele Alli played for Turkish club Beşiktaş in 2023. The club was sponsored by a website selling cryptocurrency, which became popular in a country where the local currency plummeted in value.

The Australian women's team are known as the CommBank Matildas, an unusual sponsorship deal where the official nickname of the team incorporates the name of a bank.

which also added its name to the club's Nou Camp stadium, two rather more conventional sponsorship deals. The year 2017 also marked the end of Barcelona's golden era. The club sold Neymar to PSG for €222 million, the French club's Qatari owners smashing the world transfer record in an example of nation-state largesse driving up fees and wages for the entire sport. Losing a star for a huge fee needn't be a disaster and many clubs have thrived after reinvesting such a windfall wisely. But Barcelona did not, overpaying for players like Ousmane Dembélé from Borussia Dortmund and Philippe Coutinho from Liverpool, who were signed for a combined fee of more than €300 million. Both transfers failed and many more did after that. The club spent more than €1 billion on transfers between 2014 and 2019, more than any club in the world, its debt pile getting bigger and bigger but falling behind its European rivals on the pitch. 'Every year we were a little bit worse,' admitted captain Gerard Piqué.[21]

Messi's levels did not drop on the pitch and his power at the club continued to grow, with Barcelona paying increasingly ludicrous wages to cling onto him. Then, in 2021, it finally happened. After seventeen years in the first team, Messi left Barcelona. The Argentinian announced his intention to join Neymar in Paris during a tear-filled press conference, saying he had no choice because of the Spanish league's spending controls which were tightening around the profligate club.[22] The club he loved was crippled by debt and Barcelona was eventually forced to undertake a series of exotic financial manoeuvres to stay afloat.

In recent years the Catalan club has seen some domestic success, but the overall outlook is gloomier than it was in the early 2010s, especially since Real Madrid have won repeated Champions Leagues. Barcelona have mortgaged off their future and are undergoing expensive stadium renovations to keep up with their fiercest rivals, who completed a stunning revamp of their Estadio Bernabéu in 2024. La Liga as a whole has fallen behind the Premier League in economic and footballing terms. Although Qatar Airways' stint at Barcelona was brief, it demonstrated the club's shift from the morally virtuous position of remaining sponsor-free, of being *més que un club*, that was eventually deemed unrealistic by the cold hard economic reality of modern football. Member-owned Barcelona are expected to compete in Europe against clubs like PSG and Manchester City, who are owned by nation-states. They might one day be joined at the top table by Saudi-owned Newcastle United. Ultimately, rather than being a pure symbol of Catalan identity, Barcelona's shirt became a vessel for the interests of Qatar, funded by its enormous gas reserves.

Beyond just Qatar Airways, it is hard to overstate the extent to which airlines – specifically Middle Eastern ones – have come to dominate football shirts in recent years. It began with Chelsea back in 1984–85, when the club were not members of England's elite. Chelsea was sponsored by Gulf Air for a single season, a company founded in 1974 by the governments of Bahrain, UAE, Qatar and Oman, with planes bought from BOAC, the predecessor to British Airways. Dubai was left out of this scheme so set up its own airline in 1985, naming it Emirates.[23] It would go on to leave Gulf Air in the dust. A key part of Emirates' global branding was sponsorship of football with its first major deal being, funnily enough, Chelsea, who carried its logo on their blue shirts from 2001 shortly before the club's takeover by Roman Abramovich, which saw almost immediate Premier League success, the club winning the league under José Mourinho in 2003–04 and 2004–05, both times with Emirates on the shirts. Emirates was replaced by Korean electronics manufacturer Samsung. No matter: the Dubai airline was on its way to becoming one of the most ubiquitous brands in world football.

Not far from Qatar, a little further along the south-eastern corner of Arabia, is the United Arab Emirates which includes both Dubai and Abu Dhabi. A century ago this place was 'the most desolate corner of a desolate land', according to academic Jim Krane, a place where the population was around 80,000 at the time of the arrival of Islam in 630 AD, and remained virtually unchanged until the 1930s.[24] Dubai and Abu Dhabi were part of the British Empire because of their strategic usefulness for securing trade routes to India and beyond, but not much happened here at all until after the Second World War. Like Qatar, the main industry was pearl diving, an industry killed off by the 1929 Wall Street Crash which reduced demand for pearls in the West, as did the advent of synthetic or 'cultured' pearls, which delivered an identical product while being cheaper to produce and far safer than holding one's breath and diving without equipment into the turbid waters of the Gulf.

Historically, the action has generally taken place on the other side of the Arabian Peninsula. It was also elsewhere in the Middle East where oil was first discovered, in northern Iraq in 1927, Bahrain in 1932, and then in Kuwait and in 1938 in Saudi Arabia, which is now thought to host around a fifth of the world's crude reserves. But things changed in the UAE in 1958 when an offshore drilling barge called the *Enterprise* parked in the shallow waters off Abu Dhabi's Das Island, part of what is now the UAE but then part of the 'Trucial States', named after the truces the British rulers struck with local leaders. After drilling into the seabed, the crew noticed black blobs rising to the surface, the oil excavation equivalent of a hole-in-one. An engineer described it as a 'nice, sweet crude'.[25] It quickly became apparent that the barren lands of Abu Dhabi, ignored by tribes and empires for centuries, sat atop a vast sea of oil.

The importance of crude oil as a tool of state power was established during and in the immediate aftermath of the First World War.[26] In the century since, oil, and its newer cousin gas, have completely transformed those countries fortunate enough to have reserves. As we saw in the opening chapter, oil and gas have largely displaced coal, which is dirty and harder to transport. Oil and gas have done amazing things for us, fuelling cars and planes and giving humans more freedom to travel than ever before, as well as powering factories we work in and heating homes we live in. They are a big part of why we live far more comfortably, on average, than our parents and grandparents did. However, this embrace of fossil fuels – so called because they are formed by the prolonged squashing of dead animals into solids, liquids or gases, the carbon transferring from an organic form to a form in which it can be burnt for energy – has come at a cost. Our world is heating quicker than ever as burnt carbon becomes carbon dioxide, a gas which traps the earth's heat and causes temperatures to rise. The summit of world football often feels like one long advert for fossil fuel-producing countries and fossil fuel-burning industries, particularly airlines.

Dubai eventually discovered it had some oil reserves but very little compared to its neighbour Abu Dhabi. '[Dubai's] production peaked in 1991, so it had the need to try to diversify and build something else,' explains academic Kristian Ulrichsen, who says Crown Prince Mohammed Bin Salman is now trying to do the same thing thirty years later in Saudi Arabia. 'Dubai identified tourism as being something that they could lead on in the mid-to-late 1990s.' The idea of tourism in this inhospitable part of the world would have seemed bizarre a few decades earlier, but the rise of air-conditioning and desalination changed everything. Dubai carved out a niche as a place to travel for shopping and partying, not just for Europeans looking for winter sun but also people from around the Middle East who want to let their hair down in a way that may be tricky in their home country. Alcohol is readily available in Dubai, unlike in Qatar, a far more sedate and culturally conservative place where it is only served in hotel bars at great expense. Supposedly this is only for foreign tourists, though on the one evening I relaxed on my Doha hotel's roof terrace with a solo pint of lager costing twice what it does in London, I spotted two men furtively drinking beers while wearing the thobe, the Qatari national dress consisting of an ankle-length white robe and head covering, which a sign on the door explicitly banned drinkers from wearing. Qatari 'ladies' were banned from entering the bar at all. On my one brief visit to Dubai many years ago, I had a beer in a normal bar and gawped at the spectacular fountains which spray out water alongside synchronised light shows, with one of the most multicultural crowds it is possible to imagine anywhere in the world in human history gathering around to watch and take photos. Although Dubai's rulers might be relaxed about things like alcohol and dress codes, the same liberalism is not extended to the political sphere where there is virtually no freedom of expression and dissidents are routinely locked up with little explanation.

'Diversification' is a word that crops up a great deal in the sorts of countries that buy football teams and sponsor their shirts, meaning the building of a diverse economy that is not just overly dependent on fossil fuels. Dubai is the king of diversification, pivoting away from oil and gas as the sole driver of national revenue. Dubai's oil-rich neighbours like Abu Dhabi, Saudi Arabia and Kuwait used their sudden riches to subsidise cushy lifestyles for citizens and fund sluggish bureaucracies, or their leaders parked cash in overseas investments.[27] Dubai's rulers were more far-sighted, investing its relatively modest oil windfall in ways that would help the emirate become a global travel and logistics hub. The Jebel Ali port, the world's biggest man-made harbour, became the US Navy's main overseas port. Dubai ruler Sheikh Rashid's investment gambles in the fifties, sixties and seventies triggered a wave of private investment and established Dubai as the Middle East's capital of commerce. At the same time, Sheikh Zayed, leader of Abu Dhabi and the overall leader of the UAE, was showering a grateful public in cash. 'I think it's interesting to think about the UAE as having two different poles,' explains Kristian Ulrichsen. 'Dubai is a sort of soft-power hub. It's aspirational. They want to attract people who want to come and live and work and do business and party, especially people from across the Middle East, whereas Abu Dhabi is more of a hard-power hub. It does the security, foreign policy, defence.'

A key part of the story of Dubai's diversification is its airline. Its maiden flight was in 1985, the year Gulf Air adorned the shirts of Chelsea. Emirates' starting costs were helped by a $90 million gift from Dubai's royal family. It grew slowly but earned a reputation for flying to places in Asia and Africa which other airlines avoided. It also managed to ride out the 9/11 attacks which hit the demand for air travel globally. Its rivals say Emirates benefits from being based in an autocracy. Its business model is no doubt helped by the fact it pays no corporation tax, and its Dubai-based staff pay no income tax. Emirates also lowers its costs by employing a migrant workforce paid little compared to its commercial rivals in Europe and North America. Its advocates contend it has, in the past, given money back to the Emirati treasury.[28] There is no doubt an inextricable link between airline and government. When asked why the company sponsors football, Emirates senior vice president Boutros Boutros has said 'our mission was not just Emirates Airline, but Dubai itself. Sports sponsorship captures peoples' emotion ... So, when you invite your agent to an event which enables him to go and shake hands with Arsène Wenger, you will own him forever. You explain to him all about Dubai, what Emirates is all about, you interact and you become friends. No medium can give this to you except for sponsorship.'[29] Sportswashing is defined by journalist Miguel Delaney as 'the centrally planned political use of sport to normalise autocratic states for the purpose of perpetuating their authoritarian structures without the need for reform.' Delaney argues the rhetoric of 'economic diversification' is a smokescreen. 'The obvious question is what they are trying to diversify for? The answer, put bluntly, is to keep dictatorships going'.[30] This can mean deals like the many clubs sponsored by Emirates, as well as ownership situations like Manchester City, Newcastle and Paris Saint-Germain.

The list of shirts to have been sponsored by Emirates is almost a roll call of Europe's footballing elite. The company became the main sponsor on the shirt of Arsenal in 2006, AC Milan in 2010 and Real Madrid in 2013. Olympique Lyonnais, who dominated French football in the 2000s before Qatari bought PSG, joined the Emirates family in 2020. Between 2006 and 2020, Emirates also sponsored Hamburg, who rather let the side down by being relegated to Germany's second division, prompting Emirates to terminate the deal. The airline has also long sponsored the shirts of Benfica, Portugal's most decorated club. Real Madrid and AC Milan have won more European Cups than any other and, when the two played each other in a Champions League game in November 2024, the logo of the Dubai-based airline was on all twenty-two players' shirts, as well as being plastered all over the Bernabéu Stadium. Real Madrid's deal with Emirates meant that between 2013 and 2015, at the peak of 'Messi vs Ronaldo', El Clásico was one big advert for two Gulf airlines, Messi's Qatar vs Ronaldo's Dubai, our two shirts for this chapter. Real Madrid are the world's biggest football club on many metrics. They have won comfortably the most Champions League trophies. They have the most social media followers. They are the most valuable financially according to *Forbes*. Real Madrid have had a sponsorship deal with Emirates since 2011 and the company name has been on the shirts since 2013. It is rarely commented on as an example of sportswashing but the prominence of the airline on Madrid shirts, and those of other top clubs, gives the company millions of walking billboards in every country in the world, and means Emirates is now associated more with glamorous athletes than pollution or workers' rights. Madrid's astonishing run of six Champions League wins in 11 years from 2014 to 2024 has been one long advertisement for Dubai's national airline. Emirates is now so universal that it just fades into the background of football, barely noticeable in its extended prominence. The airline also sponsors England's FA Cup, a competition synonymous with part-timers slogging it out on muddy pitches with the hope of a giant-killing against highly paid professionals, before big names battle it out in the final to lift the famous trophy at a Wembley Stadium which is bedecked in red Emirates branding for the occasion.

It is not only the glamour clubs of Western Europe that carry the Emirates logo. Étoile Sportive du Sahel are the most decorated club in Tunisia, and the country's first side to participate in the FIFA Club World Cup. Ahmed Adala, a sports journalist with radio station Mosaïque FM based in the capital Tunis, told me that Étoile desperately needed a big-money foreign sponsorship in the summer of 2023 given the club's high levels of debt, administrative issues and a transfer ban, with the African Football Confederation ordering the Tunisian side to get its house in order before it could take part in the AFC Champions League. Along came Emirates. 'For fans and for local media, [the Emirates sponsorship] was a great deal and a success for the club president and his marketing department,' says Adala. 'This contract gave the club an opportunity to get some money and resolve some of its financial problems.' Étoile marked the deal with a friendly match against fellow Emirates club AC Milan at the Italian side's training ground. The airline also sponsors the top-flight division in its home country, the UAE Pro League.

As well as the football shirts sponsored by Emirates, from Sousse in Tunisia to Madrid, the airline gives its name to a major landmark in the UK's capital city. I lived in north London for a couple of years and would occasionally play squash at a leisure centre behind Arsenal's stadium: the Emirates. The name has been attached to the stadium ever since it opened in 2006, transcending sport and becoming part of the map of London. As a new stadium, its naming rights held a lot of value. If the name ever changed, many people would still surely continue to know it as the Emirates. It would be a tougher pitch to get a sponsor to pay to attach their name to Anfield or Old Trafford. Both names are so strongly seared into the brains of English football fans that a new name would be ignored by anyone not contractually mandated to use it. Arsenal's stadium, though, was new so the name stuck, and most of the capital's eight million people are likely to be familiar with the Emirates as a place where football is played whether they follow the sport or not, in the same way people know Twickenham is the home of English rugby, and Lord's is where cricket is played. A similar phenomenon is at play in Manchester. A half-hour walk away from Piccadilly station, through the districts of Ancoats and New Islington which were derelict wastelands before Abu Dhabi's takeover of Manchester City, lies the site of one of Europe's premier sports and entertainment districts: the Etihad. With its distinctive concrete columns towering above the low-rise housing of east Manchester, the name of Etihad Airways, carried on the front of Manchester City's shirts since the year after the Abu Dhabi takeover in 2008, again transcends sport, becoming a landmark in an English city that feels distantly removed from a far-off Gulf emirate, and certainly from any political sensitivities or human rights controversies. In 2025, Real Madrid played Arsenal in the quarter-finals of the UEFA Champions League. Every player was wearing an Emirates branded shirt, and the first leg was played at the Emirates Stadium, though this was barely remarked upon.

It is interesting to compare all this with Qatar, which has spent far more money on sport than Dubai and received far more criticism for it. American academic John Krzyzaniak has compared the UAE's sporting efforts with those of Qatar as well as Azerbaijan which has invested billions into sport, hosting Formula 1 races as well as the inaugural European Games in 2015. This was a strange tournament which cost vast amounts to host and included Lady Gaga as the star turn of the opening ceremony, but left little impression on the sporting public. 'The United Arab Emirates' sport-as-soft-power strategy stands in stark contrast to that of Azerbaijan and Qatar,' says Krzyzaniak. 'Whereas the latter two countries have used a wide variety of sporting engagements to accrue soft power, the former has relied almost exclusively on sponsorships.'[31] He notes that hosting mega-events has put the spotlight on Qatar and Azerbaijan, with sports journalists suddenly flooded with messages from human rights activists imploring them to look beyond the glitzy stadiums to the murky stories beyond. In 2019, the Azerbaijani capital of Baku hosted a Europa League final between Chelsea and Arsenal. The great expense involved in travelling from London to the Caspian Sea means the stadium was mostly empty, embarrassing for one of club football's set piece events. Even worse was the controversy surrounding Arsenal's Armenian midfielder

Henrikh Mkhitaryan. Armenia and Azerbaijan have bad relations, frequently breaking out into war, and citizens are generally banned from entering each other's countries. The government told Mkhitaryan he would be safe, but ultimately Mkhitaryan and his club decided against him travelling, generating a torrent of negative publicity for the Azerbaijani government.[32] Dubai and the rest of the UAE have not hosted events on this scale and seem to have dodged a lot of the controversy while spending a fraction of the cash. Gay Gooners, Arsenal's LGBT fan club, see no contradiction in lifting their group's banner in the Emirates stadium in shirts sponsored by Emirates, the state airline of a country that imprisons gay people with impunity. Meanwhile, Arsenal's sleeve sponsor in recent years has been Visit Rwanda, the tourist board of a country accused of many human rights abuses and in a humanitarian crisis in the Democratic Republic of Congo. Arsenal's shirt, of course, is far from the only one which might give fans moral dilemmas. Most fans, of course, simply do not think about all this. They did not get into the sport to wrestle with complex geopolitical issues, and resent being asked to think about all this in something that is supposed to be an escape from the real world.

Dubai's involvement in sport has been good value. Its airline is now strongly associated with the glamour of elite football in exchange for spending in the hundreds of millions of dollars, rather than the hundreds of billions that Qatar has spent, with a fraction of the controversy and criticism. But whenever the topic of sportswashing rears its head, remember that the reason these states get involved in football is not about the present, about their reputations, about making them looking good to the West. It is about the future. It is about ensuring these regimes still exist in a world where the oil and gas have run out.

7

DEMOCRACY'S LIMITS

Prisoners of Robben Island & Newcastle United

'Sport has the power to change the world . . . it has the power to inspire. It has the power to unite people in a way that little else does. It speaks to youth in a language they understand. Sport can create hope where once there was only despair. It is more powerful than government in breaking down racial barriers.'

Nelson Mandela

In January 2025, just off the southern tip of Africa, I took a boat to Robben Island, the place where Nelson Mandela was held prisoner during his struggle against apartheid in South Africa. From the boat I watched Cape Town recede into the distance, the city's glitzy waterfront overlooked by the long flat summit of Table Mountain. I was taking a boat to learn more about a football shirt – or rather some football shirts – which are very different to the others referenced in this book. This example is not a replica garment worn by a specific team but rather a collection of shirts picked up cheaply from a Cape Town sportswear shop many decades ago, which tell a bigger story about how football can be a force for good. But just as football can be a democratic force, it can be an anti-democratic force too, and the power of fandom can be exploited by totalitarian regimes. This is exemplified in another shirt worn over eight thousand miles away from Cape Town in Newcastle in northern England, where a green shirt worn in recent years has honoured Newcastle's owners – the bloodthirsty regime of Saudi Arabia.

Football is huge in South Africa, especially the Premier League, with ties running deep in a widely English-speaking country that was part of the British Empire. While in Cape Town I took in an international cricket match at the iconic Newlands Stadium, which has a stunning view of Table Mountain and where the beers are less than a third of the price that they are back home in England. The match between South Africa and Pakistan happened to be the same day that Liverpool were playing Manchester United in the Premier League, and literally dozens of fans in the cricket stadium were wearing shirts of one of the clubs. During a break in play, pictures of fans wearing the respective shirts flashed up on the screen, to a chorus of cheers and boos. I spotted a smattering of Manchester City, Arsenal and Chelsea shirts as well in my time in South Africa, although Manchester United were comfortably ahead despite the team's dire form at the time. Like the fans I met in India, these South African Premier League fans were deeply engaged, and eager to talk about the manager's recent press conferences and choices of substitutions. A couple of United fans I spoke to cite Quinton Fortune, a South African midfielder who had a bit-part role for the club between 1999 and 2006 during the golden era under Sir Alex Ferguson, as a reason for supporting the club. On the Cape Town waterfront, in among the shops, bars and seafood restaurants, is a big public screen which shows live games and highlights of the Premier League. While heading home one evening I was surprised to not only see but also hear loud commentary of Brentford vs Southampton, hardly one of the league's glamour ties.

As I took the boat across nine miles of shark-infested and choppy waters to Robben Island, football was on my mind in more ways than one. Looking back at Cape Town's skyline, glittering in the summer sun, one of the most prominent sights is the 58,000 seater Cape Town Stadium which hosted several games at the 2010 World Cup including the Netherlands' 3–2 semi-final victory over Uruguay. (The Dutch would go on to lose 1–0 in the ill-tempered final against Spain in Johannesburg.) These days it is home to Cape Town City FC, though the locals I speak to seem far more interested in a league eight thousand miles away than their domestic league.

After the half-hour boat journey I landed on Robben Island where it was hot but windy, an inhospitable place even at the height of the southern hemisphere summer. Cape Town is beautiful but Robben Island is somewhat bleak, chosen as a prison location because it is virtually impossible to escape from. On a tour, we bounced around the island in a little bus, hearing from a charismatic former political activist who shared stories of meeting Mandela and how the prisoners used to be given backbreaking work excavating limestone in the island's quarry, begging their captors for sunglasses to shield their eyes from the sun's glaring reflection. Many prisoners developed eye problems which they carried through the rest of their life. Our tour guide for the cells was a former prisoner named Terrance Phiri. He was seventeen when imprisoned for sabotage against the apartheid regime, and now in his early sixties, gives tours of his former prison. He showed us Mandela's former cell, a tiny room with just a mat on the floor, a cup, and a toilet bucket. After this we stood outside and listened to Phiri explain the importance of a featureless rocky pitch with two football goals on it – a pitch that plays an important role in the history of this young democracy.

There is only one photograph in existence of football being played on Robben Island, taken in 1969. It is fuzzy and black and white, showing a dozen or so players on the same pitch I visited fifty-six years later. Twenty or so people are watching the game on the sidelines, all of them black. The photo was taken by the apartheid regime's jailers as part of orchestrated propaganda to show that all was well in what became the world's most infamous political prison in the 1970s and 1980s. Over time, football on Robben Island developed from a haphazard and disorganised kickabout into something more organised, making the shirts worn in that grainy photo a symbol of the fight against the racist system which governed the country for decades.

White Europeans first started living in what is now South Africa in 1652 when Cape Town was settled by the Dutch East India Company. The waves of Dutch settlers developed their own distinctive culture and a new language, Afrikaans, as well as French Huguenot incomers, who quickly assimilated with the Afrikaaners. Over the next three centuries they were followed by other Europeans including English-speakers from the British Empire. White settlers built up the cities of Cape Town, Johannesburg and Pretoria while often fighting wars against black Africans. However, the South Africa Act 1909, a law passed in London, laid the legal foundations for apartheid. In the Second World War, South Africa was a self-governing dominion of the British Empire and played a role providing supplies to ships and war materials for the war effort. All this growing industry needed labour, so large numbers of black South Africans moved to the cities for the first time, often living in shoddy accommodation on the outskirts of town. Some concessions to the black population, such as increasing wages and some working rights, led whites to formally mobilise on ethnic lines for the first time and the explicitly racist National Party was formed and won the general election of 1948. Black people had long been discriminated against in South Africa, but the new government began implementing a formal system of apartheid – Afrikaans for 'separateness' – which disenfranchised non-whites and introduced legal discrimination in every layer of life, from employment to education, housing to transport. 'Whites Only' signs popped up all over the country.

Robben Island had been used as a makeshift prison since the eighteenth century as a home for hardened 'common law' prisoners, such as murderers, gang leaders and other violent criminals. By the early 1960s, political prisoners of the apartheid regime were being sent there too, all of them black. These included Mandela, the anti-apartheid activist arrested while on the run in 1962 and eventually sentenced for organising an illegal strike and for his role in the militant organisation uMkhonto we Sizwe (MK).[1] He spent virtually his whole time on Robben Island in solitary confinement before being released in 1990, and going on to become the first-ever black president of South Africa and the first-ever leader of the country as a multi-racial democracy.

Those on the island who were not isolated from others searched for a semblance of community in a place that robbed them of their dignity. This came in the form of football. While prisoners sometimes tried to play games and sports, the equipment was regularly confiscated by the warders. One football-mad prisoner, Tony Suze, realised it was easy to bundle up and bind together some shirts as a makeshift ball. Players would kick it around the yard before hiding it whenever guards appeared. If they searched the cells, the rags could be quickly pulled apart.

Football had long been popular among black South Africans as well as among coloureds, a South African term for multiracial communities with mixed African, European and Asian ancestry. Whites, though, preferred cricket and rugby. Football leagues sprang up around South Africa in the 1920s and 1930s, when famous clubs such as Orlando Pirates – from the Johannesburg suburb of Soweto that was key to the struggle against apartheid

– were founded. Players like Steve 'Kalamazoo' Mokone, who played in Europe for Coventry City and Torino, became famous across South Africa. In 1956, when the formal apartheid system was just eight years old, a coloured team from Western Province played a one-off friendly against the province's all-white side who had just won the Currie Cup, a tournament restricted to whites only.[2] Captained by Basil D'Oliveira, the coloured team won 5–1. Symbolically, this was like a win for Indian side Mohun Bagan over an East Yorkshire regiment team in 1911, with both victories undermining a political system predicated on racial superiority. After the win, black South Africans rejoiced across the country.

After the apartheid regime consolidated its control in the 1950s, international pressure started growing. The country was banned from taking part in the 1964 Olympic Games because of a rule mandating participants to disavow racial prejudice. Soon, the apartheid issue was engulfing international sport. Footballer-turned-cricketer D'Oliveira, from the coloured community, had moved to England to escape apartheid and played for the national team. When England were due to tour South Africa in the winter of 1968, the apartheid government worked behind the scenes to ensure D'Oliveira would not be selected. He was dropped from the tour by England selectors, who spuriously claimed the decision was based on cricketing merit. There was public outcry in England. When another player was injured ahead of the tour and had to withdraw, D'Oliveira was selected and South African politicians, including Prime Minister John Vorster, claimed the move was politically motivated.[3] Attempts at a compromise failed and the tour was cancelled. The fall-out led to the 1970 tour of England by South Africa being called off, and the exclusion of apartheid South Africa from formal international cricket became official policy of the International Cricket Conference – although unauthorised 'rebel' tours still went ahead, with participants sometimes sanctioned. Like cricket, and unlike football, rugby was another sport where South Africa were among the world's best teams. It took a little longer for sporting sanctions to bite in rugby, with tours continuing into the 1970s, but by the 1980s, these had largely halted, and the country was excluded from the first two World Cups in 1983 and 1987.

In late 1964, the prisoners on Robben Island made a simple request: to be allowed to play football. It was met with derision by guards and repeatedly rejected. By this point, with opposition to apartheid becoming a cause célèbre around the world, the Red Cross was a frequent visitor to Robben Island, and the pressure was mounting on the South African government to at least give the appearance of treating prisoners well. Therefore in December 1967, after three years of asking, the chief warder granted prisoners permission to play for thirty minutes every Saturday.

Many prisoners who shared their testimonies after leaving Robben Island have indicated this was a significant moment, even if the quality of the football was low at first. The games proved hugely popular and evolved into more than just a kickabout. Men steeped in organised political struggle formed the Makana Football Association, named after a Xhosa warrior-prophet who was sent to the island by the British in 1819 for opposing colonialism. The prisoners set up a highly formalised set of rules governing how the leagues and teams operated, including even a rudimentary player transfer system. Players communicated with each other about the league in the form of written letters, using 'addresses' giving the sender's and receiver's cell number. The definitive account of football on Robben Island is by the academic Chuck Korr who has interviewed many of the former prisoners:

These rules represented something quite remarkable on Robben Island. The men, themselves imprisoned by a judicial system that granted them few if any rights, were ensuring that there was a full range of appeal available to football players. The prisoners were making sure that they created a system within which the sport would operate that was fair, equitable, and based upon the twin ideals of justice and democracy – in other words, one that was the absolute reverse of apartheid.[4]

The first seven clubs were formed along party lines, political allegiances on the mainland translating to the island football teams. They played in different coloured kits based on what was available in the Cape Town sports shops that provided the gear – Gunners in black and white, Ditshitshidi in maroon and white, Rangers in royal blue and gold, Hotspurs in green and white, Dynamo in maroon and black, Mphatlalatsane in green and gold, Bucks in black and gold and Black Eagles in navy and sky blue.

Another club, Manong FC, was admitted to the association before the first full season and was the first to select players irrespective of party allegiance, based solely on sporting merit. Members of the African National Congress and Pan Africanist Congress of Azania, two rival anti-apartheid groups, would play on the same team, its handwritten constitution enshrining the principle of equality. 'In most non-Robben Island contexts, "indiscrimination" refers to race, gender, religion or nationality but in the cells, it had a different meaning,' writes Chuck Korr. 'The members of Manong FC would not be chosen along political lines: ANC and PAC members would play together in the same team.'[5] This team, helped by picking its players from a larger pool than others, won the first-ever league championship in 1970 while playing in maroon and gold. Acquiring this kit involved negotiating with the chief warder who placed orders through the Cape Town sports shops. Prisoners worked together to transform scrubland into a lush playing field. Many of the warders, who usually treated prisoners as subhuman, became interested in the game as the quality improved and it became exciting as a spectator sport.

As well as creating a curiously formal system of rules amid the prison squalor, football on Robben Island also helped break down some of the barriers between warders and prisoners. One unlikely duo of jailer and prisoner remained friends after the end of apartheid and the pair were giving joint tours well into the twenty-first century. The prisoners who played football on Robben Island included Jacob Zuma, the tough-tackling captain of Rangers who went on to become president of South Africa, as well as the fantastically named Tokyo Sexwale, who became a prominent businessman and politician.

Many others who played football on Robben Island had key roles in the struggle against apartheid and in the fledgling democracy that followed. Sport was important in the early years when South African democracy was fragile, and many believed the country would break out into ethnic warfare. Under the leadership of Mandela this never happened. He preached the virtue of reconciliation rather than vengeance, a mindset exemplified at the 1995 Rugby World Cup, which South Africa hosted. The Rugby World Cup took place just a year after the country's first democratic elections. Rugby, and the 'Springboks' team, was historically the sport of the white population and many black people were deeply sceptical of it. Therefore, it was hugely symbolic when Mandela publicly backed the team, which had just one non-white player in Chester Williams. South Africa won the tournament, and Mandela wore a green-and-gold Springboks jersey when presenting winning captain Francois Pienaar with the trophy. Fifteen years later South

Africa hosted the 2010 World Cup. FIFA had long been desperate to take the tournament to Africa, and Mandela furiously lobbied world leaders and FIFA executives. The tournament was deemed a success, with fears about safety and logistics ill-founded.

South Africa today has deep problems with corruption and unemployment, while electricity blackouts have become common in recent years. The righteousness of the anti-apartheid cause does not absolve South Africa's leaders of their failings decades later. But still, the story of football on Robben Island, and what is represented by those football shirts bought from those sports shops around Cape Town many decades ago, is an inspirational one. Zooming out, it forms part of a story of democracy's spread across the world. In the 1990s, the number of democracies in the world grew rapidly, not just in Africa, but also the many countries of the former USSR and Yugoslavia which held elections for the first time, as totalitarian regimes crumbled. According to the Pew Research Center, the number of democracies in the world grew from forty-seven in 1988 to eighty-five a decade later.[6] The trend continued, if at a slower pace, after that.

But over the last decade or so, something has happened that would perhaps surprise a time-traveller from the late 1990s. The number of democracies plateaued, and indeed many places have become less democratic. A February 2025 report by the Economist Intelligence Unit found that democracy peaked in 2006, but had steadily declined around the world since, with autocracies growing in strength and number. Democracy is not a binary classification, and scholars use the term 'democratic backsliding' to describe a place where elections may exist but, by some measures, such as freedom of speech or control of the media, things are getting worse. At the end of the Cold War, it seemed like democratisation was an inevitable trend, with countries sure to embrace free elections once they reached a certain level of wealth. As we will see in Chapter 8, the opposite has happened with China, while India, the world's biggest democracy, has become markedly less free in recent years as Narendra Modi consolidates power in concerning ways. Things have gone backwards in Russia and Turkey too, among many other places. There are also still plenty of countries which have never been democratic and have never looked especially likely to achieve that status. In these places, rather than a symbol of democratic resistance, football can be used to boost authoritarian power. Nowhere is this truer than in Saudi Arabia.

I like Newcastle. I like the city, the people, and don't mind the football team, despite being a fan of another English club often in direct competition. My brother attended university there, so I have visited a few times, including in November 2014 when he got tickets to see Newcastle United play Liverpool. The home side won 1–0 with a late goal from Ayoze Pérez. St James' Park was loud, very loud. It is one of the biggest stadiums in English football, somewhat shabby after years of neglect, but a special place to watch a game, with steep banks of seats rising off the pitch and the fans among the noisiest around. What makes Newcastle special is that it is a one-club city. Most English cities have at least two professional clubs, creating exciting rivalries but diluting local support. If a Manchester or north London team wins a trophy, roughly half the locals are livid. But the city of Newcastle and Newcastle United Football Club feel almost one and the same. Unusually for an English stadium, St James' Park is right in the centre of the city, perched on a hill a short walk from the main train station. Fans call it the 'Cathedral on a Hill' – a grandiose description but fitting when witnessed first-hand.

The club's die-hard supporters have long offered more energy from the stands than they've received back from the players on the pitch, though, their last major trophy coming way back in 1969. Between 2007 and 2021, Newcastle toiled under the neglectful ownership of sportswear tycoon Mike Ashley, a man hated by fans for putting little money into the club and showing few signs of caring about anything aside from making a profit. The team habitually underachieved but continued to attract big crowds throughout an era that included two relegations. Newcastle long felt like a sleeping giant. Any sense the club were plucky underdogs changed, though, when Ashley sold the club to the sovereign wealth fund of the state of Saudi Arabia, the Public Investment Fund (PIF). This gave Newcastle access to the deepest pockets in world football. On the day the takeover was confirmed there was a spontaneous party outside St James' Park, with several fans donning headdresses and waving Saudi flags.

Saudi Arabia is named after its first king, Ibn Saud, who unified the country in 1932 when its population numbered fewer than three million. That figure remained virtually static for 200 years. Everything changed in 1938 when the country discovered it was sitting on a vast sea of oil. The monarchy largely invested this windfall into subsidies for the local population and generous social services, and the population shot up from six million in 1970 to thirty-two million in 2015.[7] Life expectancy rose dramatically, and these days is comparable with European countries. There was some dissent against the monarchy, peaking in the late 1970s, but this was crushed as the monarchy allied itself with conservative Wahabi clerics. Since then, Saudi Arabia has been a deeply repressive place. Recent decades have seen gross human rights violations, including underage executions, the persecution of political dissidents and women, and terrible treatment of LGBT people.[8] Successive monarchs stayed in power by doling out subsidies and maintaining a wealthy yet stagnant society. Since Ibn Saud's death in 1953, the monarchy passed between his sons who were born decades apart thanks to the first king having numerous wives, which had the effect of keeping power in the hands of increasingly elderly men. King Abdullah died in 2015 and was replaced by his brother King Salman, then aged seventy-nine. The sons of Ibn Saud were getting too old and it was time for the next generation. The emergence of King Salman's son, Mohammed bin Salman (MBS), born in 1985, has changed everything.

Shortly after his father became king, MBS outmanoeuvred older relatives to become the country's de facto leader as crown prince and prime minister. MBS rose to prominence as a different kind of Saudi prince, motivated not just by enriching himself and family members, but also by an ambitious vision for Saudi Arabia's future. He knows the oil reserves will not last forever and has advocated for 'diversification' – that word again – by pouring money into solar and nuclear energy, as well as investing oil wealth abroad. Saudi has splashed the cash on so-called 'giga projects', such as Neom, a sci-fi-like city in the desert, as well as the world's largest theme park and a new Red Sea holiday resort which is keen to compete with and challenge Sharm el-Sheikh in Egypt on the other side of the Red Sea.

A key plank of Saudi investment has been football, as Christopher Davidson, an academic and expert on the Gulf region, explains. '[Saudi Arabia] needs the world to know about these places and the best way to do that is with billboard advertising in Premier League matches beamed around the world,' he says, also pointing out that getting young men into sport has two ulterior benefits. First, it's good for their health in a country struggling with the problem of obesity. Second, it gives restless youths an identity different to their religious or tribal one. 'Historically, the biggest fear has been religious extremism or tribal backlash,' says Davidson. 'Basically, if you can get Saudis supporting a football team, that's a secular and safe type of competitive identity.'

In January 2016, Bin Salman announced Vision 2030, a plan to turn Saudi Arabia into a 'global investment powerhouse'. Bin Salman's vehicle for change is the PIF, long a sleepy government-owned investor that bailed out local businesses with royal connections. He made it face outwards, turning it into a tool to project Saudi wealth and power globally. He also took charge of Saudi Aramco, the oil company producing 42 per cent of the country's wealth and used its profits to benefit the public by providing free electricity. MBS thought that Saudi Arabia's shifting demographics made change essential. Poverty was rising and well-educated people were struggling to find work, creating the potential for instability.

PIF invested in American companies, buying up $3.5 billion of Uber shares in June 2016, which was followed by the fund purchasing big stakes in Disney, Tesla and more. The USA, long a close military ally, sold weapons and other hardware to the Saudis.[9] 'The Saudi regime knows that the rest of the world doesn't think too highly of them in terms of the human rights record, and I don't think they care,' said Christopher Davidson. 'People will do business with them because they have sovereign wealth at their disposal.' In an era when the Western European countries which long-dominated the world economy have struggled to maintain economic growth, Saudi Arabia and other Gulf states are appealing as a source of cash for investment, a place where the money flows as freely as the oil that comes out of the ground. This has attracted criticism in the West because of Saudi's dire human rights record, but it hasn't had much of an impact. 'They feel very insulated from international criticism,' says Davidson. 'They see it as a necessary cost of doing business around the world.'

Saudi Arabia took a conservative turn after the 1979 Mecca siege by Islamists, which led the Al Saud family to cede power to hardliners. The same year, many Saudis joined the fight against the Soviet Union in Afghanistan, including Osama bin Laden, who went on to found Al-Qaeda.[10] Bin Salman has impressed Western audiences by advocating a return to 'moderate, open-minded Islam', a shift from ultra-conservative Wahhabism. Positive steps have included ending the ban on women driving, and permitting the existence of cinemas, concerts and co-educational classrooms, as well as reducing the power of the religious police. Bin Salman has criticised Wahabi scholars, but his Saudi Arabia has not changed as much as Western investors wished was the case. In 2017, he moved against his critics, turning the Ritz-Carlton hotel into a prison for Saudi billionaires, some charged with corruption and reportedly beaten. 'Never have so many billionaires, titans of finance who could move heaven and earth with their immense wealth, been deprived of their liberty and treasure so abruptly,' write Bradley Hope and Justin Scheck in *Blood and Oil*, their seminal analysis of bin Salman's ruthless quest for power. Following the so-called 'Sheikhdown', they say, MBS 'controlled all branches of the military, the police, the intelligence agencies and all government ministries, and held controlling stakes in many of the country's largest businesses through government holding companies. He wasn't the king, but he was one of the most powerful men on earth.'[11]

The Sheikhdown came weeks after Davos in the Desert, an investment conference attended by a significant number of big Western companies, who ended up embarrassed following the news. There doubtless was plenty of corruption going on before bin Salman's purge, but when the whole system is built around a royal family living lavishly thanks to state largesse, with no democratic constraints whatsoever, it is hard to know where to draw the line between acceptable conduct and corruption. The purge, although popular with less wealthy Saudis, consolidated the power of the autocratic MBS. While he was open to some social liberalisation, democratic changes were viewed entirely differently. Of all the new liberal developments, the right to criticise MBS was not one of them, as Hope and Scheck explain:

> 'In Mohammed's Kingdom of Saudi Arabia, reforms could only come from the top, lest citizens come to believe they could obtain their rights through protest or openly criticise the royal family. For all his liberal views, Mohammed was in general agreement with his uncles, aunts, brothers, and cousins on one thing: It was best for the Al Saud to run things. Even if the activists and the prince agreed that women should be allowed to drive, people who publicly opposed his government, especially those who took their grievances abroad, were being locked up.[12]

The Sheikhdown increased not just MBS's power but also the scale of the wealth controlled by the PIF, with the assets of many seized companies transferred to the investment fund, which grew from controlling $84 billion of assets in 2014 to nearly a trillion dollars by 2025.[13] But Saudi's growing role in the world economy has not coincided with political freedom. 'It has gone backwards if anything. It's more autocratic than before,' Christopher Davidson said. 'Saudi Arabia before bin Salman had several key power blocs, powerful individual ministers, princes, businessmen and so on, but he has now made clear that all roads lead to him. We have a more socially and economically liberal state by far, but a more autocratic state. The danger of this modern day sultanistic system is that sultanistic rulers are prone to very rash decision making because everyone around them is saying yes. That could be foreign policy disasters, we might see it with Neom or these white elephants in the desert, or the World Cup itself may be a gross overstepping of Saudi Arabia's ambitions.'

For a long time, it was hoped that social media, popular with Saudi youth, could be a catalyst for democracy. The opposite has happened, though, and the internet has become a tool for government surveillance. The ultimate example of the limits of Saudi modernisation came in 2018 when journalist Jamal Khashoggi was murdered. A critic of bin Salman, Khashoggi was lured to the Saudi consulate in Istanbul and brutally slaughtered by Saudi government agents who drugged him and dismembered his body. UN investigator Agnès Callamard called it a 'premeditated execution' ordered, or at least condoned, by the crown prince.[14] The murder turned him into an international pariah, with Germany and France imposing sanctions. For a long time after that, bin Salman barely travelled outside the kingdom. His close ally Yasir Al-Rumayyan, chairman of both Newcastle United and the PIF-owned LIV Golf project, has become the international face of Saudi's sports investments.

Al-Rumayyan has appeared at St James' Park a handful of times, and paraded the League Cup trophy on the Wembley pitch after the club's victory in March 2025, which was the culmination of an excellent first few years for the Saudi ownership.[15] Under English manager Eddie Howe, the club's fortunes turned around dramatically, first avoiding relegation and then qualifying for the Champions League for the first time in two decades, then beating Liverpool 2–1 in the League Cup final to win the club's first domestic trophy since 1955, with local lad Dan Burn scoring the crucial first goal. Newcastle spent heavily, but avoided signing the kind of international superstars such as Neymar that some thought they would target in the immediate aftermath of the takeover. Instead, they built a team around an English core, supplemented by pricy international signings like Alexander Isak and Bruno Guimarães. The new regime was 'at pains to run the club in as far from a brash manner as possible,' wrote *Times* journalist Alyson Rudd.[16] This is easier to do when you are winning. It has not all been plain-sailing for Newcastle under Saudi ownership, with the club hampered by the Premier League's Profit and Sustainability Rules (PSR). These place limits of expenditure compared with revenue, in part to prevent this exact scenario – a state-owned club blowing everyone else out of the water in the transfer market and driving fees and wages up for everyone else. The rules have also held back Aston Villa. Newcastle and Villa fans point out that Manchester City were not subject to the same rules when they made the leap from relegation-fodder to the top table while being bankrolled by a different flavour of Middle Eastern oil money, or Chelsea with Abramovich's oil money a decade earlier.

The colour green has long had deep associations with Islam. It is mentioned several times in the Quran, as reportedly the Prophet Muhammad's favourite colour and representing the gardens of paradise. The Saudi Arabian flag is all green with the shahada – the Islamic declaration of faith – written in white in Arabic above a sword. Green and white are the colours in which the national football team play. As of 2022, so too do Newcastle United, at least for some games. The club now has a green-and-white third kit is symbolic of a takeover deal that is, at its heart, a state project. The club's owners have explicitly tied Newcastle United to the state of Saudi Arabia, including hosting training camps in the country and two international friendlies involving the Saudi national team at St James' Park. My former *Athletic* colleague Jacob Whitehead watched Saudi Arabia lose to Costa Rica in Newcastle in September

2023. 'What was on display was a symbiotic relationship that extends far beyond the friendly itself,' he said.[17]

Newcastle fans' support for their club, particularly online, has at times crossed over into overt support for Saudi Arabia, throwing up some jarring moments. Eddie Howe, regarded as a thoughtful manager, has struggled when asked about Saudi human rights abuses. In March 2022, the country made headlines by carrying out eighty-one executions in a single day, the largest number in years.[18] Half of those killed were from the Shia minority group and Amnesty International condemned the mass execution as an exercise in silencing dissent rather than dishing out punishments for crimes. The country's opaque justice system makes it impossible to take at face value Saudi claims that those executed were guilty of serious offences. Asked about this in a press conference, Howe was caught between the rock of basic human rights and the hard place of criticising the people who employ him. 'From my perspective – and I've always maintained this – my specialist subject is football,' he said, awkwardly. 'It's what I know, it's what I've trained to do. As soon as I deviate from that into an area where I don't feel qualified to have a huge opinion, I think I go into dangerous ground, so I prefer to stick to what I believe I know.'[19] Newcastle fans often deflect criticism by pointing out wrongdoing by Western governments, legitimate topics for discussion, but Western governments do not own football clubs for propaganda reasons. In some cases on social media, Newcastle fans have disturbingly seemed to side with Saudi state propaganda rather than human rights charities.

As a fan of a club of a similar stature, I understand the thrill of going from Premier League also-rans to the Champions League, and that football fans have bonds with their team which run far deeper than whoever the current owners might be. It is a connection with a place and with people. Nevertheless, some fans' attempts to defend their club's new situation have involved mental gymnastics. 'Hypocrisy' is usually seen as a negative thing, but sometimes it may be better to accept conflicting views – loving Newcastle United while condemning Saudi executions – rather than attempting to defend the indefensible. Some Newcastle fans have argued, for example, that it is wrong to use the products of companies like Uber, Disney or Tesla, which have all taken Saudi investment, while criticising Newcastle. This is not analogous, though. Those investments were made for financial reasons. The Newcastle one was not. People who take Uber taxis or watch Disney films do not wear replica shirts in Saudi colours to show their support for the investors of the company whose product they are using. Football is different. It is rarely a way to make profits, but it is a vehicle for prestige and identity, precisely the reason Saudi's PIF bought Newcastle. The loyalty of Newcastle fans helps boost Saudi's global image far more cheaply and authentically than the trolls or bots which other autocratic regimes, like Russia, have used in recent years. Fan devotion is a powerful thing – the ties run so deep that few will ever forsake their club, no matter the sins of the owner. In the aftermath of the club's League Cup win in March 2025, few people mentioned Saudi Arabia. Indeed it seemed churlish given the raw emotion on display among a devoted fan base that had been starved of glory for so long. But two things can be true at the same time. First, Newcastle earned their win, and their fans deserve to enjoy it. Secondly, Saudi cash helped buy it, and the club is now a tool in projecting Saudi power. It was nice to see the huge crowd celebrating on the city's Town Moor a fortnight after the win. Still, I raised an eyebrow when I received an email that same week from a London-based PR agency promoting Visit Saudi, the country's tourist board which is run by a government ministry. 'To mark Newcastle United's first major win in decades, Saudi has released a limited-time travel invitation for UK visitors, a symbolic gesture that connects football to travel in an emotional way.'

Other defenders of Newcastle have pointed out that many clubs, including Arsenal, Liverpool and Manchester United, have American majority-owners and that the USA has had some contentious policies and leaders, to put it mildly. This is all true, but in democratic societies, private individuals are distinct from their governments. This is not the case in Gulf monarchies. Some have also claimed that partnering with Newcastle could help drive positive change in Saudi Arabia. 'We owe it to ourselves and the wider world to listen to the evidence about human-rights abuses in Saudi, to educate ourselves and know what we're getting into,' wrote club legend Alan Shearer when the takeover was confirmed. 'It's important to be mindful about sportswashing and what that actually means.'[20] Eighteen months later, at the end of the 2022–23 season when Newcastle qualified for the Champions League, Shearer wrote a gushing article entitled 'Dear Eddie . . . Thank you, for all of it'. The piece thanked the manager for 'allowing us to reclaim our streets; people smiling, restaurants buzzing, bars buzzing, an entire city a beehive of buzzing, connected to the club again, one and indivisible, alive and awash with happiness'. There was no mention of Saudi Arabia.[21]

Towards the bitter end of the Mike Ashley era, Newcastle struggled to fill its stadium, which was highly unusual for such a passionately supported club. For many fans, a big-money takeover seemed only a positive thing, not only as a way to buy great footballers and improve the under-achieving team, but because the region sorely needed financial investment. Saudi Arabia's stature was rising as oil prices did in the 1970s, but Newcastle was falling into relative decline as the UK's manufacturing and coal-mining industries collapsed, with little springing up in their place. The north-east of England has the lowest life expectancy in the UK, and higher child poverty and unemployment rates than most places. Between 2010 and 2024, Newcastle City Council was forced to make £335 million in cuts, hitting public services hard.[22]

Local leaders were desperate for investment regardless of its source. Pat Ritchie, the council's chief executive when the Premier League initially blocked the Saudi takeover in August 2020, even wrote to the league advocating for a compromise, describing the deal as 'transformational' and highlighting PIF's long-term commitment to the city. Newcastle United is the only club in its city and is the dominant cultural force in a large region, making it difficult for local politicians to antagonise the club and its fanbase. Chi Onwurah, Labour MP for the constituency of Newcastle upon Tyne Central and West, spoke vaguely about human rights ahead of the takeover, but nevertheless pressed the Premier League to approve the deal. 'There's the beggars-can't-be-choosers aspect,' Alex Niven, an academic and Newcastle fan, has said. 'People feel that finally someone's investing in the region. It doesn't feel like the right kind of investment given Saudi Arabia's record. But for most, the alternative is remaining the most socio-economically depressed part of the country for another forty years.'[23]

The takeover bid was formalised in April 2020 and met strong opposition due to an ongoing dispute between Qatar and Saudi Arabia, which saw the latter illegally pirating the Qatari broadcaster beIN Sports. The Saudis pulled out of the deal, with Premier League chief executive Richard Masters later saying it failed the league's test for new owners due to 'insufficient legal separation between the PIF and the Saudi Arabian government', making the Saudi government a 'shadow director'.[24] This was problematic because Premier

League rules prohibit ownership by entities engaged in conduct outside the UK that would be illegal if committed within the UK. For Saudi Arabia, that list is long. According to Human Rights Watch, 'abusive practices in detention centres including torture and mistreatment, prolonged arbitrary detention, and asset confiscation without clear legal process, remain pervasive'.[25] The legal wrangling continued for over a year, but on 6 October 2021, with Qatari–Saudi relations improving, Saudi Arabia lifted the beIN Sports ban which unlocked the takeover deal. It turned out that TV piracy, not human rights, was the issue holding things up.

A day later, the takeover was confirmed, with PIF taking an 80 per cent stake in the club, the rest held by UK-based investors managing day-to-day operations. PIF's share gradually increased to 90 per cent in the following years. While some saw the jubilant reactions as harmless fun, others disagreed. 'Newcastle is the closest thing to sportswashing I can think of,' said Kristian Ulrichsen of Rice University. 'The sight of thousands of Newcastle fans celebrating the takeover was a dream come true for Saudi Arabia.'

In the statement confirming the deal, the Premier League said it had received 'legally binding assurances' that Saudi Arabia would not control Newcastle United.[26] These three words could end up being the most significant in modern English football history. In a 2021 article for *The Athletic* that I worked on with Adam Crafton – who has done so much work in this area, including revealing how the UK government lobbied behind the scenes to facilitate the takeover – we reported that KARV Communications, a firm hired by PIF, disclosed that the fund's 'communications goals' include creating a 'clear distinction' between PIF and the Saudi political leadership and 'underscoring the business-only purpose' of the fund.[27] While PIF's purpose may be to generate returns, those profits benefit the Saudi state. It has never been clear what those 'assurances' are or how on earth the Premier League, a British company, could 'legally bind' the PIF or the state of Saudi Arabia.

With vast wealth at its disposal, Newcastle spent £400 million on transfers in the two years post-takeover, although the financial rules have made their ascent slower than some predicted at the time of the takeover. However, it remains true that Newcastle could soon rival state-backed clubs like Manchester City and Paris Saint-Germain for European and global supremacy. Nation-states' bottomless pockets will drive up wages across the board, meaning that, to keep up, other clubs will demand more money from fans via tickets and TV subscriptions.

The club ownership maintains this is not a state takeover. 'Human rights we take very seriously, but our partner is PIF, not the Saudi state,' Newcastle co-owner Amanda Staveley declared shortly after the takeover. 'The separation issue has been resolved. It's not sportswashing; it's investment.'[28] Staveley has since moved on but the Saudis are still there, the Premier League having waved through the takeover in 2021 after changing its mind on this key issue. Initially rejecting the takeover a year earlier, the Premier League said: 'PIF's directors are appointed by royal decree, and its board is composed almost exclusively of Saudi government ministers. The PIF Law places it under a government ministry. Its function is to serve the national interest of Saudi Arabia.'[29] The board's chairman is Mohammed bin Salman, while the fund's governor and Newcastle's chairman is his close ally Yasir Al-Rumayyan. The PIF website states that the fund 'reports to the Council of Economic and Development Affairs', a body established by royal decree and that is headed by bin Salman. While legally separate from the government, this means little in an authoritarian state where all power derives from the absolute monarch, like Manchester City's ownership being technically a private company distinct from the Abu Dhabi government.

Lobbyists are paid handsomely to argue for this 'separation' and have had some success. Not even the most die-hard Newcastle fans try to argue that Saudi Arabia is a haven for human rights, but they do say PIF is separate from the state. PIF itself appeared to undermine the 'separation' argument in a US court case in February 2023, as part of the legal dispute between LIV Golf and the PGA Tour. Lawyers representing PIF said it is 'a sovereign instrumentality of the Kingdom of Saudi Arabia' and that Al-Rumayyan is a 'sitting minister of the government'.[30] The Premier League has said it has been convinced that Newcastle's owners are separate from the Saudi state, but PIF itself has since argued the opposite.

Public entertainment was largely banned in Saudi following the 1979 attack on Mecca, after which the country headed in a more conservative direction, but things have changed under MBS. It all began in December 2018, when Riyadh hosted a Formula E race, with Enrique Iglesias performing and Wayne Rooney in attendance. Since then, PIF has become the largest investor in global sports.[31] The list of Saudi sports investments is ever-growing. Saudi Arabia's plans are nothing short of a quest for world sporting domination. In October 2021, the same month that PIF bought Newcastle, it invested $2 billion in the breakaway LIV Golf, offering huge prize money to stars like Phil Mickelson, Dustin Johnson and Brooks Koepka. After two years of resistance from the PGA Tour, LIV won, merging with the PGA in a new entity funded and chaired by PIF.

Saudi Arabia has also spent huge sums hosting heavyweight boxing bouts, WWE wrestling events and, since 2021, a Formula 1 Grand Prix in Jeddah. The kingdom's ambitions extend to top events in cricket, horse racing and tennis. Minky Worden, director of global initiatives at the charity Human Rights Watch, says Saudi Arabia has a strategy to use 'sports teams, athletes and major sporting events in the country to distract from its national human rights crises'.

But football remains the biggest focus. It began with Newcastle but has grown much bigger. Despite Saudi Arabia's frequent qualification for the World Cup since 1994, its domestic league had little international profile until January 2023, when Cristiano Ronaldo signed for Al-Nassr FC, a move which kicked off a Saudi football revolution. That same summer, PIF took direct control of four clubs – Al-Ahli, Al-Ittihad, Al-Hilal and Al-Nassr – which prompted a massive spending spree, with stars like Neymar, Karim Benzema, Sadio Mané and N'Golo Kanté joining Ronaldo, the most-followed person in the world on social media, helping drive interest in the league. The Saudi Pro League spent $957 million in the summer transfer window, second only to the Premier League.[32] Almost a billion dollars of Saudi state cash was pumped into the global football ecosystem, gratefully received by agents working on commission and by European clubs looking to shift ageing players.

Back in 2016, it was China that upended world football's transfer market before that bubble quickly burst. The USA, India and other Middle Eastern countries have also splashed the cash on international superstars in the past, but there are reasons to think the Saudi shift will be more enduring. Leading figures have been smart in pumping state money into four different clubs, ensuring that the championship is likely to remain competitive rather than be dominated by one or two clubs in the way that Guangzhou Evergrande won everything in China before their demise. As well as ageing superstars like Ronaldo, players in their prime have also moved to Saudi, such as Wolves' Portuguese midfielder Rúben Neves (26) and Aston Villa's French winger Moussa Diaby (25) and Colombian striker John Durán (21). Although the Saudi Pro League is bankrolled by the state, it is worth noting that the country has more of a domestic football culture than, for example, Qatar, and some clubs do get decent attendances. The national side aren't complete no-hopers - they upset Argentina 2–1 in the 2022 World Cup, a stunning result largely forgotten because Messi's side went on to lift the trophy.

The Saudi Pro League is a prelude to the main event: the 2034 World Cup in Saudi Arabia. Football is desperate for cash to cover rising player wages and tournament expansions, and Saudi Arabia has the resources to help. The 2026 World Cup in the USA, Canada and Mexico is the first to feature forty-eight teams. Expanded tournaments require more infrastructure, and Saudi Arabia is one of the few places capable of meeting such demands, hosting the 2023 Club World Cup, the 2027 Asia Cup, and the Italian and Spanish Super Cups, hosting top teams like Real Madrid, Barcelona, Juventus, and Inter Milan. FIFA is becoming increasingly reliant on Saudi cash. Aramco, the state oil company, is now a FIFA sponsor, rumoured to be the organisation's biggest ever. Like Gazprom's sponsorship of Schalke, this deal is not about selling fuel but about projecting state power. The Trump White House has had a close alliance with Saudi Arabia and MBS, and supported each others' bids, with Jared Kushner, Trump's son-in-law, a key figure.

To better understand Saudi Arabia's shift from football non-entity to Premier League owners to World Cup host, I spoke to Miles Coleman, a documentary producer who spent two and a half years making the Netflix mini-series *FIFA Uncovered*, interviewing senior football figures all over the world. The series was televised a few days before the Qatar World Cup began, throwing up huge ethical question marks over both that tournament and, more broadly, FIFA. I met Coleman in November 2022 in a BBC radio studio when we both appeared on a panel discussion about politics and the World Cup. We stayed in touch afterwards and he was insistent that the 2034 tournament would go to Saudi Arabia, something few were saying at the time, based on the sources he developed making the documentary. He turned out to be completely correct.

'There were a few things that I saw that indicated Saudi was the next frontier,' he told me two years later, explaining that Qatar's true goal in hosting the World Cup was to become 'uninvadable' – building deep ties with the USA and other Western powers to hold off aggressive neighbours like Saudi. 'If Saudi Arabia invaded Qatar tomorrow, the first calls they'd have would be the US, UK and German embassies saying "Hang on",' he says. 'Every major military power has a vested interest in keeping it safe. You are now in for a world of trouble if you invade Qatar. Hosting the World Cup is expensive, but less so than building an army.'

The Qatar World Cup led to Saudi Arabia feeling wrong-footed and outsmarted by its tiny rival. 'You can talk about fancy geopolitical terms, but the people I spoke to said that the Saudis were annoyed. The idea they were gazumped by their little cousin annoyed them,' Coleman explained. 'The other factor in all of this is that FIFA was running out of money . . . They were living World Cup to World Cup. They woke up the morning after the [Qatar] World Cup and said "All right, where's our new funding coming from?" And the last pool of money in the world is Saudi Arabia. FIFA were desperate for one last big payday.'

Running FIFA has become increasingly expensive, with massive staff numbers and officials still enjoying five-star hotels a decade on from the FBI's infamous corruption raid on a Swiss hotel. Its accounts still lack transparency, to put it mildly. Saudi Arabia was initially mentioned as a possible host of the 2030 World Cup, but two out of three tournaments being held in the Gulf was deemed unnecessarily controversial. The Saudis went for 2034 instead, leaving Spain, Morocco and Portugal to have a clear run at 2030, with South American countries hosting some early games to commemorate the centenary of the first tournament in Uruguay. It certainly seems strange that a region with little football heritage is hosting two World Cups in quick succession. 'I think there is a real sense of embarrassment among the rank of file who I met,' Coleman says. 'These are people who love football, forced into a position where they are defending a government that has done appalling things.'

He also points out that a constitutional innovation designed to make things more transparent has benefited Saudi Arabia. Before the Qatar World Cup bidding scandal, the host was decided on by an executive committee of thirty or so football bigwigs from around the world. This process awarded the 2018 tournament to Russia and 2022 to Qatar, and the corruption allegations have never gone away. 'FIFA said "We'll change the structure so every association head from around the world can vote",' says Coleman. 'That's great news for Saudis.' The Saudi state started splashing the cash all around the world. In 2024, it signed a 'multi-year global partnership' with CONCACAF, North and Central America's football confederation. The same year it announced a 'global partnership' with FIFA which will see the Aramco logo adorn pitches for World Cup qualifiers and other matches across the globe. Saudi money now pours into football in almost every country in the world – and every country gets a vote.

Coleman is South African and points out the contrast between the 2010 World Cup in South Africa and the 2034 event in Saudi Arabia. The 2010 World Cup saw few memorable matches, Spain's 1–0 final win better remembered for seeing fourteen yellow cards and one red than for exciting football. The tournament is perhaps best remembered for the background din of the vuvuzelas, the plastic horns blown by locals throughout every match. Nevertheless, this World Cup remains a symbol of South Africa moving beyond apartheid. Today, it is a deeply flawed country, but a vast improvement on what preceded it by virtue of being built on the principles of multi-racial democracy. The shirts worn by the footballers of Robben Island symbolise South Africa's fight for democracy, a cause that animated the world. The 2010 World Cup is one of the crowning glories of Mandela's struggle, South Africa's road to freedom, and an era when more and more countries were embracing democracy. By contrast, the 2034 World Cup in Saudi Arabia, and the green-and-white shirts of Newcastle United, show that democracy is not inevitable. Just as football can help spread democratic ideas, it can also be a tool to consolidate power in the hands of autocrats.

8

CHINA'S RISE AND RETREAT

West Bromwich Albion & Guangzhou Evergrande

'I think there was a lot of luck involved. Because now, about our national team, I'm not so sure about their level.'
President Xi Jinping overheard speaking to his Thai counterpart after a 2–1 China win during a World Cup qualifier, November 2023

This chapter tells the story of football in China. Unlike many of the other countries discussed in this book, I have not been there. Visiting as a journalist is extremely tricky these days. But I wanted to tell the story of a place where more than one in six of the world's population live, and has a fascinating recent history when it comes to football, which traces the story of the country's broader rise and retreat from the global stage. I did this with the help of experts, books, and an interviewee familiar with the inner circles of Chinese football whose identity I cannot reveal for that person's own safety. The story is told through two football shirts: one in the English Midlands and one in the Chinese city of Guangzhou.

I grew up watching *Football Focus* on the BBC, a show that often broadcasts interviews with a specific visual format. The journalist would interview a player or manager inside an empty stadium, sitting in the stands with the bright green pitch in the back of the shot. Despite some time in football journalism, I had never managed to do an interview in a location like this, but finally got the opportunity to feel like I was on *Football Focus* when I spoke to Caroline Parker in April 2024 inside an empty Select Car Leasing Stadium. This is the home of Reading FC, just outside London. Reading is Parker's local club and the one she has supported all her life. I was interviewing her after Reading had drawn 1–1 with Lincoln City in League One, the third tier of English football, a feisty encounter with a decent crowd. We met in a hospitality box after the full-time whistle and sat outside in the spring sunshine. Throughout the game, fans had been chanting 'Stand up if you hate Dai Yongge', Reading's Chinese owner who had become despised by the fanbase.

Back in the mid-2000s, this place was known as the Madejski Stadium, named after the local businessman who had bankrolled the club's success. For a brief time, this was one of England's most exciting places to watch football. In the 2005–06 season, Reading topped the Championship with 106 points, the highest total ever recorded in a professional season in England. The following year was even better with the club reaching the dizzy heights of eighth in the Premier League, missing out on qualification for European football by a single point. The club were relegated the following season, though, and became something of a 'yo-yo club' between the top two divisions with two promotions and two relegations between 2006 and 2013. May 2017 would turn out to be a momentous month for Reading. After finishing third in the league, the club reached the Championship play-offs, putting them close to reaching the top flight once more. Reading edged past Fulham in the semi-final on 16 May to reach the final. The following day came some more big news. A Chinese brother and sister, Dai Yongge and Dai Xiu Li, who had made their money converting air-raid shelters into shopping centres as China's economy boomed in the 2000s, completed a takeover of the club. Reading lost the final a week later. Since then, everything that could possibly go wrong has gone wrong.

'We've slowly watched this man destroy our club,' Parker told me, describing how the two siblings had come in on a wave of optimism, but everything since had been a disaster, the club falling into England's third tier while battling repeated points deductions for financial irregularities. The club had become a basket case, with its absentee owner at the heart of all the problems. Early promises of vast wealth flowing from China have dried up, payments to staff and the taxman have been missed, the women's team has been liquidated, and a once-proud club have been driven to a state of despair following the owner's wasteful spending in his failed pursuit of the Premier League's TV riches. 'It's a really sorry tale of someone who's bet the house on black, came up red, lost interest and just had terrible advice and really shouldn't be anywhere near running a football club.'

If one good thing has come out of this for Parker, it is that she has built up a community of football fans and experts trying to figure out what is going on, not just at Reading but at other English clubs with similar absentee owners. She is now a campaigner fighting to change the laws governing football in the UK. 'There are so many problem clubs,' she says. 'There's a massive gap in the regulations.' Parker has watched from afar as two other clubs owned by Dai Yongee, in China and Belgium, have gone into liquidation. 'Reading fans are rightly concerned that we are going to be the hat-trick.' She says the 'lowest moment' was when the club's Bearwood training ground was reported to have been sold to Wycombe Wanderers, a historically smaller club located nearby.[1] The deal collapsed when eagle-eyed fans noticed some legal small print saying that the site could only be used for Reading FC.[2]

Describing the situation of many English clubs below the Premier League, Parker keeps returning to the metaphor of the casino. 'Football just attracts these lunatics, but the thing is if you don't make it a sustainable business, you're encouraging gamblers.' In March 2025, the English Football League took the dramatic step of disqualifying Dai Yongge as a director under the league's ownership test, requiring him to sell the club. This is not just a story about English football regulation, the story of Reading and several other English clubs tells a bigger global story, though. Our shirt for this chapter is not Reading, but another English club a hundred miles away which a decade ago had not just a Chinese owner but also a Chinese sponsor. This shirt has not aged well.

One week after my Reading trip, I went to the home of West Bromwich Albion in England's West Midlands. The Hawthorns is just a few miles from where I grew up in Birmingham, but as a fan of rivals Aston Villa it was not somewhere I had ever been before. I went with my friend John, a lifelong fan of the club known as the Baggies, famous for having some of English football's first black stars in the 1970s. Like Reading, West Brom have long been a yo-yo team bouncing between the Premier League and the second tier, the peak being eight consecutive seasons in the top flight between 2010 and 2018, including an eighth-place finish in 2012–13, helped by the goals of a teenage Romelu Lukaku.

The last few years have not been so kind. The game I saw was against Watford FC, another yo-yo club, in what was West Brom's third consecutive season outside the top flight. After a poor start to the season the club were chasing the play-off places under young Spanish coach Carlos Corberán. After conceding two quick goals, the mood turned gloomy, but after a dramatic late comeback the game finished 2–2 and the Hawthorns was bouncing. The crowd sang their peculiar anthem, 'The Lord Is My Shepherd' a well-known Christian hymn. This is not because of fans' religious affinity but is a joke running back to the 1980s. Football matches were always traditionally played on a Saturday, but one game was moved to Sunday because of a public strike. The West Brom crowd started singing a hymn because Sunday is church day, and it stuck. English football is full of quirky stories like this. Everton walk out to 'Z-Cars', an endearing but old fashioned folk tune which is one of the least intimidating songs you could possibly imagine. It is the theme of a 1960s cop show. Someone played it once and it stuck.

Just like Reading, West Brom has been hobbled by Chinese ownership. As I did on some of my other research trips for this book I went to the match looking out for fans wearing one very specific replica shirt from their recent past: the version of West Brom's navy blue-and-white vertical striped kit from the 2017–18 season, the last in that run of eight consecutive Premier League campaigns, which saw the side finish bottom of the league. The front of this shirt features the word 'Palm', alongside Chinese Mandarin writing. There are many examples of Premier League shirts with Chinese on them promoting dubious betting companies as we saw in Chapter 3. This is something very different.

The Palm Eco-Town Development Company is headquartered in Guangzhou, a huge city in southern China near Hong Kong.[3] In 1985, 2.4 million people lived there. This number doubled in the following decade and doubled again in the ten years after that.[4] Many other Chinese cities saw similar growth as the country's economy exploded in the late twentieth and early twenty-first centuries, with vast numbers of people relocating from the country's rural interior to the swelling cities. The property industry boomed, with companies like Palm building new places for people to live. In 2014, the head of Palm, Guochuan Lai, stepped down to focus on 'private investment projects'.[5] One of these was West Bromwich

Albion. In the summer of 2016, he became the club's controlling shareholder, taking an 88 per cent stake. After an initial burst of enthusiasm, including funnelling money into the club by putting his company's logo on the team shirt, West Brom were relegated, and Lai appeared to lose interest. The sense that he was no longer engaged in the day-to-day running of the club got worse during the Covid pandemic, which cut China off from the rest of the world.

In June 2022, a sign that something strange was going on came buried in the club's 2020–21 financial accounts, which made grim reading for every club in England due to the pandemic. This document showed that Lai had taken out a £5 million loan from the club to fund one of his other businesses in China.[6] He then missed a deadline to pay this back. While football fans often complain about their owners not spending as much cash as they'd like on transfers, this goes far beyond that. Owners borrowing money from their club to fund completely unrelated projects is exactly what Reading fan Caroline Parker means when she talks about 'problem clubs', enabled by what campaigners see as gaps in regulations governing how football clubs operate. Things got even messier when the club took out a big loan to cover 'football operations'. The amount was £20 million, climbing to £28 million when interest was added.[7] While the details of the loans and Lai's other companies were complex, the essence was straightforward. Guochuan Lai owned a venerable institution – one of the Football League's founding members – and had stopped putting in cash, then started borrowing money to keep the lights on.

There is little fans can do in this situation. No owner can be forced to sell a club, and finding a buyer is often difficult. Football is rarely a profitable industry. Fans of Reading, West Brom and other clubs have been forced to become experts in corporate accounting, Chinese business law and other subjects completely unrelated to football. Just like at Reading, activist West Brom fans immersed themselves in the details, which are tricky to understand not just because of the language barrier but because of China's opaque legal system and business structures. In June 2023, a group called Action for Albion published a startling graphic detailing West Brom's ownership structure and how it related to Lai's web of companies. It alleged that 15.8 per cent of the club was ultimately owned by the Chinese state.[8] Further to this, campaigners heard from people who had done business in China about how making losses on investments is socially taboo in the country. People often cling on to assets hoping they will inflate in value against all logic, rather than cut their losses by selling up. There was no chance of Lai turning a profit on the rumoured £175 million he paid Jeremy Peace for the club in 2016, by all accounts an overvaluation, with the club now in a far worse state on and off the pitch.[9]

The Championship is one of the most bizarre and fascinating divisions in world football. The wages are higher than many top divisions around Europe meaning there are a lot of good players, the gameplay is often more high-octane and unpredictable than the tactically refined Premier League, and the gulf between top and bottom narrower. Financially, though, the league is a basket case. This is because owning a Premier League club is hugely appealing to rich people around the world but there are only twenty such clubs at one time, they rarely go on sale, and if they do the prices are eye-watering. Sir Jim Ratcliffe and his Ineos group bought little more than a quarter of Manchester United for $1.65 billion in 2024.[10] Buying a struggling Championship club and getting them promoted is more financially feasible, but this is far easier said than done, especially as clubs relegated from the top flight receive so-called 'parachute payments' to soften the landing, which give them a huge advantage over their rivals. Being competitive on the pitch often involves spending more money than is coming in. Both Reading and West Brom had seasons where they spent far more on wages than they were bringing in in revenue. That isn't sustainable for long. The Championship is a casino where most gamblers lose.

At the peak of the Chinese football bubble in the mid-2010s, the West Midlands became ground zero for Chinese football's global expansion. At one point, all four of the region's biggest clubs – West Brom, Birmingham City, Wolverhampton Wanderers and Aston Villa – had Chinese owners. Further south, Reading and Southampton were in the same situation. Wolves, owned by the Fosun conglomerate, would be the only one of these whose owners would stick it out beyond 2024.

Aston Villa's experience of Chinese ownership was disastrous although mercifully brief. In May 2016, following Villa's humiliating relegation from the Premier League, the club was sold by Randy Lerner, the American finance boss who had owned the club for a decade. The Lerner years started brightly before he lost interest and stopped spending, desperate for a way out after pouring a quarter of a billion pounds into the club with little in the way of return, later saying 'the Premier League cost me my nervous system'.[11] He sold up to a little-known Chinese businessman called Tony Xia who invested heavily to start with, but then seemed to be facing problems, apparently unable to move his cash from China to the UK. At the time the UK had closer relations to China than would be the case later. In 2015, Chinese leader Xi Jinping made a state visit to the UK in which a reported £30 billion worth of commercial deals were reached. Prime Minister Theresa May visited Beijing in 2018, but by this time, beneath the surface, there were some strange things going on when it came to Chinese investment in the UK. Keith Wyness had the unenviable task of being Villa's chief executive in this period. '(Xia) was trying to pick the team from watching the game on TV, claimed he played football at Oxford University which he never had done, claimed he had a degree from Harvard which he never had,' Wyness told me. The media reporting at the time of the takeover went big on Xia's academic background, for example the BBC reported that 'Dr Xia spent six years at Harvard and Massachusetts Institute of Technology, including five months at Oxford University, before returning to China'. In an interview on the club website a year later, Xia spoke of his time spent 'doing my PhD at Harvard'. Later, Xia asked the club for help with a UK visa and the paperwork asked for proof of the Harvard doctorate. 'Xia repeatedly made excuses about being unable to find the document, and the visa idea was quietly abandoned,' says Wyness. Remarkably, Xia wanted to open a Villa Park branch of the Confucius Institute, a state chain of cultural promotion organisations linked to the Communist Party, he told me. 'If you do any research, that is a real red flag . . . this is the Chinese state. I stood up against that and said you shouldn't do that at Villa Park.' After eighteen months of this, with things improving slightly on the pitch in Villa's second season in the Championship, Xia became unable or unwilling to move his money out of China. Villa were close to the brink. 'We never got a penny from him after February 2018,' says Wyness. 'He left us high and dry with no money . . . the taps were turned off. If it had leaked out to any of the suppliers that there was no money, you'd have had no pies to sell on Saturday and the risk of the whole thing collapsing.'

The darkest day in a dark decade for Villa came on 5 June 2018, shortly after the club lost the play-off final to Fulham and failed to win promotion back to the Premier League. Villa then missed the deadline for a £4 million tax bill and was faced with a winding-up order by the taxman and the very real threat of going out of business. Miraculously a pair of billionaires – American Wes Edens and Egyptian Nassef Sawiris – came to Villa's rescue and the club's subsequent rise has been remarkable.

Birmingham City, Villa's biggest rivals, had their greatest moment in modern history in March 2011 when the club stunned Arsenal to win the League Cup. Three months later the club's then owner, Hong Kong businessman Carson Yeung, was arrested in connection with alleged money laundering. He was convicted and imprisoned in 2014 while he still owned the club.[12] It was a case of out of the frying pan and into the fire for the Blues, who were sold to Trillion Trophy Asia, an investment vehicle registered in the British Virgin Islands by Paul Suen, a Chinese businessman. Around a quarter of the club was then sold to a Cambodian company. It was not clear who ultimately owned the club, or their motive in doing so, and the details were shrouded in mystery, an opaque web of offshore financial vehicles and people who had no public presence in the UK. The club's salvation, like others in recent years in English football, came from the USA.[13] Knighthead Capital Management bought the club in 2023, with NFL star Tom Brady a minority investor. The club has big ambitions including a proposal for a huge new stadium, which would vastly improve an area close to where I grew up but, as a fan of the club's fierce rivals, I hope it goes badly.

Florida-based businessman Shilen Patel bought West Brom from Guochuan Lai in February 2024. When I visited two months later the ghost of Lai had been exorcised and, unlike at Reading, there were no anti-ownership chants, although fans still wandered around the concourse wearing the logo of Palm. With a couple of exceptions, notably Wolves, Chinese money has almost vanished from the English game. This rise and retreat fits a wider pattern, with the winding path of Chinese politics and Chinese football closely mirroring each other.

In the 1990s and 2000s, China was inching away from the global periphery on its way to becoming an economic and military superpower. Chinese football was doing the same. China was admitted to FIFA back in 1952 and regained its membership after briefly being booted out due to a dispute over Taiwan, but Chinese football went into retreat under the leadership of Mao Zedong. Western culture, including competitive sport, was seen as a capitalist evil, contaminating the ideological purity of Chinese communism.[14] In 1976, as the country was beginning to re-engage with the world under the leadership of Deng Xiaoping, China joined FIFA again. The New York Cosmos, filled with ageing stars including Pelé and Franz Beckenbauer, was the first international team to tour the country a year later, West Bromwich Albion and Inter Milan touring the following year.[15] In 1983, Watford, an unfashionable English team from a commuter town on the edge of London, were the guests for a three-game, post-season tour sponsored by the London Export Corporation, which was eyeing up the potential of the Chinese market to sell textile goods, just as Europe was beginning to be flooded by imports from China and other Asian countries. Watford were managed by future England manager Graham Taylor. The team had surprisingly finished second in England's top division under the chairmanship of pop superstar and local boy Elton John. The team drew huge crowds in China, playing before 80,000 people in Beijing and bringing a splash of celebrity to dour post-Mao China. Martin Amis, who later became one of the UK's most celebrated novelists, reported on the tour for the *Observer* newspaper.[16] He said Watford were treated politely by their hosts but the crowd went wild when Lü Hongxiang scored for the Chinese in a 3–1 defeat. The extra-curricular activities were groundbreaking as well. Two years before Wham! became the first Western pop group to tour China, Elton John sang in the Great Hall of the People. 'Their quivering chopsticks negotiated the usual menu of fish stomachs, sea-slugs and ancient eggs,' wrote Amis. In Shanghai, the locals appreciated a spirited performance as their team narrowly lost 2–1. Back in Beijing, Watford were joined by two of their stars, John Barnes and Luther Blissett, who had missed the early games because of England national team duties. With their two stars, Watford hammered the Chinese side 5–1. Amis wrote of the crowd's 'climbing anger' as well as 'selective and unmistakable' hostility towards Barnes and Blissett, who are both black. Outside the stadium the Watford bus was 'cursed, barracked and gestured at' as it drove away. The game was also notable for the identity of one of the faces in the crowd. Xi Jinping, then a junior official, drove 170 miles from Zhengding in Hebei province to watch the game. He was sorely disappointed by the result and privately vowed to do something about it one day. He would get the opportunity when he became president of China.

Cameron Wilson is a Scottish football journalist who has lived in China for two decades and is a passionate Shanghai Shenhua fan. He says Chinese football has an authentic fan culture, which sometimes exhibits itself in ways which might surprise people. 'There's a lot of things expressed which you wouldn't see expressed elsewhere,' he says. 'That's what makes it so interesting.' He tells the story of how back in 2014, Shanghai Shenhua became Shanghai Greenland, adopting the name of a real-estate developer that at one point was the largest in the world, with huge overseas investments in cities like London, Los Angeles and Sydney. The name change threw up a rare example of public protest in modern China. After the takeover, Greenland filled a wedge of the stadium with employees in green corporate T-shirts. But fans' groups, led by the Blue Devils, kept silent for nineteen minutes before unveiling a banner quoting

Xi Jinping: 'abandoning tradition is tantamount to severing your spiritual lifeline'. This was a provocative gesture, and the police waded into the crowd to confiscate the banner. There were some scuffles and angry chanting, though no arrests were made.[17]

Ultimately, the protesters got their wish and the club was named Shanghai Greenland Shenhua, later ditching 'Greenland' after clubs were made to abandon corporate names in 2020. 'The very fact that so many people could gather in one place at one time and not be policed to death and move on, as the innumerable laws against public assembly and association required, was a rare breath of collective freedom,' notes football historian David Goldblatt, who explains that fans at other clubs made their voices heard too. 'While many of these new groups amount to no more than a few dozen young men, claiming their small patch of the stands and producing their own T-shirts and banners, such organisational autonomy remains a rare and precious psychic space in contemporary China.'[18] Football is often a tool used by dictators in repressing their people but can also function as a valve for popular dissent, with the stands acting as a place for limited protest, providing space for democratic ideas to permeate. Fans played a role in overthrowing autocrats like Hosni Mubarak in Egypt in 2011 and Slobodan Milošević in Yugoslavia a decade earlier. In China, though, football dissent has never gone much further than the terraces.

A low point in Chinese football was a 2–1 home defeat in 1985 to Hong Kong, which was administered by the UK until 1997. The game culminated in a riot known as the '519 football hooligan event'. Chinese fans were incandescent following the embarrassing defeat, raining debris on the Hong Kong players, who were besieged in the ground before they could be evacuated by police. Outside the ground fans smashed up buildings and buses, and assaulted police officers. After this, Chinese football saw the need to improve things on and off the pitch and began to cautiously experiment with some capitalist principles during the 1990s, just as it did in business and other walks life. The government set up two companies, the Chinese Super League Company and Chinese Football Company, to start running football independently from the state, a model that was clearly not working. In the short term, the changes appeared effective – the high-water mark for Chinese football was in 2002 when the country qualified for the World Cup hosted by neighbouring South Korea and Japan. The squad featured two players, Li Tie and Sun Jihai, who played in the Premier League for Everton and Manchester City respectively. China made little impact on the World Cup, losing group games against Costa Rica, Brazil and Turkey without scoring a goal, but 2002 was seen at the time as the beginning of an exciting new era for football in China, long seen as a sleeping giant because of the country's huge population. But it was not a new era, it was a high water mark.

The same year, China saw the 'black whistle riots' where fans of Shaanxi burned seats inside a stadium before smashing police vehicles and setting a bus alight, after a referee allowed the visiting Qingdao team to equalise through a penalty allegedly awarded beyond the end of injury time. Match-fixing has long hung heavy over Chinese football.[19] It was a catalyst for deeper reform. The 2000s were a time of China liberalising and opening up to the world, the country joining the World Trade Organization in 2001 and hosting the Beijing Olympics in 2008. Still, in the post-Olympic glow, the quality of Chinese football seemed to go backwards, with the country failing to qualify for the World Cup after 2002 and no players since Sun Jihai and Li Tie becoming established in the Premier League. 'Football, increasingly doomed in the shadow of the country's Olympic triumphs and its infatuation with Yao Ming, the NBA and basketball, looked doomed to occupy a marginal and rather unsavoury place in the Chinese sports landscape,' writes David Goldblatt. 'That, however, was to calculate the future without the presence of Xi Jinping.'[20]

Soon after becoming party leader and president in 2013, the man who watched that defeat against Watford all those years ago began talking about football on the world stage. He had previously visited Bayer Leverkusen in Germany in 2009 and said he wanted to 'improve' the game in China by incorporating it into his wider anti-corruption reforms.[21] China's rapid growth between 2003 and 2013 under previous president Hu Jintao had happened alongside eye-watering levels of corruption, as rival cliques vied for control of local governments and state-controlled industries, which they used to try to grab a piece of the fast-growing economic pie for themselves. Football was corrupt too. Anti-graft measures saw multiple big clubs relegated and stripped of titles. In 2012, two previous heads of the Chinese Football Association were jailed, along with four players and referee Lu Jun who had previously been known as the 'golden whistle' for his perceived clean reputation.[22] Dalian Shide, one of the country's most successful teams in the late 1990s and 2000s, was owned by Xu Ming, a close associate of Bo Xilai, a politician known as Xi's biggest rival for the top job but got obscenely rich and made too many enemies. His wife was implicated in the mysterious death of a British businessman in a hotel room, which became an international scandal that brought down Bo, along with his football owner friend. Dalian Shide disappeared completely.

Xi kept up his footballing diplomacy, though. He was presented with a Lionel Messi shirt in Argentina, and met Dutch goalkeeping legend Edwin van der Sar on a trip to the Netherlands. On his UK state visit in 2015, he visited Manchester City's training ground, taking a famous selfie with UK prime minister David Cameron and City striker Sergio Agüero. Somewhat ludicrously, Sun Jihai, a member of the Chinese 2002 World Cup squad who had had an unremarkable couple of seasons with Manchester City before they became an elite team under Emirati ownership, was admitted to the National Football Museum's English Football Hall of Fame. A UK politician called this a 'grubby little fix' to buy Chinese influence.[23] These days the name Sun Jihai does not appear on the museum's website.

Also in 2015, China published a fifty-point reform programme for the nation's football, written in the baffling jargon of the Chinese Communist Party. It contained three of Xi's concrete wishes: for China to soon qualify for another World Cup; for China to host the World Cup one day; and for China to win the trophy by 2050.[24] This pricked the ears of the country's new rich, people like Dai Yongge and Guochuan Lai, eager to ingratiate themselves with Xi by investing in clubs like Reading and West Brom. Observers of Chinese football explain that the rush of investment by the Chinese new rich into football was not necessarily directed explicitly from the top but done to curry favour with a leader who they all knew cared deeply about the game. If Chinese-owned clubs played in the Premier League and competed for trophies, that would bring glory to China, a smart goal for any businessman in a country where the lines between the private sector and the state are thin at best.

On the domestic front, cash suddenly began pouring into the Chinese Super League, which until then had been a backwater of world football. It began attracting ageing stars like Didier Drogba, Nicolas Anelka and Adriano. In 2015 and 2016, the transfer policy changed, no longer just providing faded superstars one last pay day. Several Brazilians in their prime went to China, such as Hulk and Alex Teixeira, as well as Colombian striker Jackson Martínez. In the 2016 summer transfer window, more money was spent by clubs in China than anywhere else. Chelsea manager Antonio Conte called the league a 'danger' to the European elite after having star Brazilian midfielder Oscar poached by Shanghai SIPG for £60 million fee.[25] Plenty of elite managers went there too, including World Cup winners Luiz Felipe 'Big Phil' Scolari, Marcello Lippi and Fabio Cannavaro. In China, in those heady years of the mid-2010s, football was opening up and booming, and plenty of other things were too.

China's rapid economic growth was built on urbanisation. Hundreds of millions of peasants became city dwellers in the late twentieth century and the beginning of the twenty-first. Cities exploded in size and this new urban population needed somewhere to live. The construction company Evergrande was founded in 1996 by Hui Ka Yan, who grew up poor in the Chinese countryside. He spotted a gap in the market as the country was dismantling its system of state-provided housing and embracing an economic system that has become known as state capitalism. Before the millennium, people in Chinese cities generally lived in apartments provided by their employer, alongside people they worked with in factories, and sending their children to the same factory school. A private property market created a new economic sector from scratch, with vast opportunity for investment and growth. In 1996, about one-third of Chinese people lived in cities. In 2025, around two-thirds of a far bigger overall population did so, and the proportion keeps growing.[26] Companies like Evergrande started buying up land from local governments, who raised money in the short term without realising land values were about to explode. Many of those who did figure out this pattern got very rich indeed, and China's new rich were ostentatious in their displays of wealth. It was all a long way from the hair-shirted communist ideals of Mao.

At the start of the new millennium, China was embracing elements of free-wheeling capitalism as a member of the World Trade Organization. The 2008 Beijing Olympics showed off a new China open to the world. The country was less affected by the financial crisis that devastated the American and European property markets, which seemed to validate Chinese beliefs about the superiority of their political and economic system compared to the West.[27] Before then, many in the West assumed that economic liberalisation would go hand-in-hand with political liberalisation, like it had in the Soviet Union when Mikhail Gorbachev's dismantling of communism's state-owned industries set off a runaway train of events which led to the USSR's collapse. Chinese rulers saw a different path was possible. They observed the Arab Spring closely as the Middle East's repressive dictatorships eventually reasserted themselves against calls for democracy, with leaders realising that many people would put up with autocracy if it came with stability and security. Desmond Shum is the author of *Red Roulette*, one of the few insider accounts of communist China. He argues that the Chinese Communist Party inherently leans towards repression and control but opened up after the 1970s out of economic necessity because of the devastation of the Cultural Revolution. Things changed when China's economy started growing quickly, which meant politics could again tighten. 'Anytime the party can afford to swing towards repression, it will,' he says.[28]

Evergrande's initial public offering (IPO) in 2009 made Hui Ka Yan one of the country's richest men. The following year the company made its move into football by buying Guangzhou FC, a club in the second tier of Chinese football that had a proud history but had also seen a series of gambling and match-fixing scandals. As was common in China at the time, the club took on the company's name and became Guangzhou Evergrande FC. Naturally, shirt sponsorship followed too, and the club's red shirt was emblazoned with the Evergrande logo in English and Mandarin. This is the shirt that tells the story of this chapter, alongside West Bromwich Albion's dalliance with Palm.

The new era saw the club splurge on some of the biggest stars in Chinese football, including national team captain Zheng Zhi, who played in Scotland for Celtic and in the Premier League for Charlton Athletic, and Gao Lin, poached from Shanghai Shenhua, who would become Guangzhou Evergrande's all-time top scorer. Then came the moves for international players like Jackson Martínez, signed from Atlético Madrid, and Paulinho, who played for Tottenham and Barcelona. Guangzhou Evergrande rapidly became the dominant force in Chinese football, winning seven consecutive Chinese Super League titles between 2011 and 2017. Even more impressively they won the Asian Football Confederation's Champions League in 2013 and 2015, edging out teams from more established footballing nations in the Middle East as well as South Korea and Japan. This gave them the opportunity to play in the FIFA Club World Cup, competing against the likes of Bayern Munich and Barcelona. The team had big-name managers: Cannavaro, Lippi and Scolari. In 2014, the huge Alibaba retail group bought half of the club for $1.2 billion.

Guangzhou Evergrande followed the trajectory of the company which gave it its name, dominating club football in a place that increasingly felt like the future of the global game. Hui Ka Yan also became a government adviser, seen on stage at party events, the celebrated face of one of the country's biggest companies. But, just like China's own boom, it would not last for ever because of what was going on behind the scenes. A small elite in China was growing more and more wealthy, spooking Xi into thinking the property boom was creating new threats, not in the form of a popular uprising but in the form of powerful businessmen who could one day move against him. Xi was an admirer of his neighbour Vladimir Putin. Russia was a country where oligarchs like Chelsea owner Roman Abramovich had been free to get as rich as they liked, so long as they obediently supported the government and didn't cause political problems. Xi liked this idea.

He was keen to reassert the power of the party and weaken the power of these wealthy businessmen, often using corruption as a pretext to clamp down. Just like in Russia, corruption is a very real problem in China but has also often been used by leaders to purge their enemies. In March 2018, something happened that attracted little attention in the West but might be looked back upon in hindsight as one of the key global events of that decade. The National People's Congress voted to remove the provision that the president can serve government two consecutive terms, solidifying China's status as a totalitarian dictatorship. This was a journey few would have predicted following the anti-government Tiananmen Square protests in 1989, a year when dictatorships were tumbling in Eastern Europe. Chinese autocracy was not just surviving, it was getting stronger.[29]

In 2018, the same year that Xi became China's indefinite ruler, red lights started blinking on the dashboard of Evergrande. In November, China's central bank named it as one of a handful of huge companies that posed 'systemic risk' to China's financial system, because it owed money to so many banks and other companies.[30] Just as an overheated property market had spilled over into the broader US economy in 2008, the same thing was happening in China a decade later. Like the US with its subprime mortgages, Evergrande had extended far beyond its original purpose of providing housing for China's burgeoning urban workforce and had moved into financial speculation, evidenced in Guangzhou Evergrande's shirts, which started carrying the logo of HDFAX, the company's financial services platform. Evergrande was hugely valuable as long as land values kept going up but ruinous if they did not. But they did not.

Urbanisation in China was slowing in pace by the mid-2010s. The population was growing less quickly as the effects of the 'one-child policy' took effect. Because of this, Evergrande's business model shifted from building and selling homes to something far more complex. The company was borrowing to buy land, selling homes on sites before they were built, and using this cash to pay lenders. The company turned to unorthodox ways of raising funds. Reuters reported that one Evergrande subsidiary encouraged staff to use their wages to buy financial products directly from the group's wealth management unit, which was helping fund further property development. Evergrande properties were 'sold as speculative investment, not sold as a place to live', says Anne Stevenson-Yang, marketing principal of J Capital Research. People invest in financial products because they think the value of them will go up. 'The confidence game will only work as long as people keep buying.'[31]

At its peak the property industry made up around one quarter of the value of the world's second largest economy. Then, suddenly, it didn't. In 2020, when the Covid pandemic hit China and then the world, Evergrande had more than 2,300 building developments in China, 200,000 staff, and 3.8 million more were working as contractors.[32] In chasing expansion, Evergrande had racked up $300 billion in debt, a figure equivalent to 2 or 3 per cent of China's entire economy. As domestic demand slowed down as the pandemic took its toll, the government implemented strict rules aimed at restricting developers' ability to borrow money. President Xi seemed personally angry at China's property tycoons for how their industry had behaved. He began emphasising the importance of what he called the 'real economy', as opposed to 'the fictitious economy', saying 'houses are for living in, not for speculation'.³³ Once the masters of China's boom, the country's property moguls were now associated with capitalist greed. China's tighter borrowing rules triggered a crisis for Evergrande. Rather than being a cyclical downturn of the sort that come and go, the issues here were structural, a consequence of China's demographic changes and slowing economic growth, with the country unable to maintain the pace it set while growing rapidly from a base of virtually nothing. China's urban population growth is now projected to slow dramatically before falling from the 2040s.³⁴ All of a sudden, there was too much housing and not enough people who wanted to buy it in a country where housing had been the most expensive in the world relative to local wages. A property boom became a property bust. This was devastating to companies like Evergrande.

In August 2021, crowds gathered at the company headquarters in Guangzhou, the city also home of the Palm developments that sponsored West Brom. Those protesting workers were demanding the repayment of cash they had put into Evergrande financial products, and construction workers halted projects as payments went overdue.³⁵ Protests of any sort are rare in China and this did not put Evergrande's bosses in the governing party's good books. The central bank summoned executives and issued a warning. The company then missed more payments, and Hui Ka Yan sold his personal assets to raise cash, including London's most expensive property near Hyde Park.³⁶ The company's vast debt pile raised worries that Evergrande would become China's version of Lehman Brothers, the American bank whose demise in 2008 sparked a global crisis. Evergrande shares were listed on the Hong Kong Stock Exchange and its credit rating was downgraded. In January 2024, after various attempts to find solutions by selling assets and restructuring the debt, Evergrande was issued a liquidation order by a Hong Kong court. The company collapsed under a mountain of debt, admitting in the later legal wranglings to vastly overstating its revenues, alongside other financial misconduct.[37]

A dramatic symbol of all this was Guangzhou Evergrande's abandoned stadium. It was once planned to be the world's largest and one of its most expensive, with a striking lotus flower shape that wowed the footballing world when the designs were first unveiled. But it has been abandoned mid-build and the land taken over by a government body because of Evergrande's yawning debts.[38] In the space of a decade, Guangzhou Evergrande went from obscurity, to becoming the best team on the continent and host to foreign stars, and then to bankruptcy and an abandoned mega-stadium. The club was relegated in 2022. A glimpse into that lost world of the recent past can be seen on an unofficial Instagram page for Guangzhou Evergrande fans, a mixture of nostalgia and rage.

> 'Guangzhou has not won enough as long as you don't disband, I will continue to support 🖤 🖤 🖤'

> 'Bookies' dogs go to hell.'

> 'The mortgage bubble burst.'

Guangzhou Evergrande was not the only Chinese club with deep ties to the country's housing crash. Indeed, in 2021, the year the crisis hit, eleven of the sixteen teams in the top division were owned by property developers with many like Guangzhou Evergrande carrying the name of the company. Beijing Renhe was owned by Dai Yongge, owner of Reading FC and the Renhe chain of shopping centres. The club was dissolved in March 2021.[39]

Clubs carrying company names is not unique to China. There

are a few top European teams named after the companies that founded them, such as Bayer Leverkusen (pharmaceuticals) and PSV Eindhoven (named after Philips electronics), as well as the Red Bull soft drinks empire which owns several clubs around the world, including Red Bull New York in the USA and Red Bull Salzburg in Austria. But nowhere did the trend become as widespread as China. Riding on the back of the property boom in the 1990s and 2000s, many clubs took the names of finance firms and real-estate developers. In 2020, though, the Chinese Football Association announced a new policy. All clubs must be 'neutral' and could no longer feature companies in their names. This had been in the pipeline for a while and is a healthy idea in sports governance, helping shift the perception that a club is the plaything of a company or an oligarch and instead belongs to the fans and the community. But the main reason for the change in China was that the property industry had become toxic.

Because of the problems afflicting the property sector, many clubs faced financial crises in the early 2020s, exacerbated by the effects of the Covid pandemic. Since then dozens of professional clubs have folded amid financial irregularities, such as unpaid player wages. Football journalist Cameron Wilson told me the pandemic also saw lots of foreign players returning home, worsening the quality of the league. The rise of the Chinese Super League in the mid-2010s did not change the structural reasons why China lags far behind not just Europe but other Asian countries when it comes to football. China has gone back to the footballing periphery. 'There's not a grassroots football culture,' Wilson says. 'There's too much pressure in society, kids have to do homework twenty-four hours a day and a lot of Chinese parents think playing football is a frivolous pursuit.'

Simon Chadwick has the impressive job title of professor of sport and geopolitical economy at SKEMA Business School in Paris. He is a particular expert on China, having taught a course in Beijing for a few years, though has not returned since before the pandemic. This is a common situation for China-watchers who have found their work harder since Covid, which triggered a retreat from the international stage. The country's 'Zero Covid' policy saw China locking down harder and longer than anywhere else in the world, the pandemic giving the government an excuse to extend its surveillance and control even deeper, ostensibly while fighting Xi's battle against corruption. 'Corruption is endemic within Chinese society,' explains Chadwick. 'When Xi came to power, one of his platforms was the eradication of corruption.'

However, defining corruption in China is notoriously difficult because of the culture of *guanxi* – the tradition of connections and informal gift-giving, a major feature of Chinese society. It is virtually impossible to do business without giving gifts and assiduously cultivating contacts over a long period of time, in ways that may seem corrupt in other cultures. It means everyone with business or political power in China has skeletons in their closet that could be used to accuse them of corruption. 'What you and I think is corrupt may not be what the Chinese government or the Chinese legal system think is corrupt,' Chadwick told me. In democracies, there is a degree of transparency about the legal process, so if somebody is accused of corruption, it is at least possible to know what the evidence is, and how credible it is, even if miscarriages of justice still happen. In China, a totalitarian regime where the courts are inseparable from the governing party, there is no such credibility. It is extremely difficult to distinguish genuine cases of corruption, undoubtedly a huge problem, from politically motivated axe-grinding. 'Most people are never going to question it because if you question the corruption purge, essentially you're questioning the Chinese state.' Despite frequently interacting with course administrators in China and students who come to Europe to take his courses, Chadwick says the learning generally goes in one direction. 'People in China are just not going to answer questions,' he says. 'Over the last twenty-five years, I've had Chinese students in my classrooms and none of them talk about anything.' This is not because of their intelligence or abilities, but because they know the state has eyes everywhere.

Cameron Wilson agrees that it is difficult to separate state corruption from political grudges. 'I didn't really know what "rule of law" meant until I got to China. The rule of law basically means there are laws which are written down and everybody must follow them, including the government, whereas in China, the government just makes the rules and interprets them as they please. I know in the West people really don't trust the institutions and the media, but it's still way more reliable than the Chinese system in this way. For example, you can walk into a court and you can watch. Everything is transparent. In China, you can't do that. It's not transparent. There's no due process.' As a Westerner, Wilson can say these things. He was speaking to me while on a trip outside China, so there was no question of breaking Chinese laws. For Chinese people, dissent is almost impossible, with social media and electronic communications monitored just as scrupulously as the print media and TV bulletins.

An example of the opacity of China's legal system is demonstrated in the peculiar case of Li Tie who starred in the only Chinese squad to reach the World Cup back in 2002. He was unusual as a Chinese player who saw some success in Europe, playing for Everton in most of their games during the 2002–03 Premier League season when the club came seventh under David Moyes. This was a bright era for the Merseyside club, with a young Wayne Rooney coming through the youth ranks and Everton turning the corner from a relegation-battling side to one that would finish near the top of the table regularly under Moyes. I spoke to David Unsworth who played alongside Li in that Everton side. 'He was tidy on the ball, skilful, he fitted right in,' Unsworth told me. 'He didn't try to segregate himself as a foreign player. He enjoyed the banter and had a laugh. He was an absolute diamond of a bloke.'[40]

That season was Li Tie's peak in England, though, before he was plagued by injuries. He returned to China in 2008 as a player, then moved into management, eventually replacing 2006 World Cup winner Marcello Lippi as manager of the Chinese national team. Despite China's vast population, the national team has got worse since that sole World Cup appearance in 2002. In 2021, Li Tie's team failed to qualify for Qatar and he was sacked. A year later, the country's public prosecutor issued a bombshell statement: 'Li Tie, the former head coach of the Chinese national men's football team, was suspected of accepting bribes, offering bribes, offering bribes at the unit, accepting bribes of non-state employees, and offering bribes to non-state employees.' He confessed to paying three million yuan to become the coach, and said he achieved promotion as a club manager by fixing matches. Other top Chinese officials were also accused of taking bribes. In a documentary broadcast on state TV, Li Tie and others made televised confessions. 'I am very sorry. I should have kept my head down and followed the right path,' the 46-year-old mumbled. 'There were certain things that were customary in football at the time.' In December 2024, he was sentenced to twenty years in prison for bribery.[41] His former boss Chen Xuyuan, president of the CFA, was sentenced to life.

Because I have not been to China, I wanted to speak to someone actually from the country, alongside reading books and speaking to Western experts. After trying countless people through various routes and receiving radio silence, I managed to speak to and meet one person who has worked in the inner circle of Chinese sport, with intimate knowledge of how things operate. I promised this person I would not reveal their name or any aspect of their identity, including where in the world I met them. 'If I talk too much, I might endanger people's lives,' they said. 'People will get longer added to their prison sentences.'

The insider, who had met Li Tie many times over the years, explained how the world of politics and the inner workings of the Chinese Communist Party are unavoidable in Chinese sport. 'Every decision at the sporting level is decided by the sports ministry.' They explained that the avalanche of private cash into Chinese football in the 2000s and the 2010s in Europe was not about savvy investment or a personal love of football. 'People want to please the government. Football always loses money, but they get favourable treatment such as loans from the government.'

It is simply impossible to know for certain whether Li Tie was genuinely corrupt, whether he exhibited *guanxi*, the culture of gift-giving, or if he has been completely framed. 'Nobody has any real faith in the actual truthfulness, the veracity, of the legal system,' says Cameron Wilson. The insider I spoke to speculates that Li may be a scapegoat for the broader failures of the Chinese football project which might otherwise be aimed at President Xi, but criticising the leader is strongly taboo in Chinese society. 'In a totalitarian state, there is one boss, whatever decision he wants to make, he makes ... I feel very sorry and sad for what has happened to Li Tie, because he's probably the best coach China could produce.' They say the Chinese public likely take Li's confession at face value for the most part, with many ordinary people justifiably furious at the corrupt officials they encounter on a local level, believing corruption to be endemic throughout the Chinese state. People in the football industry, though, are sceptical of the charges. 'There is a good rule in authoritarian states: "When you see people on TV doing confessions, be suspicious".'

After decades on the rise, Chinese football is now in retreat, with Xi Jinping losing interest and the game no longer a source of national pride. Money has not made the national side better. The 2023 Asian Cup was supposed to take place in China but was moved because of the country's zero-Covid policy. It was relocated to an Asian Football Confederation member that did have the infrastructure in place: Qatar. Bailing on this tournament with just three months' warning was a significant blow to China's ambitions as a serious footballing nation. Their performance on the pitch was embarrassing, too. A country with a population of 1.4 billion people failed to qualify from a group including Qatar (2.7 million), Lebanon (5.5 million) and Tajikistan (10 million). China failed to score a single goal. This came a few months after humiliating defeats against Syria, Uzbekistan and Oman. The Asian Cup is a neat demonstration of how little population correlates to footballing success. In the same tournament, India, which had recently overtaken China as the world's most populous country, also finished bottom of their group without scoring. In January 2025, Guangzhou Evergrande – renamed Guangzhou FC – were refused permission to play in the domestic league by the Chinese Football Association because of unpaid debts.

When it comes to football, China seems to have abandoned ship, retreating to the things it is good at. While the country is still an economic powerhouse and a key player in world affairs, it is far more insular than it was before the Covid pandemic, less interested in Western culture and traditions. This can be exhibited in absentee owners stranded in the lower rungs of English football and the wistful comments on the Instagram page of Guangzhou Evergrande, the fans who remember the glory days of Chinese football, hoping one day China will take football seriously again.

9

THE OTHER HALF

England Women's Goalkeeper Shirt & SC Corinthians SP

'The game of football is quite unsuitable for females and ought not to be encouraged.'

Football Association, 1921

In July 2021, I was in a hotel room in Malta, which I chose for a holiday because it was one of the few places on the 'green list' of countries that British tourists could visit under the Covid pandemic restrictions at the time. I had flown out the day after the traumatic experience of watching England lose the Euros final against Italy at Wembley. Still a little devastated a couple of days later, I was scrolling through my phone when I saw a message in *The Athletic* journalists' WhatsApp group. Colleague Nancy Froston had told the group that tickets were on sale for the UEFA European Women's Championship in England the following summer, sharing a link to buy them. At that point I had watched a couple of England women's games at major tournaments on TV. The semi-final defeat against the USA in 2019 had felt like a relatively big cultural event. But I couldn't recall watching any women's football in my childhood, despite being obsessed with the men's game. Given my line of work at the time, my overall knowledge of the women's game was embarrassingly limited.

I'm always up for live sport, though, so on seeing that tickets to the Wembley final were available for the ludicrously low price of £10 each, I bought several and then didn't think about it too much for a year. It turned out I had snagged one of the greatest bargains of my life. The summer of 2022 was when women's football truly broke through and conquered the mainstream in England, the hosts not only reaching the final but winning it, going one better than the men I had watched in the same stadium a year earlier. I watched Chloe Kelly's extra-time winner against Germany from behind one of the goals, celebrating wildly with 90,000 other England fans when the Lionesses lifted the trophy. One of those Lionesses was Mary Earps, the England goalkeeper at the centre of controversy the following year when her shirt was not available for fans to purchase. To many observers this was a symbol of long-standing disrespect towards the women's game. That goalkeeper shirt is one of two which tell the story of this chapter: the recent rise of women's football, which tracks the rise of women's rights around the world more broadly. Things are improving, although not everywhere, and not all is rosy. Another shirt – a purple one worn by Corinthians in Brazil – shows how women's football is reaching new places, as shown by the rapid development of the global game between the 2019 World Cup and the tournament in 2023, when several traditionally weaker sides did surprisingly well and the long-dominant USA crashed out early.

The status of women's football is changing fast. The Euros summer of 2022 wasn't really the year it became mainstream, though. That had already happened before, a century earlier, before it was rudely interrupted.

Football grew out of the factories of England's industrial Midlands and North as a working man's game, although many women took a keen interest from the start. An English women's team played Scottish counterparts in 1881. The English side won 3–0 in Edinburgh, but a second game five days later was abandoned after hundreds of men mobbed the pitch, forcing the players to flee on a horse-drawn bus. 'The players were roughly jostled and had prematurely to take refuge in the omnibus which had conveyed them to the ground,' said the *Nottinghamshire Guardian*. 'Their troubles were not, however, yet ended, for the crowd tore up the (wooden) stakes and threw them at the departing vehicle, and but for the presence of the police, some bodily injury to the females might have occurred.'[1] The early women footballers were not only ignored and patronised, but also faced outright hostility for their involvement in an activity that society deemed unladylike. After 2,000 women turned up to a Preston North End game in the 1880s, the club had to rescind an offer of free entry for 'ladies' for fear of losing revenue.[2] Women soon began organising games across the country, including a North London vs South London game in the Crouch End area of the city in 1895 which attracted 10,000 fans and was organised by a woman named Nettie Honeyball. A few years earlier, she told an interviewer from *Sketch* magazine that she set up matches 'with the fixed resolve of proving to the world that women are not the ornamental and useless creatures men have pictures of'.[3] Honeyball is thought to be a pseudonym, although we can't be quite sure as much of the origin story of women's football is shrouded in mystery, given limited record-keeping and a lack of interest from football's male administrators.

The history of women's football mirrors broader changes in women's role in society. Women's football shirts tell the story of how women's rights have, steadily but unevenly, improved around the world over time. By the early twentieth century in Britain, traditional gender roles were beginning to change because of industrialisation, women were stepping out of the home and into the workplace, and out of the fields and into the cities. The First World War accelerated this shift as men were called to fight, and working women became vital to the war effort. 'Wartime gave women a bit of leeway when it came to occupations and pastimes that had previously been the sole domain of men,' writes Carrie Dunn, a women's football writer. 'Women were needed to do the jobs vacated by men who had joined the armed forces, and it seems to have been tacitly accepted that women were also going to do other typically "male" things.'[4] With no men's football during the war the women's game became more prominent and began attracting huge crowds. The standout team was Dick, Kerr Ladies, a factory team from Preston in Lancashire named after a company which made trams and train engines.

In August 2024, I visited the National Football Museum in the centre of Manchester, got the obligatory photograph with replicas of the Premier League and Women's Super League trophies, then headed on past the trophies and up the Astroturf stairs to the main exhibition. Immediately on the right one of the first exhibits is a cabinet dedicated to a woman named Lily Parr. She was the first superstar female footballer, scoring more than 1,000 goals for Dick, Kerr Ladies between 1920 and 1951. Legend has it she once broke the arm of a male goalkeeper who doubted her abilities with a particularly powerful shot.[5] Immediately after the war when Parr started playing, women's football was thriving, peaking in 1921 when a huge crowd watched Dick, Kerr Ladies beat St Helens Ladies 4–0 at Goodison Park, home of Everton FC. There were 53,000 tickets sold with the gate receipts raising cash for injured ex-servicemen, and more than 10,000 fans were said to have been turned away. This attendance record for domestic women's football in the UK would not be beaten for 102 years – not until May 2023, when 60,000 fans watched Arsenal play Wolfsburg in the semi-final of the Champions League at the Emirates Stadium. (Crowds have been even higher in recent years outside England, with 90,000 watching Barcelona Femení at the Camp Nou on several occasions.) I was at that Arsenal game, having been offered a ticket at the last minute by a friend who is a fan of Arsenal's men's team, and knew little about the women's game but was curious. The stadium was completely full with the vast majority of those in attendance women and girls, making the crowd noises notably higher in pitch compared to what I was used to hearing in male-dominated stadiums. I went along simply to experience a fun afternoon out with no skin in the game, but this put me very much in the minority. The crowd was a sea of Arsenal shirts, on the back of which were names like England captain Leah Williamson, with fans singing different chants for different players. The collective ecstasy of Arsenal's early lead was matched by the agony of a late Wolfsburg winner deep into injury time.

Between these two great moments for women's football in England – Goodison Park in 1920 and then the Emirates in 2023 – there is a gaping void. The reason becomes clear when reading the open pages of an old leather-bound book displayed in the Lily Parr cabinet at the National Football Museum. It contains the typed minutes of an FA Consultative Committee meeting which took place in 1921, the year after the Goodison game. 'Complaints having been made as to football being played by women,' it reads, 'Council felt impelled to express the strong opinion that the game of football is quite unsuitable for females and should not be encouraged.'

This killed the women's game in its tracks. It was effectively a ban, requesting that FA-affiliated clubs 'refuse the use of their grounds for (women's) matches,' justifying this with spurious concerns about the 'appropriation' of gate receipts which were 'excessively' used for expenses, rather than charitable causes. That bombshell dropped at a time when women's football was booming and new leagues were being formed to capitalise on the hype. But now men were home from the war, there was a feeling that football should return to how it was: a man's game. 'There is a general feeling that football is no game for women,' said the *Sheffield Daily Telegraph*. 'It is too strenuous.'[6] The idea that women's bodies could not handle sport was widespread at the time. In 1927, the first women's edition of the annual boat race between Oxford and Cambridge universities saw a baying mob of hecklers who thought the event was unfeminine, with one newspaper explaining that rowing's physical exertions were bad for women's 'insides'.[7]

The ban on using FA-affiliated grounds did not amount to a direct ban on women playing football recreationally, but it killed the game as a serious competitive sport. The Dick, Kerr Ladies went on a US tour in 1922, but after that were forced to play in more obscure and ill-suited locations and the club fell into decline. France and Spain introduced similar bans, followed by West Germany where a law pronounced the sport as 'essentially alien to the nature of women ... in the fight for the ball, the feminine grace vanishes – body and soul will inevitably suffer harm'.[8] Women did continue to play football, though. Matches had been played in the US as early as 1918 and the game was prevalent in colleges in the 1920s and 1930s.[9] But the years between the 1920s and the 1970s were the dark ages of women's football. Dick, Kerr Ladies folded in 1965 due to lack of players, just a year before the England men's World Cup win would inspire countless girls as well as boys to play the game. There were women's teams playing in the era of the ban, such as Corinthian Ladies in Manchester, but they struggled to find pitches and opponents. It was not until the FA ban was lifted in 1971 that organised women's football would slowly rise from the ashes.

I was inculcated with a deep love of men's football practically from birth, and have enthusiastically cheered on women athletes at the Olympics, such as fellow West Midlander Denise Lewis who visited my school shortly after winning gold in the heptathlon in Sydney in 2000. Other British athletes like Kelly Holmes and Paula Radcliffe were household names in my childhood too. Aside from athletics, though, and perhaps tennis, women athletes were not especially visible when I was growing up. I am a keen cricket fan as well but it was not until 2023 that I went to my first women's game at Edgbaston Stadium in Birmingham, my second-favourite sporting venue in the world. The clash between old rivals England and Australia was entertaining and high in quality, and a far cheaper alternative to a men's game that, like football, is getting extortionate to watch.

Women's sport, and women's football specifically, has had little purchase on the popular imagination until very recently, but I have come to appreciate that this is not the natural order of things. It is not some sort of logical consequence of the two sexes' respective talents, as some of the game's more cantankerous critics would have you believe. The suppression of women's football was an intentional act, artificially choking demand for a product that was booming. Moya Dodd is an Australian lawyer and former captain of the women's national team who was one of the first women to serve on the FIFA Council. She is quoted in Sue Anstiss's book *Game On* as saying:

> There were deliberate measures to exclude women ... That was the world we lived in for pretty much all of the twentieth century, and it has taken a hundred years for us to get back to the point where you are seeing once again tens of thousands of people in stadiums watching women's sport. The whole idea that there is no demand to watch women play sport is the biggest fallacy that has been sold to us. It is not something that occurred naturally. It is something that occurred because of the active suppression and eradication of women from the sporting landscape.[10]

We are still a long way off women's football becoming anywhere close to men's football in terms of viewing figures, revenue or cultural ubiquity. But perhaps that is the wrong way of thinking about things. Instead of constantly comparing the women's game with something that has followed a very different path, we should look at it for what it is. Right now, women's football is booming on its own terms, although the game's advocates are keen not to sugarcoat the difficulties of a game running on a shoestring, and with far smaller crowds compared to men's football. Things are changing quickly, though, and the rising prominence of women's football is not some act of charity or atonement for the sins of the past, but because lots of people enjoy it.

One of the appeals of women's football is that there is less of a gulf between fans and their heroes compared to the men's game. 'Players have needed fans to help justify their right to be able to build a career from the game, which has resulted in a closeness between fans and players,' writes journalist Suzanne Wrack. 'After every fixture, players will spend up to an hour, sometimes more, talking to fans, signing autographs and taking photos, rain or shine. This has in part been helped by the many years of the game being part-time and amateur in nature. Players have the same struggles as fans. The overwhelming majority live fairly modestly and still wonder how they will pay the bills.'[11]

One of the challenges of the new game is to embrace greater professionalism and higher standards, and attract more investment without losing the distinctive qualities that brought fans to women's football in the first place. Up until very recently, football at every level, everywhere in the world – professional players, grassroots players, crowds – has been dominated by men, leaving a huge untapped demand for football played by half of the global population that is female. The road to football becoming even more of a universal sport than it already is by fully embracing the women's game may be a bumpy one, with twists and turns along the way, but the overall direction is clearly positive.

Few names in women's football are bigger than England and former Manchester United goalkeeper Mary Earps. She was one of the breakout stars of England's successful Euro 2022 campaign, selected for the team of the tournament after some excellent performances, including winning the player of the match award in England's semi-final win over Sweden, stopping Sofia Jakobsson with her outstretched left leg in the first minute, then scooping out a looping Stina Blackstenius shot while backpedalling towards her own net. Earps also made a brilliant double-save on her goal-line in the final against Germany, lifting the trophy in front of me on the Wembley turf after conceding only two goals in six games. A year later at the World Cup in Australia and New Zealand, Earps was even better, conceding just four goals in seven games and saving a penalty in the final, although this wasn't enough to prevent England falling to a 1–0 defeat against Spain, a game also remembered for Spanish football federation president Luis Rubiales' inappropriate attempt to kiss Jenni Hermoso and the ensuing fall-out which lasted weeks and became the catalyst for an important conversation about sexism and abuse of power. In 2025, Rubiales was convicted of sexual assault and fined €10,800. Despite losing the final, Earps won the Golden Glove award for best keeper and was also named the BBC's 2023 Sports Personality of the Year, previously won by the likes of Bobby Moore, David Beckham, Andy Murray and Lewis Hamilton. In 2022, Earps's teammate Beth Mead had won the award for her goalscoring accomplishments at the Euros, making it two consecutive wins for women's football, a sport that had never been named in the top three in the sixty-nine previous years the prize had been awarded. With tennis player Emma Raducanu winning in 2021 and Olympic gold medallist track runner Keely Hodgkinson in 2024, it made it four wins in a row for female athletes. Mary Earps's emergence as a public figure was helped by something else that happened during the 2023 World Cup, a saga that started at an eve-of-tournament press conference, involving a football shirt, one of our two for this chapter.

'I can't really sugarcoat this any other way, so I'm not going to try – it's hugely disappointing and hurtful,' Earps told the startled crowd of journalists. She was explaining that her fans could not buy the replica version of her goalkeeping shirt, even though they could buy outfield shirts. A teammate's young niece had asked for an Earps shirt, but was told kit manufacturer Nike could not help. 'It's something I've been fighting behind closed doors, desperately trying to find a solution with the FA and Nike,' Earps announced, explaining that she had been told it was impossible, despite the firm's huge sponsorship deal with England's men's and women's teams said to be worth £400 million over twelve years. 'It's the young kids I'm most concerned about. It's that they're going to say, "Mum, Dad, can I have a Mary Earps shirt?" and they'll say,

"I can't, but I can get an Alessia Russo No. 23 or a Rachel Daly No. 9." And so, what you're saying is that goalkeeping isn't important, but you can be a striker if you want.'[12]

Some cynics noted that Earps had a sponsorship deal with Adidas at the time, later switching to Puma, so had no qualms about bashing Nike. But her words struck a nerve. Once the tournament kicked off, Earps focused on her football, but the debate rumbled on. The day after England lost the final in Sydney, with Earps awarded the Golden Glove, Nike acknowledged the 'unprecedented passion and interest in women's football this year', adding that the company had not served 'those fans who wished to show their passion and support to the squad's goalkeepers'.[13] Nike announced it would immediately start selling the goalkeeper shirt for England, and a handful of other nations, in 'limited quantities' while committing to selling more keeper shirts for women's tournaments in the future.

It is significant that a female goalkeeper has become such an icon. Those who denigrate women's football have often picked on keepers. A couple of aspects of the women's game have made this position an occasional issue. The disparity between the best teams and the weakest has often been larger than in the men's game where even the worst teams at World Cups will be made up of well remunerated full-time professionals. This gap in ability can be particularly apparent when it comes to the most exposed position on the pitch. At the 2019 World Cup, the USA beat Thailand 13–0, the largest-ever victory at a men's or women's World Cup finals. Thailand's goalkeeper, the 5 foot 5 inches-tall Sukanya Chor Charoenying, was consoled by US star Carli Lloyd after the game. Emma Hayes is the most successful manager ever in English women's club football before she moved Stateside to manage the US national team. After the 13–0 result, while still at Chelsea, she wrote a column suggesting smaller goals and smaller pitches might be a good idea, given that women athletes jump over smaller hurdles in track and field, and basketball players use a smaller ball. 'We frequently hear the criticism, even from advocates of women's football, that the standard between the posts lets it down,' wrote Hayes. 'But is this anything to do with the quality of goalkeeping or the basic science of size and space?'[14]

At the next World Cup in 2023, though, with women's football having had four more years to develop around the world, Earps and other goalkeepers were some of the tournament's stand-out performers. 'Goalkeepers really only get attention when it's something ridiculous we've done, an obvious error,' said Chloe Morgan, who has kept goal for Crystal Palace and Tottenham in the Women's Super League. She highlighted how many goalkeeper performances at the World Cup were 'incredible', singling out the Netherlands' Daphne van Domselaar, Nigeria's Chiamaka Nnadozie and Sweden's Zećira Mušović for praise.[15]

Before the tournament, some had suggested the tournament's expansion from twenty-four teams to thirty-two would increase the number of unfair match-ups that reflect badly on the women's game. The opposite happened, though, with many smaller nations putting in strong performances against the traditional heavyweights. There was no equivalent of that 13–0. The biggest margin of victory was seven goals, the same as at the men's World Cup the previous year, and most games were tight battles. Two-time winners Germany were sensationally beaten by Colombia in the group stage after conceding a last-minute winner in a 2–1 defeat in one of the biggest World Cup upsets of all time, with Linda Caicedo's dummy and curling shot voted the goal of the tournament. The USA, winners of four of the first eight tournaments and never failing to reach a semi-final, lost in the round of 16 to Sweden on penalties. Megan Rapinoe, an icon of the sport and a huge name in the US known for her spats with Donald Trump as well as her sporting prowess, missing the crucial spot-kick. Countries outside North America and Western Europe have long struggled to be competitive at the Women's World Cup, but there were signs this was starting to change too. Strong performers included Jamaica, who had to fundraise online to pay for their travel, Morocco, who reached the knockouts in their first-ever tournament, and hosts Australia, who made their maiden appearance in the semi-finals.

Shortly after Earps won the Golden Glove following the 2023 World Cup final, a mural of her appeared, on a wall just off Sir Matt Busby Way near Old Trafford. Her arms are spread wide with fists clenched, her mouth wide open, roaring in joy beneath the slogan 'Welcome to Manchester' against a red backdrop. As well as Earps's sporting achievements, she has become a public figure because of her charisma and outspoken attitude. She has also become a cult figure on social media, making and recording all her videos herself, and has a clothing range featuring her slogan, 'Be unapologetically yourself'.[16] The Premier League's top teams have only been taking their women's teams more seriously for a few years, and several signed genuinely famous faces to attach to their existing global brands, such as Sam Kerr at Chelsea, Leah Williamson at Arsenal and Earps, who moved from Manchester United to Paris Saint-Germain in 2024. I have been to watch Aston Villa Women, who are a long way off attracting the crowds of Arsenal and Chelsea but have had a big boost in the past couple of years through the arrival of prominent Lioness Rachel Daly.

At Manchester United Women's games, fans can be seen wearing the 'Earps 1' shirt which now carries a deeper symbolism. Journalist Flo Lloyd-Hughes is critical of Nike's role in the Earps saga and says the industry is still catching up with how quickly the women's game is growing and changing. 'Women's football is still exploring how to cater to the sizing that fans want. In my experience personally, and a lot of people I know, they don't want the women's fit, they want the men's straight cut.' She explains that there is sometimes an inaccurate assumption that women fans always want figure-hugging clothing. Another issue, says Lloyd-Hughes, is that fans sometimes order a shirt with their favourite player's name and number on the back, but receive the wrong style of lettering – for example, Premier League badges on a Women's Super League shirt.

Women's football can sometimes fail to capitalise on its own hype. At the 2019 World Cup in France, fans complained of not being able to buy merchandise meaning money left on the table. Things were better at the Euros in England three years later, but some of the host country's games were held in stadiums with a capacity of just 20,000 or 30,000 fans, which could have been filled several times over given the excitement the tournament generated. This is often a tricky balancing act because the atmosphere is always better in a full smaller stadium than a half-empty larger one, but it's not ideal to turn away potential paying customers. The appeal of women's football is growing so quickly that it's difficult to know where to host games. Although many Women's Super League clubs are playing most or all of their games at the men's stadiums now, average attendances are nowhere near those of the men's matches, although the picture is changing rapidly. In the 2023–24 season, Arsenal women had a higher average attendance than several clubs in the men's Premier League.

Flo Lloyd-Hughes has observed one possible reason that Nike got the Earps issue so wrong. 'The model that exists [in women's football] is much more in line with US sports where we see it's a more individual-driven league, and we see fans that are much more drawn to individual players,' she says. 'Obviously, we've had that in men's football with Messi and Ronaldo, and how fans have followed them rather than the teams they played for. But I think we see that across the board in women's football. People love the individual players and where they end up.' Icons like Mary Earps, Leah Williamson and Megan Rapinoe are arguably more important to the women's game than the biggest male stars are to their sport, where clubs have longer histories, and ties to teams run through the generations. In women's football, ties are looser and potential new fans are waiting to be won over, which is exciting in its own way.

Back in the early 1970s, a couple of things happened to improve the outlook for the women's game. The English FA's ban was lifted to little initial fanfare. In 1970 in Italy, and the following year in Mexico, the unofficial women's world championships took place with no help from FIFA or governing bodies. The Mexican Football Federation tried to stop the tournament but two private stadiums in the country, including the Azteca which had hosted the men's 1970 World Cup final, volunteered to host. Around 100,000 Mexicans came to watch a clash between the hosts and Argentina. Even more watched the final of the Campeonato de Fútbol Femenil, which Mexico lost 3–0 to Denmark. These were astonishing numbers given none of the players were familiar to the fans who went to watch. There was still some way to go on the path to women's football being taken seriously, though. 'The goalposts were painted pink,' writes Suzanne Wrack, 'and women security guards, translators and other officials wore pink uniforms, while players had their hair, make-up and false eyelashes done before talking to the press and meeting the rapt public after the game. The players wore hot pants and bright colours to show off their bodies.'[17] (Former FIFA boss Sepp Blatter once notoriously suggested 'tighter shorts' to boost interest in the women's game.[18]) Still, the crowd numbers showed that interest in women's football was out there, that the game had huge untapped potential. The following year elsewhere in the Americas – this time in the US Congress – came a change that would unwittingly give a massive boost to women's football in the US and beyond.

Title IX is one of a list of amendments to an education bill passed by the US Congress, signed into law by President Richard Nixon on 23 June 1972. It is only thirty-seven words long and is elegant in its simplicity: 'No person in the United States shall, on the basis of sex, be excluded from participation in, be denied the benefits of, or be subjected to discrimination under any education program or activity receiving Federal financial assistance.' The law effectively banned sex discrimination in educational institutions which received government funding. It was not intended to reshape competitive sport in the USA, but that is what it did, and no sport more so than soccer. After Title IX, colleges felt pressure to create sporting opportunities for women to comply with the new law. Soccer was useful because the game's big squads helped schools quickly meet requirements to offer a similar number of opportunities to women as men. Also, it was cheap. Playing football requires little money or equipment, just a pitch, two goals and a ball. According to research by the *New York Times*, the sport was virtually non-existent in US high schools before 1972, but by the turn of the millennium was one of the most popular sports in the country, with hundreds of thousands of girls playing at school, and more than 20,000 a year playing in the organised college system, benefiting from elite facilities and coaching.[19]

Mia Hamm, the first women's football superstar of the modern era, began her career at the University of North Carolina at Chapel

Hill. The team began its life playing against high-school girls because there weren't enough nearby colleges to play against. But then women's football teams were being set up in colleges across the US and an increasingly intricate women's football ecosystem started to emerge. Within a couple of decades the women's football scene in the US was huge and well organised and had started producing some excellent players. The US Women's National Team (USWNT) played its first match in 1985, losing 1–0 to Italy. This got little attention, but subsequent progress was fast. Six years later, the US won the '1st FIFA World Championship for Women's Football for the M&M's Cup', a tournament later acknowledged as the first-ever Women's World Cup after FIFA belatedly bestowed that honour on the competition. Few in the US noticed, though, nor the tournament in Sweden four years later which saw the US come third and Norway the winners. Things began to change after the 1996 Olympics in Atlanta, when women's soccer debuted as an event. The US won the gold medal in front of huge crowds. Soccer continued its surge in the public consciousness when the USWNT won the World Cup for a second time in 1999, beating China on home soil at a packed-out Rose Bowl in Pasadena, the venue where Brazil had won the men's World Cup five years earlier. One iconic football shirt – or the lack of it – became symbolic in the rise of women's football. After slotting home the winning penalty in her all-white kit, US forward Brandi Chastain whipped off her shirt, roaring with joy in her black sports bra. Chastain's celebration was echoed twenty-three years later when Chloe Kelly poked in England's winning goal in the Euros final before taking her top off and running around the Wembley grass in her white sports bra, arms outstretched, the picture appearing on the front page of every English newspaper the next day. 'I loved watching men, women, boys and girls jump up and down with sheer delight when Chloe's ball rolled past the line,' Chastain told me. 'There was no significance about gender, just that England had scored. This euphoria is ubiquitous.'

Just as Earps's goalkeeper shirt symbolises the fight for women's football kit to be taken seriously, the images of Chastain and Kelly are symbols of something bigger too – unselfconscious joy at sporting achievement, and a rejection of the backward attitudes about women's capabilities that have stunted the game's progress. Suzanne Wrack argues that female footballers past and present have been motivated by the same thing as men: simply enjoying the game. However, the very act of women playing football 'is a feminist one', she writes. 'Picking up a ball and heading to a patch of grass violates everything society expects of women.'

The increasing prominence of women's football reflects a global shift towards gender equality more broadly. It is important not to be glib or complacent about this because the journey is uneven and progress can often go into reverse – think about how women's rights in Iran got worse after the 1979 revolution, how abortion rights have deteriorated in the USA over the past decade, or the dire situation in Afghanistan since the 2021 seizure of power by the Taliban, who have even prevented girls from going to school. But the overall picture is one of progress. 'Our World in Data' is an organisation that tracks social changes around the world using public data. It has found that in 1990 just six countries had laws against domestic violence and 45 against employment discrimination. In 2023 those figures were 164 and 161 respectively (although enforcement is another matter). The expansion of contraception and changing social conventions about family life has given women opportunities beyond motherhood and domestic labour. Maternal deaths have plummeted. Women are far more represented than in the recent past in politics, business and the rest of public life in almost every country in the world. The gap between boys and girls in primary education, significant as recently as the 1990s, has virtually closed, while slightly more women around the world go to university. The gender pay gap is far lower than it used to be in countries that measure it accurately. To reiterate, things are much better than they were, but progress is not inevitable, and the world is still far from a gender equal place. Our World in Data uses the phrase 'the world is awful, the world is much better, the world can be much better' to reflect this. Women's football is a microcosm of these global changes. Just as the overall picture is getting better, there are still plenty of bleak problems too, like the abuse female players and pundits get on social media.

Because women have historically been discriminated against in every country in the world, women's football has long been associated with activism, far more so than the men's game. There is a high number of LGBT players at every level of women's football, something that became a big talking point when Visit Saudi, the country's tourist board, was signed up by FIFA as a major sponsor of the 2023 Women's World Cup, despite homosexuality being illegal in the country, along with women's rights in general being poor. Samantha Lewis is a writer for ABC Sport in Australia. 'The backlash was so immediate and intense that, within a few weeks, there was a revision of the brand's presence in the tournament,' she told me. 'They were largely removed from public view, such as advertising hoardings surrounding the fields, but they were still included in FIFA's larger suite of tournament partners.'

The USWNT has also been at the forefront of debates about equal pay with the team's high-profile players frequently speaking out on the issue. The US is in an unusual position when it comes to football because of the relative status of the two national teams. 'The women are better known than the men,' journalist Pardeep Cattry told me. 'We don't have a ton of household names that are soccer players in our country, but the ones that are are women,' she says, reeling off the names of Mia Hamm, Megan Rapinoe and Chloe Morgan. Cattry explains that the USWNT has historically been particularly strong, not just because of Title IX, but because US Soccer was the first national federation to truly take the women's game seriously. 'They decided first, "Hey, let's do this". US Soccer had the financial but also structural advantage of giving a bit more credence to women's sports.'

At that Arsenal vs Wolfsburg match I was watching in May 2023, extra-time was looming when Laura Wienroither, an Austrian defender who had come on as a substitute for Arsenal, suddenly fell to the ground. There was no clear reason. She simply collapsed with nobody around her, always an ominous sign in football. Immediately, I and many others in the sell-out crowd thought of the same terrifying three letter acronym: ACL.

The anterior cruciate ligament in the knee connects the femur, the thigh bone, to the tibia, the shin bone. An ACL rupture can come from simply turning sharply or landing awkwardly after a jump. It is one of the most devastating injuries possible for a professional footballer, with full recovery taking a year or more. ACL ruptures have long been a rare but present risk at the top of the men's game, but the women's game has had something of an ACL epidemic. Remarkably, Wienroither was the fourth Arsenal player during that 2022–23 season to get the same injury, alongside a trio of the greatest women players of modern times: Dutch striker Vivianne Miedema, the all-time leading goal scorer in the WSL; Beth Mead, the Golden Boot winner in England's victorious

Euro 2022 campaign; and stylish centre-back Leah Williamson, the poster girl of English football as captain of her national team and an eloquent voice in the media. All tore their ACLs that season and missed that summer's World Cup in Australia and New Zealand, alongside twenty-five or so other players from around the world with the same injury. 'At least we will all be in the gym together,' posted Miedema on Instagram, alongside a treatment room selfie of the four of them. 'PS, ACL group is full now. Please no more.' Sam Kerr, captain of Chelsea and the face of women's football in Australia, suffered the same injury a few months later.

Many studies show ACL injuries are far more common in women than in men. There are various theories as to why, including the shape of women's lower bodies putting different pressure on the knees, and hormonal fluctuations weakening the knee ligaments at certain points of the menstrual cycle. Some top women's teams have adjusted players' training schedules to factor this in, but much remains not fully understood. One clear contributory factor is workload. While professional male footballers have been playing packed calendars for decades, for women this is all relatively new, and many have not grown up putting their bodies through this level of intensity. 'Boys are doing gym work and learning basic running mechanics at the age of six,' England and Chelsea star Fran Kirby has said. 'When I was coaching at Reading, the grassroots girls couldn't even access a gym. The most important thing is teaching young girls the basic mechanics of being a footballer and being a sportsperson.'[20]

The reason women's sport exists as a separate category is because there are profound physical differences between the sexes. The average man is taller and heavier than the average woman. Men tend to have more muscle and women more body fat. Women tend to have more strength in the lower half of their body, men more in their upper half. The average man is stronger, even when compared to a woman of the same size and weight. This is because men have, on average, higher bone density. A growing body of research shows that the profound physiological differences between the sexes are more complex than 'men are stronger', with the sexes quite evenly matched in ultra-endurance races. Women also have greater endurance than men when it comes to illness and physical hardship, exhibited by the higher survival rates of baby girls, women's better survival rates in famine and droughts, and the vastly higher numbers of women in the extremely high age brackets.[21]

Women's sports science experts often make the point that women have historically been viewed simply as 'small men', despite their physiology being completely different in ways that science is still establishing. Remarkably, even at the top level, many women play in football boots designed for men, which are widely thought to increase the risk of injury. Running shoes for women can be bought in any high-street store, specially designed to account for women's weight distribution and running gait, but football lags behind. Caroline Criado Perez's 2018 book *Invisible Women* notes all the ways that women are disadvantaged in a world designed for men.[22] A morbid example is that women are more likely to die in car crashes because test dummies are based on the average man, with seatbelts and airbags often not as protective of a woman's smaller body. Football kits have been designed by and for men until very recently and it is only now, with the issue becoming important to manufacturers' bottom lines, that change is starting to happen, and more brands are releasing women's boots, as well as kits, like that of Mary Earps.

Michael Cox is a former colleague of mine at *The Athletic* who has written two bestselling books about football tactics – *Zonal Marking* and *The Mixer* – and has played a significant role in popularising in-depth tactical analysis, first as a blogger and then in mainstream journalism. He is a rare example of a journalist who made his name covering the men's game but who is equally interested in women's football. He says the two versions of the sport are different, but that does not mean one is better or worse. 'Because the women's game is slower – it's probably 60–70 per cent of the speed of the men's game – I think the tactics become clearer,' he explained to me. 'If I'm at a game, it's much easier to see on first viewing what's happening, what the key battles are, the systems and that kind of thing. Premier League football is just so fast that it can be quite difficult to work it out. I think the slower tempo and slightly less physicality means you get certain types of player who can really thrive in the women's game that maybe struggle a bit in the men's game.' He singles out Keira Walsh, England's key midfielder who moved from Manchester City to Barcelona in 2022 before winning a continental quadruple with the Spanish club in the 2023–24 season. 'She's almost an Andrea Pirlo kind of figure, which the England men's side are really lacking – a deep-lying passer,' likening Walsh to the classy Italian who was a key figure in the Italian men's 2006 World Cup win, as well winning countless trophies with AC Milan and Juventus.

The success of unexpected teams at the 2023 Women's World Cup showed that women's football is becoming an ever-more global game. The following year at a FIFA Congress in Bangkok, the 2027 host was announced. A joint bid from three traditional women's football powerhouses – Belgium, the Netherlands and Germany – was beaten into second place. The winner, by 119 votes to 78, was Brazil,[23] which became the first country to host the

Women's World Cup on a continent home to just 5 per cent of the world's population that has provided 45 per cent of men's World Cup winners: five titles for Brazil, three for Argentina and two for Uruguay.

Women's football in Brazil, like everywhere else, has a history of suppression. Between 1941 and 1979, the country banned women outright from playing sports deemed incompatible with 'the female nature'. This was a period when the men's team lifted the World Cup three times. Throughout Pelé's football career, perhaps the greatest there has ever been, women's football was illegal in his country.

One of the first women's matches in Brazil took place between São Paulo and Corinthians in 1982, with 68,000 supporters showing up despite the São Paulo Football Federation attempting to ban it. Legendary male player Sócrates, who was at Corinthians at the time, spoke out in favour of the match. Organised women's football picked up throughout the 1980s with the national team founded in 1988, sending a squad to the inaugural World Cup. Brazil beat Japan 1–0 in their first group game but lost 5–0 to the USA and 2–0 to Sweden. This all took some getting used to for a country whose men's team would expect to win those match-ups easily. At the 1995 World Cup in Sweden, players wore ridiculously baggy kits, seemingly the ones the men had won the World Cup in the year prior. Brazil did no better. However, at the following tournament in the US, the Brazilian women achieved an impressive third-place finish, and the team went one better in 2007, finishing as runners-up after losing 2–0 to Germany in the final in Shanghai. Brazil have become a solid team in women's football, winning three Copa América trophies this century as well as three Olympic silver medals. It is thanks in large part to perhaps the greatest-ever woman to play the game: Marta.

The Maracanã Stadium in Rio de Janeiro is the spiritual home of Brazilian football. It hosted the biggest football crowd ever when an estimated 200,000 people watched the national team's shocking 2–1 loss to Uruguay in the 1950 World Cup final. On the route towards the stadium is a wall of fame which immortalises the male heroes of Brazilian football, as well as a handful of illustrious foreigners, including Argentinians Diego Maradona and Lionel Messi. In 2018, the first woman added her footprints. Marta Vieira da Silva's powerful left foot helped her win FIFA World Player of the Year five years on the trot between 2006 and 2010, and once again in 2018. Scoring 119 goals in 204 appearances for Brazil before retiring from international football in 2024, Marta played a huge role in driving interest in the women's game in this football-obsessed country.

Brazil's men's clubs, which have fanatical followings, are gradually seeing the appeal of taking the women's game seriously, which takes us on to the second shirt in this chapter. In the 2021–22 season, Corinthians, the team that played that match in the 1980s which would kickstart women's football in Brazil as a serious force, unveiled a new third shirt made by Nike just one year before the company would get itself into sticky waters over the Mary Earps debacle. The shirt, worn by the men's and women's teams, was mostly purple, a colour that has been associated with feminism throughout history. 'Women's football is a fundamental part of Corinthians' sport,' Duilio Monteiro Alves, president of Corinthians, announced. 'We are very proud to be pioneers in Brazil by debuting an official shirt with the women's team.'[24]

Marketing gimmick or not, the shirt tapped into a key aspect of Brazilian football which might seem unbelievable to a European fan: Corinthians claim that more than half of their supporters – 53 per cent to be precise – are women. The club's female fans are known as the *'minas'*, with *'Respeita as minas'* ('Respect the minas') inscribed on the neck of that Nike Corinthians shirt. As I saw in Colombia, South American football crowds are far more gender-balanced than in Europe despite the limited traction gained by the women's game itself. Maurício Alencar is an Anglo-Brazilian football journalist. 'Brazilian football crowds have never been as largely male-dominated as games I've been to in Europe,' he explained. 'Growing up, when in England I was used to going to matches solely with my dad, in Brazil, it would feel strange going to a match without my sister, female cousins and aunties. I think there is a strong family fan culture in Brazil and it's a key part of the wider passion for football.' Sometimes this has fed through to kits. In addition to Corinthians' purple shirt, Cruzeiro have played in a special-edition shirt to mark International Women's Day, while several other clubs have released pink shirts in support of breast cancer awareness.

Júlia Belas Trindade is a Brazilian football journalist who explains that the Corinthians women's team have had great success, winning five Copa Libertadores championships denoting the best women's team on the continent, which contributed to the club doing more to promote the team, a virtuous circle increasing respect from fans of the men's team. 'They organise themselves, they go to games, they watch the team play, they support the players on social media,' she explained to me, adding that purple has another symbolism too. 'There's this expression in Brazil, if you're passionate about something, you're so passionate that you get purple, like your face gets too red, it gets purple. Corinthians fans used to say that they were *Corinthians roxo*, purple Corinthians.' The men's team had a purple shirt in the past because of this reason. Belas Trindade agrees that the *minas* of Corinthians have a proud history, and women fans in the stands are far more prominent than elsewhere in the world, but there are problems too. 'There's a lot of machismo in Brazil and in South American culture in general. We talk a lot about the fact that you shouldn't go to the stadium wearing short shorts or tight clothes because you draw attention, and people will comment.'

While Corinthians have managed to capture a wave of enthusiasm, this is an exception rather than the rule, and general apathy towards the women's game in Brazil extends to the national team. 'I feel like people have this idea that because Brazil are great in the men's game, they will be great in the women's game as well. It's always a struggle to have these huge expectations: "You're Brazilian, you have Marta. How come you haven't won a World Cup yet?" The idea in Brazil is that when we win something important, like the World Cup or the Olympics, then we will have the support we need. That proved to be true with Corinthians, when they started winning everything, they started gaining more and more support from the fans. But why should it be like this?'

While women's football in South America has some distance to go to catch up with Europe and the US in infrastructure terms, the fact that women have long attended men's football in large numbers suggests there is huge room for the game to grow if Brazil can get it right, although there is apprehension as well as excitement about the 2027 World Cup. Brazil hosted the 2014 men's World Cup, which proved to be a traumatising experience. The team was under intense pressure to win the tournament on home soil with the help of golden boy Neymar, seen as heir to legendary Brazilian strikers Pelé and Ronaldo. He got injured during Brazil's win over Colombia in the quarter-finals and in the following game against Germany, the hosts capitulated spectacularly, losing 7–1 with five of Germany's goals coming in the first half-hour. This was more than a defeat, it was like a collective national meltdown with the entire world watching. It was one of the most shocking results in football history.

Off the pitch the tournament had issues too, with protests against the amount of money spent at a time of economic strife. Stadium construction was plagued by accidents, budget overruns and delays. Two years after the tournament, just before Rio de Janeiro was set to host the Olympics, the country added political drama to economic chaos as President Dilma Rousseff was impeached two months before the games began. What should be remembered as a golden era for the country, hosting the world's two biggest sporting events in close proximity, was traumatic. 'With everything that happened with Brazil hosting the Olympic Games and the men's World Cup,' says Flo Lloyd-Hughes, 'I do worry that [hosting the Women's World Cup in 2027] might not necessarily be prioritised at a time the country is experiencing a lot of economic hardship. It has all the potential of being an iconic tournament because it's in Brazil. It's just there's always that question mark of will they deliver it? Will it be in the right stadiums? And everything like that. With a men's World Cup, you kind of know that whatever happens, it will be delivered, and it will be good. But with a Women's World Cup, I think there's a fear of making sure it's the best it can be.'

Júlia Belas Trindade says it sometimes feels that the country's footballing authorities do not give the game the respect it deserves, such as organising two friendly games in October 2024 against Colombia in the state of Espírito Santo which has little football tradition. Only a week's warning was given, meaning the attendance was poor. This sort of thing is common in women's football, Trindade says, with unsuitable locations and kick-off times chosen to fit around men's matches. She says it sometimes feels like there is an 'active attempt' to undermine the women's game. Nevertheless, she is excited to welcome the world to her country in 2027. 'The World Cup is important because it acts as a catalyst for this change. It has been changing, and I don't think that the development of women's football will go back to the dark times when no one even knew we had a women's team in most clubs in Brazil. At the same time, it's difficult to grow a game when you have so much expectation with so little investment.'

Whatever happens in Brazil, the march of women's football is relentless, and mirrors the uneven yet steady improvement in gender equality around the world. The women's game is breaking out of its heartlands, attracting bigger crowds by the year, and getting more and more interest from fans and brands as exemplified by the shirt of Mary Earps and what it represents, and the purple shirt of Corinthians. This is all the start of a return to the natural order of things, a thriving women's game existing alongside the men's game, as was the case before women's football was rudely interrupted by the men from England's Football Association.

10

BORDERS

Rangers FC & Club Deportivo Palestino

'There's a thing in a football ground called a 90-minute bigot, someone who has got a friend of an opposite religion next door to them. But for that 90 minutes, they shout foul, religious abuse at each other.'
　　　　　Lawrence Macintyre, head of safety for Rangers FC, 2005

Celtic Park on a European night is quite something. Most British stadiums have one section or stand that is vocal, but most fans are quiet for most of the game. At Celtic for a big occasion there is noisy singing on all four sides throughout, the crowd particularly fired up for European games because Scottish domestic opponents often provide feeble competition. Instead of sitting in the press box for the game between Celtic and Shakhtar Donetsk in October 2022, I was in the away end with a couple of hundred Ukrainians, many of whom had just moved as refugees to Scotland after Russian tanks rolled into Ukraine eight months earlier. Varya, Donetsk who had been in Scotland for seven years, took it upon herself to be the group's ringleader, marshalling her compatriots into chants.

I was here because in the autumn of 2022 I played a part in making *Away from Home*, a podcast about Shakhtar Donetsk alongside Adam Crafton, Abi Paterson and other colleagues at *The Athletic*.[1] The Ukrainian club qualified for the Champions League while their country was at war and we were given access to the team and its players through this tumultuous campaign. Way back in 2014, Shakhtar had moved from Donetsk in eastern Ukraine to the capital Kyiv after Putin invaded the Crimea region and the east of the country was plunged into war. Eight years later Putin invaded the whole of Ukraine and not even Kyiv was safe, so the team kept travelling west. While making the podcast I travelled to Split in Croatia, where Shakhtar's academy, many of them young children, travelled by bus after the outbreak of war. I also went to Warsaw in Poland, where the senior team was playing its 'home' European games, and watched Shakhtar play out a gutsy draw against Real Madrid. This followed a surprise win over RB Leipzig in Germany, so by the time Shakhtar visited Celtic Park in Glasgow in Scotland, the Champions League group was finely poised.

The game ended 1–1, a decent result for Shakhtar which guaranteed them a spot in the Europa League. After the game I met Sviatoslav, a young boy attending the game with his mother. Her English was limited but he spoke fluently, adapting quickly to his new life in Scotland, and telling me about his father on the front line in Ukraine. 'He is a warrior defender in Ukraine. His name is Kostya,' he told me, describing how he spoke to his father every day by message and video call. I asked if he had enjoyed the game. 'Man, it was so exciting,' he said. 'All that noise.'

Shakhtar is a club that moved location as borders – in practice, if not in internationally recognised law – moved around it. Celtic and their fierce Glasgow rivals Rangers are two clubs also defined by borders. This chapter will tell the story about those clubs, as well as describing another football shirt on the other side of the world in Chile, which tells the story of a border in the Middle East.

For much of human history there were no borders as we know them today. When hunter-gatherers wandered the earth looking for food they would stick to a vaguely demarcated territory but the boundaries were rather informal. This changed as humans formed sedentary communities based around farming in the 'fertile crescent' stretching from modern-day Egypt to Iraq, via southern Turkey. This was the shift from humans being a species that roamed around looking for food to one that based itself in one place, kickstarting all sorts of developments like writing, architecture and politics. City-states would plunder their neighbours and guard what was theirs meaning that borders of a sort sprung up, and they became increasingly formalised over time.

The system of borders as we know it today, though, is more recent. Between 1618 and 1648 around eight million Catholics and Protestants are thought to have died in the Thirty Years' War in Central Europe. The treaties to end that conflict, known as the Peace of Westphalia, introduced the principle of state sovereignty. This is the idea that each state, no matter how large or small, has the exclusive right to govern its own territory. The Westphalian idea of the state gradually took over the world. Sovereign states were first confined to Europe but this changed through a series of expansions, such as the end of empires after the First and Second World Wars, then the collapse of Yugoslavia and the Soviet Union.[2] The idea is exemplified in the modern United Nations charter which says 'nothing . . . shall authorise the United Nations to intervene in matters which are essentially within the domestic jurisdiction of any state'.[3] There are more countries in the world than ever before and this has had an impact on football – UEFA had thirty-one founding members in 1954 but this had increased to fifty-five by 2025. The sovereign state system underpins the international game – it is because of various quirks of history that Northern Ireland is a distinct team to Ireland, Spain to Portugal and San Marino to Italy.

Every corner of the globe is now governed by this system. Even places not under one state's control, such as international waters and the Antarctic Territory, are that way because of explicit, codified agreements between states. Every modern country has a clearly defined border which it will defend by force if necessary. Religion used to be the driver of most conflicts around the world but more recently territory and borders have been the bigger factor, such as the wars of Napoleon's imperial expansion, or the Second World War which was kickstarted by Hitler annexing a portion of neighbouring Czechoslovakia, followed by his ambitions to rewrite the borders of Europe.

Nationalism is the belief that a group of people who share things like culture, ethnicity, language, and history should also share a territory. It emerged as power shifted from hereditary monarchs to governments whose legitimacy had to stem from something else. Nationalism can be healthy if it makes states coherent but it can also get ugly. 'Ethnolinguistic groups rarely have sharp dividing lines, leading to arguments over which nation had the strongest claim to particular territories,' write Alexander C. Diener and Joshua Hagen. 'Much of European political history since 1800 involves efforts to revise the region's feudal and absolutist borders to fit this new nation-state framework.'[4]

One of the consequences of the two world wars was the end of Europe's multinational states and the rise of new ethnically homogeneous ones. Poland was 60 per cent Polish between the First and Second World Wars. The figure now stands at around 96 per cent Polish. Its borders were trimmed after the Second World War, moving Belorussians into Belarus and Ukrainians into Ukraine, while many Germans also moved back to their ethnic and linguistic homeland. Pre-war Poland's Jewish population of several million was reduced to almost zero. Germany's Jewish population fell from 522,000 in 1933 to 20,000 after the war. The Holocaust was the ultimate dark consequence of unchecked nationalism. Europe's democracies are now underpinned by rights for minorities, enshrined in law, although this system does not always work perfectly.

Most borders around the world now exist without controversy but there are a handful which are subject to ongoing tension. One is a border in the Middle East formed when a homeland was created for the Jews after the horrors of the Second World War. Another one is on the island of Ireland and it plays a big role in football on the other side of the Irish Sea.

I spent a lot of time in Scotland on holiday as a child as someone with Scottish family on both sides, so have long been a follower of the country's football. For a place of just 5.4 million people, it punches well above its weight in footballing terms. The Scottish Professional Football League has four divisions and more people attend top-flight games than in any other country in Europe per head of population.[5] Scotland was a football pioneer alongside its neighbour to the south, playing England in the first-ever international fixture in 1872. While Edinburgh is Scotland's capital and home to its cultural and political elite, Scotland's footballing capital is the somewhat larger city of Glasgow. Celtic and Rangers dominate Scottish football, with one of the pair winning the title every season since 1986, and all bar nineteen of the seasons dating all the way back to the league's beginning in 1890. The rivalry is known as the 'Old Firm', thought to come from a satirical cartoon which said the rivalry was confected by a 'firm' to benefit both sides, through increased crowds and gate receipts. Whatever the truth in that, the rivalry soon became very real.

Despite healthy crowds, even the most passionate fans of Scottish football would admit not all is rosy these days. As England's Premier League boomed and became the world's richest and most-followed league, Scottish club football fell behind in comparison. England's rise and Scotland's relative demise are two sides of the same coin. One key statistic – how much money a football club pulls in in revenue each year – tells the story of English and Scottish football's contrasting fortunes. In the 1990s Manchester United were dominant in England and Rangers were similarly successful in Scotland. In 1993, a year after the Premier League was formed, Manchester United earned £25 million more than any other club. Rangers enjoyed the second-highest revenue in the UK with £20 million, narrowly ahead of Liverpool, Arsenal and Tottenham. Fast-forward three decades and everything has changed. Manchester United and Liverpool each turn over more than half a billion pounds per year and rising, with Tottenham, Arsenal, Chelsea and Manchester City not far behind. Rangers and Celtic have seen material growth, with Rangers revenue reaching £84 million in 2023, quadruple the figure from three decades earlier. Celtic, outstripping their rivals financially as well as on the pitch, have increased revenue from just £9 million in 1993 to £120 million. In isolation that is impressive compared to many other industries – football has grown as a commercial product almost everywhere – but in relative terms Scotland has been left in the dust, with the Old Firm now having a fraction of the resources of the big English clubs.[6]

This financial divergence reflects how football has become a global commercial enterprise. Traditionally, the bulk of a football club's revenue came from selling tickets and in the early 1990s,

Rangers' home stadium of Ibrox was roughly the same size as Old Trafford and Anfield so the gate receipts were similar. This has changed a bit – English stadiums have expanded and there is more demand for expensive hospitality seats – but it is the rest of the picture that has shifted drastically. TV rights are worth far more as football is broadcast worldwide. The Premier League now has global TV deals worth billions while Scottish domestic football is of little interest to fans outside the country. In 2022, the Scottish top-flight signed a four-year deal worth £150 million, with the league's chief executive saying this was the 'first step' towards hitting a long-term target of securing a total of £50 million a season for the forty-two member clubs in the first and second tiers of Scottish football. That same season the broadcast income of Southampton, who finished bottom of England's Premier League, was double that, at just over £100 million.

When it comes to the football, less revenue means lower wages and transfer fees for Scottish teams, who therefore attract a lower calibre of player and have a weaker overall product. This is self-reinforcing as richer teams with better players can sell players for higher fees, global TV exposure allows for more lucrative commercial deals, and so on. Rangers and Celtic have been left behind – let alone the other Scottish teams. I was on holiday on Scotland's west coast in August 2023 when Aston Villa played Hibernian in the first round of the Europa Conference League. I watched my team's first European game for over a decade on Scottish TV, the game taking place in Edinburgh, a hundred or so miles from where I was. The result was a 5–0 Villa win, great from my perspective but it was almost sad to watch the vast gulf between two teams that might have given each other a good game a few decades earlier. Villa had individual players worth more than the entire Hibernian squad.

These days even Rangers and Celtic, despite having genuine global reach and far bigger fan bases than Premier League teams like Fulham, Bournemouth and Brentford, are comfortably outspent by those teams who make as much as 80 per cent of their revenue from TV money. Rangers' record signing is Norwegian striker Tore André Flo, who was signed from Chelsea all the way back in 2000 for £12 million, worth almost twice as much in today's money, but not broken since. Celtic's record signing is Arne Engels, who was signed for £11 million in 2024. The Premier League's smallest teams routinely spend double this, and even teams in England's second tier spend more sometimes.

Scottish football's decline mirrors that of other leagues across Europe outside the Big Five of England, Spain, Italy, Germany and France. Between 1985 and 1995, winners of the European Cup included Steaua București of Romania, FC Porto of Portugal, Red Star Belgrade of what was then Yugoslavia, as well as PSV Eindhoven and Ajax of the Netherlands. It's hard to imagine any of these teams coming close to winning the modern Champions League where the huge and growing financial gulf means the same clubs keep winning.

The last team outside the Big Five leagues to reach the final was Porto, who won the Champions League in 2004 while managed by a young José Mourinho. A year before Porto's stunning win in Schalke's home stadium in Gelsenkirchen, Mourinho's side won the UEFA Cup, now called the Europa League, after beating Celtic who impressively reached the final in Seville. The mid-2000s was a fine era for Scottish football. Rangers reached the final of the same tournament five years later against Zenit Saint Petersburg. Around 200,000 Rangers fans, a small fraction of them in possession of tickets, travelled the short distance south to Manchester in what is thought to be the largest travelling crowd in the history of football.

A judge, later sentencing eleven hooligans to prison, described the scenes as the 'worst night of violence and destruction suffered by Manchester city centre since the Blitz'.[7]

Neither Glasgow side won their final but with both clubs reaching these heights on the European stage at a similar time, both had strong teams and the domestic battles were often finely poised. Rangers won the league every year between 1989 and 1997 but in the period that followed, between 1998 and 2011, the two clubs won seven titles each. Back then, top players like Henrik Larsson and Chris Sutton played for Celtic, and Barry Ferguson and Ronald de Boer for Rangers, which made for some excellent games. The pair traded wins and titles, a thrilling example being the climax of the 2004–05 season which has since been immortalised as 'Helicopter Sunday'. Celtic were favourites to win the league ahead of the final round of fixtures, sitting one point ahead of Rangers meaning they needed a win against lowly Motherwell who had nothing to play for. Rangers did their bit by beating Hibernian 1–0. Celtic were leading Motherwell 1–0 until the last minute of the game but then Scott McDonald, an Australian striker who grew up a Celtic fan, scored two late goals. The Motherwell manager Terry Butcher, a legend as a player for Rangers, looks happier than his striker in the photos that followed the full-time whistle. A helicopter carrying the league trophy had been hovering over Scotland's Central Belt. It veered away from Motherwell and headed to Hibernian's stadium in Edinburgh, where the Rangers players jubilantly lifted it.[8]

Things since have generally been less exciting. If the story of the 1990s was Rangers' dominance, followed by a competitive 2000s, the pendulum has since decisively swung towards Celtic. A shoot-out win over Rangers in the Scottish League Cup final in December 2024 took Celtic's all-time trophy haul to 119, pulling ahead of Rangers for the first time in decades. (In third place was Aberdeen on just nineteen.) Rangers have fallen behind for dramatic reasons. In the 2000s, the club was battling to keep pace with Celtic while still competing in Europe, on a modest budget by continental standards. The club ran up big debts and it transpired Rangers was concealing the scale of its spending from the taxman by paying players and managers through secret companies. Financial storm clouds had been gathering for several years and it all culminated in Rangers' liquidation in 2012, the consequences of which are still being felt in Scottish football.[9] Rangers was forced to reform as a new company and start again in the fourth tier of the Scottish league system. Although Celtic fans enjoyed their bitter rival's demise, it devalued Scottish football by rendering the league utterly uncompetitive for a long time. No other team could muster anywhere near Celtic's resources and the club became dominant, winning nine titles in a row, often by ludicrous margins. Celtic won the 2017 title by thirty points, winning thirty-four games, drawing four and losing none. Other seasons were almost as emphatic.

Rangers have long since returned to the top flight and even won the title in 2021 after going a whole season unbeaten under the management of Steven Gerrard. This stopped Celtic winning 'ten in a row' which is a mystical concept in Scottish football. Celtic have won nine titles in a row twice, with runs starting in 1966 and 2012, while Rangers won nine from 1989 onwards. No club has ever managed ten. While Rangers are back as a competitive force, Celtic continue to dominate after that one slip-up. The Old Firm clubs have generally been underwhelming in Europe, though. Rangers' surprise run to the 2022 Europa League final aside, the pair have been routinely thrashed in continental competition while giving out the thrashings on the domestic front, Celtic's valiant defeat against Bayern Munich in February 2025 was their first Champions League knock-out game for over a decade, helped by a new format which puts twenty-four rather than sixteen teams through past the group stage. Generally, the Old Firm finds itself in a catch-22. They are too rich for their domestic competition but too poor to compete in Europe, a familiar fate for league champions across Europe, from Rosenborg in Norway to Red Star Belgrade in Serbia.

If any match is more than just a game and any shirts are more than just shirts, the Old Firm fits the bill. Historically speaking, the Glasgow rivalry splits the city down not just football lines but also sectarian and nationalist lines. Celtic is the club of Glasgow's Irish Catholic community. At games like the one I went to in October 2022, the green, white and orange of the Irish tricolour was proudly flown. Rangers is Glasgow's Protestant club, with fans flying the red, white and blue of the Union flag. There is a lot of history here. The story of this rivalry includes potatoes and a Dutch king, the colour green and the colour orange.

Tension between Catholics and Protestants is a thread running through British history. Britain was a Catholic country just like the rest of Western Europe until 1534 when the Pope refused to allow Henry VIII to divorce his wife Catherine of Aragon. Henry responded by renouncing the Pope's authority and setting up his own Church. The Church of England became the national religion based on the new Protestant doctrine imported from Germany which rejected the Pope's authority. After that Catholics were persecuted in England with many put to death.

The situation in Ireland, ruled by England from the twelfth century to the twentieth, was different. Catholicism remained the dominant religion there but Protestants from England and

Scotland started settling in big numbers from the seventeenth century onwards in the north where in 1690 the Protestant army of William of Orange, the Dutchman who sat on the English throne, beat the army of James II, who ended up as Britain's last Catholic king. This military victory solidified the Protestant ascendancy that continues to this day in what is now known as Northern Ireland. The island of Ireland is now split into the six counties of the north, which are part of the United Kingdom, while the remaining twenty-six in the south form the country of Ireland, which has been independent for over a century now and where Catholicism is historically dominant.

Every country in the world has a higher population than it did two centuries ago. There is one exception. Ireland's 1841 census recorded the population as 8.2 million, at a time when the Industrial Revolution was running at full speed on both sides of the Irish Sea and millions of the Irish lived in dire poverty. In parts of the country's west more than three-fifths of the houses were windowless one-room mud cabins.[10] Rural Ireland was very densely populated and as numbers boomed, the land struggled to sustain them. Locals were highly reliant on the potato crop which had been imported from the New World, easy to grow in Ireland's wet and rugged countryside and packing in far more calories per acre than traditional crops like wheat for bread. Much of the country had never industrialised and millions were subsistence farmers. In much of Ireland the concept of employment effectively did not exist, writes the historian Cecil Woodham-Smith. 'The possession of a piece of land was literally the difference between life and death'.[11]

Then came 'the blight'. Around half of the country's crop became inedible almost overnight after being infected with a type of fungus called *phytophthora infestans*. As soon as diseased potatoes were dug up they turned to slimy handfuls of rot. People started dying from starvation, and even more from diseases like cholera, dysentery and typhus. One observer wrote that 'skeletal children cried with pain, their features sharpened with hunger and their limbs wasted so that there was little left but bones. The dead were buried in mass graves, often only a few inches below ground'.[12] Around a million died and a further two million emigrated, mostly to Britain and North America. The scale of the problem was exacerbated by the British government in London which had fostered dependency on the potato crop and then turned a blind eye to Irish suffering. Ireland's population fell by a quarter in the space of five years and continued to fall for decades after that, only starting to grow again in the 1960s. Modern Ireland's population is still well below what it was in the 1840s and is far more concentrated in Dublin and other cities. Many rural areas were home to thriving communities before the famine then emptied them, never to be repopulated again.

Across the water in Scotland, Catholicism had long been banned following the Reformation in the sixteenth century although there were small numbers of holdouts in remote areas. The famine changed everything, with huge numbers of Irish Catholics making the short journey across the Irish Sea to escape the blight. My paternal grandmother's family moved from Roscommon in the middle of Ireland to the city of Dundee on Scotland's east coast. Most ended up in and around Glasgow.

One who made the journey across the Irish Sea was Brother Walfrid. He was born in May 1840 as Andrew Kerins in a village in Sligo, a rural Irish county devastated by the famine. In his early childhood, Sligo port saw 'coffin ships' full of diseased passengers depart for North America. Many of them were dead upon arrival.[13] Little is known about Brother Walfrid's early life but in

Glasgow he became a priest working in the city's East End where the poorest Irish migrants had settled. At that time Glasgow was the most densely populated city in Europe, a hotbed of squalor and deprivation. In 1888, 40 per cent of deaths were those of children under five. Celtic, the football club, was formed in the city the same year.

At that time the city of Edinburgh already had its own Catholic football team, Hibernian, who won the Scottish Cup in 1887. The win was celebrated throughout Scotland by the country's Irish communities including in Glasgow, which lacked its own Catholic team until Brother Walfrid set one up. The team had an explicitly charitable goal: to raise money to feed needy children. 'Many cases of sheer poverty are left unaided through lack of means,' said a pamphlet issued in January 1888. 'It is therefore with this principal object that we have set afloat the "Celtic", and we invite you as one of our ever-ready friends to assist in putting our new Park in proper working order for the coming football season.' The move also had a religious motivation, with Catholics wanting to keep children under the watchful eye of their own Church and away from the more numerous Protestant organisations. A week after that meeting, volunteers found land for a pitch and built the first Celtic Park in the east of the city where the Irish community was mostly based. The new club, featuring Irish immigrants and their children, was an overnight success. Celtic won their first game 5–2 against Rangers and reached the Scottish Cup final the following year, going on to win four league titles between 1892 and 1898.

Celtic's bitter rivals trace their history even further back to 1872, the year of the first international match between England and Scotland. While Celtic's links with Ireland and Catholicism were explicit from the beginning, the Rangers story is slightly different. 'There was nothing religious in the origins of Rangers,' writes William James Murray.[14] 'They were Protestant only in the sense that the vast majority of clubs in Scotland at that time were made up of Protestants.' But Protestantism and its cousin unionism – support for the British state and opposition to Irish nationalism – gradually became a more conscious identity following wider political and economic shifts. Harland & Wolff was the Belfast company that built the *Titanic* which set sail and then promptly sank in April 1912. That same year the company acquired a new shipyard in Govan in the west of Glasgow due to the political instability in Ireland, where nationalist clamour was growing stronger and stronger, alongside plenty of resistance in the north. Many Belfast workers moved with the company, and this workforce was overwhelmingly Protestant and unionist. With Irish politics febrile at the time, in Glasgow, the Protestant identity started to be defined in relation to the unionist cause which became associated with supporting Rangers and opposing Celtic.

The signing of the Anglo-Irish Treaty in 1921, ending British rule over most of the island of Ireland while solidifying Northern Ireland's position as part of the United Kingdom, calmed things down but divisions remained. From the 1920s onwards, Rangers had an unofficial policy of not signing Catholic players or employing Catholics as club staff. This remained the case throughout 'The Troubles', a period of violent sectarianism in Britain and Ireland that saw terrorist bombing campaigns on both sides of the Irish Sea, peaking in the 1970s. Football fans on both sides of the divide often sang unsavoury things, even glorifying terrorism from the Irish Republican Army or unionist counterparts like the Ulster Volunteer Force. Rangers eventually signed their first Catholic player of the modern era, the striker Mo Johnston, in 1989. Many have since played for the club including Lorenzo Amoruso, an Italian who captained the club around the time of the millennium, while other players have blessed themselves with the sign of the cross, a Catholic gesture, with no negative reaction from fans. Northern Ireland has been at relative peace since the Good Friday Agreement of 1998, but the Old Firm rivalry has remained one of the world's most vicious, with both sides frequently disciplined for sectarian chanting. Rangers have been reprimanded for their fans' singing of the 'Billy Boys', a tune about a 1920s violent street gang named after King William of Orange which features the word 'Fenian', an offensive term for Irish people.

In 1999, Donald Findlay, one of Scotland's most high-profile lawyers, had to stand down as Rangers vice-chairman after he was videoed singing the song. The club has been sanctioned for other tunes including the grim 'Famine Song'. Celtic, meanwhile, have been guilty of singing songs celebrating the Irish Republican Army, the group that killed around 1,800 people, many civilians, between 1969 and 1994. Recently Celtic fans have been condemned for booing the minute's silence observed at football matches every November to mark the UK's Remembrance Day honouring those killed in wars. To some this is a valid rejection of British imperialism, but to many others is in extremely bad taste.[15] Other incidents have included fans hoisting effigies representing rival fans and players. Celtic player Neil Lennon retired from representing Northern Ireland on the international stage after receiving death threats in 2002. A decade later two men were jailed after sending parcels containing explosive materials to Lennon, who was at this point Celtic manager. When it comes to offensive chants, the two clubs have been repeatedly upbraided by the Scottish and European footballing authorities.

The curious context to Scottish football's ugly sectarianism is that fewer and fewer Scots go to church these days. The last census revealed that a narrow majority of Scots say they have no religion for the first time ever.[16] While the rivalry is often described as sectarian, few are sincerely motivated by the disputes over prayer books and priests that inspired violence a century or two ago. Nationalism, though, in the form of opposing views on the conflict in Ireland and what should happen to the border, is alive and well. The Good Friday Agreement accepted that Northern Ireland would remain part of the UK until a majority decide otherwise in a 'border poll'. This may happen one day, but there is no sign of it being imminent or inevitable. Catholics overtook Protestants according to the 2021 census but even among many Catholics there is little appetite for opening old wounds and compromising Northern Ireland's fragile peace, with everyday issues like the economy more of a pressing concern. The situation is further complicated by the fact that the voting public in Ireland as well as Northern Ireland would have to agree to unification. While there may well be a majority for the abstract idea of independence on both sides of the border, the details could be very knotty indeed. While the issue often simmers along in the background, when Celtic play Rangers, in a fixture that often takes place five or six times a year because of how the Scottish league system works, there is a huge public platform for the two fiercely opposing views on what Northern Ireland should do next.

More recently it has been mainland Britain that has seen constitutional turmoil. In 2014, Scotland carried out a referendum on whether to become an independent country, and rejected it by 55 per cent to 45 per cent. Although the margin was decisive, 1.6 million Scots voted 'Yes', indicating they are deeply unhappy with the status quo. Support for independence rose immediately after this and for a while seemed inevitable. This has faded somewhat but the independence question has not gone away. In 2016, the UK as a whole voted to leave the EU, against the wishes of a majority in Scotland and Northern Ireland who wanted to remain. The result and subsequent legal wranglings threw up all sorts of complications given Northern Ireland's border with Ireland which remained an EU member.

Sectarianism has greatly diminished in Northern Ireland, and even more so in Scotland, but the Old Firm retains its lively and at times unsavoury character. In some recent games, away fans have not been allowed into either stadium for the Old Firm game because of ticketing disputes over fan safety. Social media has brought a whole new aspect to the rivalry, with vile slurs often traded from the comfort of bedrooms rather than in the stands or the streets. 'The remnants of sectarianism are felt in schools and workplaces where mostly good-natured humour is exchanged,' explains Jordan Campbell, a Scottish football journalist. 'But there is still the phenomenon of the "90-minute bigot".' These people 'have close friends who are from the opposite faith and support the rival team and perform a professional job,' explains Campbell. 'Yet at a football ground they can sing sectarian lyrics and shout sectarian abuse before going back to being normal citizens.' Campbell says isolated incidents should not obscure the fact that things have improved, and that matchday trouble rarely translates to sectarianism in everyday life, although progress is not inevitable. 'The concern is that a lot of the sectarian posts seen on social media seem to come from the younger generations. So, while society has improved, I am not sure that there is a direct correlation between a reduction in sectarian views and a more enlightened, younger generation of fan.'

When it comes to the two clubs' shirts, Celtic's green-and-white hoops are of course a nod to their roots. The colour green is recognised around the world in association with the 'Emerald Isle' where incessant rain dictates the colour of the countryside. Rangers' blue shirts were established even earlier than Celtic's, one of the oldest designs in world football. The club wore blue and white for their first game, an 11–0 victory over Clyde in 1872, but in the patchy historical records no reason is given for the colour blue. It was probably just what was available in a Glasgow sports shop that day, but blue has been associated with Rangers ever since.

Another colour associated with Rangers is orange. This is the colour of the Netherlands and King William who led his army to victory in the Battle of the Boyne in 1690 which solidified Protestant rule in Northern Ireland. The Dutch royal family's name, the House of Orange-Nassau, comes from the medieval principality of Orange in southern France which the Dutch inherited in the sixteenth century. Because of William, the colour is now deeply associated with Protestantism. The Orange Order is a Protestant fraternal order with lodges in Northern Ireland and beyond, which attracts controversy by marching through Catholic areas on 12 July, the anniversary of that battle more than three hundred years ago. The tricolour of Ireland's national flag – green and orange with white in the middle – is meant to symbolise peace between the island's two Christian denominations.

Orange was also the colour of a new away kit released by Rangers just after the millennium. This was a time when there was a big push by both clubs to clamp down on sectarianism following the end of The Troubles, and in response to the murder of Celtic fan Mark Scott who was killed in 1995 while walking home past a Rangers pub. Scott's death gave rise to the anti-sectarian charity Nil by Mouth. In this context, the orange kit looked like a retrograde step. 'Rangers promoted it as "tangerine", but much of the public discourse viewed the release of an orange away kit in 2002 as a dog whistle stunt that commercialised sectarianism,' explains Jordan Campbell. 'It came two years after the "Oranje Day" when the vast majority of Rangers support turned up at the national stadium Hampden Park for the Scottish Cup final against Aberdeen wearing the colour, many of them sporting the Netherlands home kit, or similar. Rangers fans said it was a tribute to their Dutch manager Dick Advocaat and the growing contingent of his countrymen in the squad such as Giovanni van Bronckhorst, Arthur Numan and Michael Mols.' There was an outcry over a move which felt 'out of kilter' with the idea of Scotland moving to a new era 'shorn of the baggage of sectarianism', says Campbell. In 2002 that orange kit was swiftly ditched, but in 2018, 2022 and 2023 the same colour was chosen for Rangers' away kit with less pushback. In other recent seasons the home goalkeeper kit has been bright orange. Barry Ferguson grew up just outside Glasgow in a diehard Rangers family and played for the club 431 times, many of them as captain. In February 2025, he was appointed Rangers manager, arriving at his launch in a bright orange pick-up truck.

On the other side of the world in Chile is another football shirt, which tells a different story about borders and nationalism, but in the Middle East.

In 1896, a Jewish Austro-Hungarian writer called Theodor Herzl wrote a pamphlet called *Der Judenstaat* – the Jewish state. It outlined the dire situation that Europe's Jews faced at the time. 'Wherever (Jews) live in perceptible numbers they are more or less persecuted'. Herzl's proposed solution was a drastic one. He argued that an ethnic group that had long been scattered across countries, a minority everywhere they went, should create its own state in which they form a majority. One proposal was to pay Argentina, a sparsely populated but fertile country which already had a sizable

Jewish population, to cede a portion of territory. The other solution was Palestine, what Herzl called 'our ever-memorable historic home ... We should there form a portion of a rampart of Europe against Asia, an outpost of civilisation as opposed to barbarism.'[17]

Though some Jews moved to Argentina, in the decades following Herzl's pamphlet more moved to Palestine, fleeing Soviet pogroms and European nationalism. They were always a minority compared to the Arab population. The 'Zionist' movement was given a huge boost in the 1910s when the Ottoman Empire collapsed following the First World War. The League of Nations gave Britain a 'mandate' to govern Palestine and Jewish migration was encouraged. In the so-called Balfour Declaration, named after the foreign secretary who signed it, the British government announced its support for a 'national home for the Jewish people' in Palestine. The Jewish population steadily grew through the twenties and thirties before the urgency of the Zionist question was forever altered by the rise of Hitler. The persecution of European Jews in the 1930s and 1940s culminated in the Holocaust when six million were murdered. This convinced many Jews that they were not safe in Europe. In 1947, a United Nations resolution split the territory into separate Arab and Jewish states, kicking off a civil war between the two groups before Israel declared independence on 14 May 1948. While the events of that year are celebrated by Israelis as the birth of their state, Palestinians call it the 'Nakba' or 'catastrophe' as many Arabs who lived there were expelled or fled, never to return.

Many people in football have been guilty of ripping off Barcelona's iconic 'more than a club' motto (me included for the title of this book). Another is Club Deportivo Palestino, a team based in the south of the Chilean capital Santiago who play their football in the country's top division. Their slogan is *'más que un equipo, todo un pueblo*' – more than a team, an entire people. The club and its supporters see themselves as representing the Palestinian cause on the world stage and this slogan can be seen on a banner flown during every game at the 8,000-capacity Estadio Municipal de La Cisterna.

The movement of Palestinians to Chile began in the mid-nineteenth century, around the same time the Irish were fleeing famine. While the population of modern Palestine is mostly Muslim, many of those who went to Chile were Arab Christians who were being treated badly by Ottoman rulers. The Crimean War, which raged between 1853 and 1856, was a driver of immigration.[18] Disputes over territory in the Holy Land between Orthodox Christians who were championed by Russia, and Catholics who were championed by France, was a threat to religious sites that were spiritually important to all Christians as well as many Jews and Muslims. Fearing they would become a pawn in this power struggle, many Palestinians uprooted their lives to migrate as far away as Latin America. Thousands arrived in the port of Buenos Aires after a month-long journey by ship, but there was an outbreak of 'Turkophobia,' discrimination against those coming from Ottoman lands, resulting in attempts to deport newcomers. As a result many ventured to Chile instead and, as legend has it, crossed the Andes on mules carrying little more than the clothes on their backs.[19] Later on, many Palestinians migrated to South America to escape being drafted into the Ottoman military where they often were sent to the front lines, sometimes unarmed, as cannon fodder during the Balkan Wars and the First World War. The 1917 Balfour Declaration which promised territory to Jews, was a further driver of migration.

In 1920, by which time Chile was home to a sizable Palestinian population, Club Deportivo Palestino was formed in Santiago.

After 1948 the country's Palestinian community grew even bigger, following the creation of Israel which turfed many Palestinians out of their homes. While many of those who arrived in Chile faced fierce racism, the community is now a major part of Chile's life and its football culture. This is true for other teams founded by migrant communities – the top division sees annual clashes known as the Clásico de Colonias between Palestino and Unión Española, founded by Spaniards in 1897, and Audax Italiano, founded by Italians in 1910.[20]

At the beginning of the twentieth century the distinction in Chile between Arab and Jewish immigrants from the Middle East was 'relatively blurry', writes historian Brenda Elsey.[21] 'The majority of Middle Eastern immigrants defined themselves as Arab, which included Jewish, Christian, and Muslim natives of Syria, Palestine, and Lebanon.' These groups would have experienced similar kinds of discrimination. A 1963 cartoon from defunct sports magazine *Estadio* features a group of hook-nosed businessmen wearing exotic clothing and hoarding piles of banknotes.[22] It looks strikingly similar to the repulsive antisemitic cartoons which spread hatred of Jewish people in Nazi Germany but is in fact depicting the Arab Christians involved in Chilean football.

Today the 500,000-strong 'Chilestinian' diaspora is the world's largest Palestinian community outside the Middle East, most with their origins in places to the south of Jerusalem like Beit Jala and Beit Sahour, as well as Bethlehem, birthplace of Jesus Christ.[23] There are striking differences between the mostly Muslim people living in the West Bank and Gaza today, and the mostly Christian Chilestinians who have assimilated into their new homeland. Many of the latter do not speak Arabic and look physically indistinguishable from the majority of Chileans who have a mixture of European and indigenous heritage. But to this day many

Chilestinians have a close affinity to their homeland and feel strongly about the conflict raging thousands of miles away, with the football club a key part of this connection. Although the club has few players of Palestinian origin these days, others are keenly aware of what playing for the club represents. 'It's more than just a club,' says Bryan Carrasco, the team's captain since 2020. 'It takes you into the history of the Palestinians.' Palestino have generally lagged far behind Chile's big two clubs, Universidad de Chile and Colo-Colo, but won the Copa Chile in 2018, the club's first trophy since winning the league four decades earlier.

In 2014, the club made headlines around the world with a football shirt. It kept the club's traditional colours – the red, black and green of the Palestine flag – but replaced the number '1' on the back of certain shirts with a silhouette map of Palestine from 1947 before the United Nations voted to partition the land. Many Israelis and Jews see this map as a provocation because it appears to deny the legitimacy of the modern Israeli state. Some Jewish organisations in Chile complained about the shirt and Patrick Kiblisky, owner of Chilean top-flight club Ñublense, filed a complaint, saying 'we cannot accept the involvement of football with politics and religion'. After the club had played three matches in the kit the Chilean FA banned it and issued a $1,300 fine. The federation said it was opposed to 'any form of political, religious, sexual, ethnic, social or racial discrimination'.[24]

Another political kit was unveiled in 2024. This shirt featured the green-and-white hoops of Celtic, as well as the club's four-leaf clover badge, and was named the 'Green Brigade' after the Celtic fan group that has vocally supported the Palestine cause inside and outside stadiums. (Members of the group were criticised for flying the flag of the Popular Front for the Liberation of Palestine (PFLP), a group recognised as a terrorist organisation by the US and the

EU but not the UK, a move which the club called 'unacceptable', removing the season tickets of some members.) Many Celtic fans identify with the Palestinian cause, viewing both conflicts through the same lens as resisting what they see as imperial oppression. In the Catholic areas of Belfast, it is common for murals to feature both Irish nationalist and Palestinian iconography. In response, some Rangers fans support Israel and murals highlighting this have popped up in unionist areas.

In Chile, politicians on both the left and the right have been broadly supportive of Palestine, perhaps reflecting the fact that Chile has a larger Palestinian than Jewish population, the opposite of the USA which has long been a firm backer of Israel. In 2011, the Chilean government made the decision to recognise Palestine as a 'free, independent and sovereign state', under the leadership of right-wing president Sebastián Piñera who visited Temple Mount in the old city of Jerusalem alongside officials from the Palestinian Authority. He was rebuked by Israeli officials for violating diplomatic protocols and subsequently apologised. Left-wing president Gabriel Boric, elected in 2022 at the age of just thirty-six, took an even more provocative stance, calling Israel a 'genocidal and murderous state' and accusing it of violating international law, which Israel denies.

The Israel–Palestine issue bubbles in the background of international affairs while periodically rearing its head and taking centre stage. This happened in 1967 when a series of Israeli military victories over its Arab neighbours meant the Jewish state controlled the West Bank and Gaza, which became known as the 'occupied territories'. Over time, Israel was condemned by much of the international community for its treatment of the Palestinians, leading to growing militancy among the region's Arab population. Peace talks were advanced in the 1990s but broke down as the situation in the region gradually worsened, with sporadic conflict disrupting an unhappy status quo in which Israel suppressed violent Palestinian militancy with increasing levels of repression. While the international community gave lip service to a 'two-state solution', this became increasingly implausible in a world where both sides were tending to the extremes, Palestinian territory controlled by violent groups, and Israeli 'settlers' making their home on Palestinian land, making peace ever-more difficult to achieve.

Then came 7 October 2023. Terrorists from Hamas, the Palestinian organisation that has gradually displaced more moderate groups, broke through the border wall between Gaza and southern Israel. It was the first invasion of Israeli territory since 1948. More than a thousand Israelis were killed, the vast majority civilians, many while attending a music festival. United Nations special rapporteur Alice Jill Edwards documented 'grave violations of international law – killings, hostage-taking, and torture, including sexual torture'.[25] This was a huge shock for the Israeli population who had lived in relative security for decades. Israel hit back, bombing Gaza for months on end, at times with a brutal lack of consideration for human life. Tens of thousands of Palestinians have been killed, with large parts of Gaza reduced to rubble by the Israeli military which has been heavily backed by the US and European allies. The war has since morphed into a wider regional conflict, with Lebanon, long a rival to Israel, getting sucked in, and the Assad regime crumbling in Syria.

The Palestinian cause has long been a cause célèbre for many, particularly, but by no means exclusively, in the Muslim world. To some of them, CD Palestino is far more than a football club, it is a means of supporting this cause from afar.

While running a half marathon in London in December 2024, I saw a young man wearing the 2014 Palestino shirt, presumably for its geopolitical message at a time when there was huge international pressure for a ceasefire in Gaza, rather than because he was a fan of a fairly obscure team based thousands of miles away. Mohamad Abdulaziz is a genuine fan of the club but he is not in Chile. He lives in Riyadh in Saudi Arabia and runs the Arabic language Facebook page for the club. He told me he first heard of Palestino in a TV report twenty-five years ago before becoming an active supporter, struggling to follow the club until he was helped by some supporters in Chile he connected with on social media. 'The matches were not shown on Middle East channels until a great fan called Omar from Santiago replied to me on Facebook and we became friends. He was my guidance on how to watch the matches live, and he even shipped me the shirts.' Abdulaziz says he feels an 'obligation' to follow Palestino and help find new fans for the club, particularly in Arab-speaking countries. 'They carry a noble message, and it has to be known to everyone around the world.'

As well as its role in Chilean football, Palestino has also played an important part in providing personnel for the Palestine national team which joined FIFA in 1998. In 2014, the team won the AFC Challenge Cup, a tournament for 'emerging countries' in the Asian Football Confederation, beating the Philippines 1–0 in the final. Palestine won their first game in the full AFC Asian Cup in January 2024, beating Hong Kong 3–0 before being knocked out by eventual champions Qatar. 'Although their on-field success has been limited the presence of a Palestinian national team allows [them] to compete and participate like any other country,' says author Glen Duerr. 'This has helped retain a sense of national identity.'[26] Several 'Chilestinians' have played for Palestine, with three former players from the Chilean club involved in qualifying for the AFC Asian Cup including Camilo Saldaña, the starting left-back in that knockout defeat against Qatar, who comes from Santiago's Palestinian community.

Modern borders have not changed often since the end of the Second World War and the decolonisation process that followed. Since then the international community has only recognised major border changes 'in response to extraordinary events, like the collapse of Yugoslavia and the Soviet Union or decades of violence as in Eritrea and South Sudan,' note academics Hagen and Diener.[27] Everyone has a different definition of extraordinary events, but as for the two borders described in this chapter, while they may change in the very long term, a continuation of an uneasy status quo seems more likely.

International football by its very nature gives a sporting dimension to the politics of borders, which are often more durable than they first appear. In Ukraine, Russian aggression is attempting to move a border westwards causing havoc for the country's football teams competing at Europe's highest level. In Northern Ireland, a fragile peace based on compromise means a border remains and is an ever present issue in the Old Firm derby. In Chile, an ethnic group upset by the creation of a border in 1948 sees football as a way to showcase their identity and support for the Palestinian cause.

11

FINANCIAL TIMES

Beşiktaş J.K. & Australia Women's Training Shirt

'My Twitter Space is about to go live to discuss my NFT project. Despite the critics, my NFTs will be the first ever that can't lose their initial value.'

Michael Owen, May 2022

'Meet me at the eagle.' Those were the instructions I was following on a late morning in January 2023 in the Beşiktaş suburb of Istanbul. Football fans will know Beşiktaş as one of the city's 'Big Three' clubs alongside Galatasaray and Fenerbahçe, a regular in European competitions and an active contributor to Turkey's fiery football culture. The eagle is the neighbourhood's symbol and an eagle statue a prominent landmark in the crowded streets not too far away from the club's stadium. The 43,000-seater arena sits beside the Dolmabahçe Palace which was once the administrative centre of the Ottoman Empire. A century ago the modern state of Turkey was built from the ashes of empire by militant secularist Mustafa Kemal Atatürk. His portrait is never far away wherever you are in Turkey. Politics is ever present in Turkish football too. Beşiktaş fans see themselves as the club of the common people of Istanbul as opposed to the elites of Galatasaray and Fenerbahçe. Beşiktaş' main fan group, the Çarşı, played a major role in anti-government protests in Istanbul's Gezi Park in 2013. More recently the group vocally opposed the Passolig, Turkey's controversial ID requirement for match-going fans.

But I wasn't in Istanbul to report on Beşiktaş or Turkish football specifically. I was here because I had finally secured a meeting – a meeting at the eagle – with an interviewee I had been searching for over the course of two years of reporting on football's grubby relationship with cryptocurrency. I had spent countless hours investigating how and why so many top athletes and teams had accepted money in exchange for promoting bizarre digital tokens which were liable to plunge in value, leaving ordinary football fans holding the bag. There were real human victims in this confusing world of charts, numbers and technological jargon, but finding them was hard. Finally, though, in this continent-straddling city, I was meeting one. Unfamiliar with Istanbul I was early for my meeting at the eagle. With time to spare, I walked to the Beşiktaş club shop and passed adverts for Bitci, a cryptocurrency exchange. I popped inside the shop and looked at the various bits of black-and-white merchandise – mugs, dog collars, golf balls. There was also a wall of football shirts. Like Newcastle United, the club play in vertical black-and-white stripes made by Adidas. The Beşiktaş badge features these same vertical stripes as well as the red-and-white crescent and star that features on the flag of Turkey, and the club's founding year of 1903. The sponsor, though, was one I had never heard of: Rain. It turned out to be another cryptocurrency exchange. This stuff was everywhere in Turkey.

For most of human history there was little 'finance' to speak of. Most people grew what they ate and ate what they grew, acquiring other goods and services through barter: 'Here's one of my sheep.

I'd like four bushels of wheat in return please.' Finding a seller who wants exactly what you have can be difficult, so money emerged as an intermediary. Empires and nations borrowed money in pursuit of their ambitions and often ran into trouble, with financial crises a key factor in bringing down the Roman Empire and others that came after.

Banks have had a long history – stashing away your gold coins somewhere safe in exchange for a paper note – but finance was far more peripheral to most people's lives than it is now. An innovation that would change everything came in the Netherlands in the 1600s. Dutch bankers figured out that so long as everyone didn't ask for their money back at the same time, banks could lend out far more money than they held in deposits, effectively creating money out of thin air. This idea, fractional reserve banking, is the foundation of modern finance.

Around 1700, things started changing more quickly. Finance was a key driver of the Industrial Revolution. People became more productive, able to do more with less such as using fertiliser and equipment to grow more food on a finite patch of land. 'Society became increasingly complex at an accelerated rate,' writes Bob Swarup in *Money Mania*, a history of financial crises.[1] 'As interactions between people as well as demand grew, money flowed into the system in response. It fuelled innovation and productivity increased dramatically.' This helped the industrialised world become far richer than before, though not without misery for lots of people living through this change, from those exploited in the colonies that provided raw materials to those labouring in terrible working conditions in Europe. Overall, though, the economic pie kept getting bigger.

'Finance' can be broadly understood as changing the time horizons of money, such as saving what you earn today for tomorrow, or spending now what you expect to earn in the future. This can mean all sorts of complicated things but also includes putting money into a piggybank, spending on a credit card, or buying a house with a mortgage. These days the word finance brings to mind pinstriped bankers, or perhaps gilet-wearing tech bros, but it is only the phenomenally wealthy who can afford to live completely without finance which gives us the ability to live comfortably without paying for everything in one go. It has brought us many benefits but can also be a dangerous beast. 'One may see the transition as akin to the transition from an oxcart to a car,' writes Bob Swarup. 'The latter will get you to where you want to go much faster, but it also has far more moving parts that can break down unexpectedly. However, that is a compromise we make willingly every time because we value the added benefits.'[2]

In the last few decades, finance has become more and more complex. The global recession of the late 2000s was triggered by American 'subprime' mortgages. These mortgages were packaged up into new financial products in ways so convoluted that even those trading them had little idea what they were. Ultimately, they were house loans that people couldn't afford to pay back. Banks were holding so little actual cash that they were unable to weather a storm and ended up needing government bailouts. The fallout would ripple around the world for years to come. 'Since the 1980s, financial activities and assets have played an increasingly dominant role in the global economy,' argues Hung Tran, a senior fellow at the Atlantic Council think tank. 'At the same time, underlying economic activity as measured by global GDP has been growing more slowly. The result has been an ever-larger gap between the volume and value of financial activity relative to the real economy. And that gap has left economies more susceptible to financial instability and crisis and more dependent on fiscal and monetary support from governments.'³ We live in financial times, and they have left their mark on football.

To understand why banks and other finance firms are attracted to sponsoring football, it helps to recap what these companies do. Big banks make money in two main ways. First, by offering bank accounts to retail customers, who are then offered profit-making products like mortgages and loans. Second, investment banking attempts to put cash in places where it will generate a return. It is, of course, all much more complicated than that, but those are the basics. Like all businesses, finance firms want new customers. Finance includes not just banks but also insurance companies such as AIA who sponsor Tottenham Hotspur, and Allianz who sponsor Bayern Munich's stadium. Football is an effective way of finding customers just like advertising in newspapers or on TV. For more than a decade, Liverpool have been sponsored by Standard Chartered, a bank headquartered in London, but which has no high-street presence in the UK. Most of its profits come from Asia, Africa and the Middle East. The bank is big in countries like Egypt, home of Mohamed Salah, Colombia, home of Luis Díaz, and Brazil, home of Roberto Firmino, players who have all starred for Liverpool in recent years.

But banking sponsors are not without controversy. Back in 2003, Newcastle announced a new sponsorship deal with Northern Rock. Like Aston Villa's deal with Rover cars at a similar time, this was seen as a wholesome relationship with a strong local brand – Northern Rock's roots go back to two English building societies founded in Newcastle in the mid-nineteenth century. But the bank no longer exists and its name is forever associated with the global financial crisis. In September 2007, it got into trouble thanks to the knock-on effects of the subprime mortgage crisis in the US. It was eventually bailed out by the UK government before being taken over by Virgin Money, which briefly replaced Northern Rock on the front of Newcastle's shirts in the 2011–12 season. Senegalese forward Papiss Cissé was wearing its logo when he scored one of the all-time great Premier League goals, a sensational curving volley against Chelsea. Northern Rock was the trigger for a wider financial meltdown which hit the UK's economy in the long term, kicking off a decade-and-a-half of stagnant wage growth. (Later on, Newcastle would have a more controversial financial sponsor in Wonga, a company offering payday loans – money lent at a very high interest rate – that has been heavily criticised by politicians and campaigners for alleged predatory lending.) Incidentally, my own team's recent improvement in fortune owes a little to the subprime mortgage crisis. In the aftermath of the collapse an American financier called Wesley Edens hoovered up lots of US property at bargain basement rates and, according to the *Wall Street Journal*, flipped a $124 million investment into $3 billion.[4] In 2018, he became co-owner of Aston Villa alongside Egyptian billionaire Nassef Sawiris, the two pumping huge sums of money into a club that was in a dire state, sparking Villa's renaissance.

A more niche example of a finance company in football relates to a training kit sponsorship deal involving the Australian women's national team, which is conventional in one sense, highly unconventional in another.

National team shirts themselves are never sponsored. This is not through any lofty anti-corporate ideals. Quite the opposite in fact. It's because FIFA and UEFA do not want sponsors competing with their own. Although shirts go sponsor-free, almost everything else in international football has a corporate logo slapped onto it, from training gear to the boards that managers speak in front of during pre-tournament press conferences. But Australians take this a step further than other countries, helped by their penchant for giving their sports teams nicknames. The men's rugby team are the Wallabies, the men's football team the Socceroos, and the women's team are the Matildas, named after 'Waltzing Matilda', the iconic 'bush ballad' that has become an unofficial national anthem.

Soccer in Australia has experienced a similar trajectory to the game in the US, albeit on a smaller scale. It is one of the few other countries to call the sport 'soccer' because of the popularity of Australian rules football, known simply as football. For a long time, soccer in Australia lagged far behind other sports, including rugby union and cricket. There has been little to shout about on a national scale for the men's team, apart from achieving the biggest victory in the history of international football with a 31–0 win over lowly American Samoa in 2001. The 1974 World Cup was Australia's only appearance in the finals until 2006 but since then the Socceroos have qualified for every tournament, reaching the knockout stage on two occasions. Both times they were unfortunate to draw the eventual champions in the round of 16, Italy in 2006 and Argentina in 2022, with both defeats coming by a single goal.

The women's side, spurred on by their talismanic captain Sam Kerr, surprised many by reaching the World Cup semi-final on home soil in 2023 in a tournament widely seen as a big success for the women's game around the world. The Matildas are sponsored by the Commonwealth Bank of Australia, known as CommBank, whose logo is visible on the players' training shirts as well as on stadium billboards when the team is playing – our second shirt for this chapter alongside Beşiktaş.

The bank has sponsored Australian women's football for a while. It was a major sponsor of the 2023 World Cup, a deal that was especially appreciated following the dramatic ditching of Visit Saudi as a sponsor just before the tournament began. What was unusual about CommBank's sponsorship announcement in November 2022 was that it went beyond sponsoring training kits. CommBank would sponsor the team's very name and from then on the national side would be the 'CommBank Matildas', the team referring to itself as this in official media channels.[5] From afar, this feels like the ultimate commodification of football. Almost everything that could be sold – billboards, shirt space, stadium names – had already been sold off, but a team's actual name feels like one of the few things left unsullied. It is not unknown for club teams to adopt the name of a sponsor, the obvious example being Red Bull, which own teams in Salzburg, Leipzig and New York – although this is somewhat different because the company directly founded those clubs rather than the relationship being a commercial association that came along later. (The German side are called RB Leipzig, not Red Bull, to get around league rules on corporate naming.)

I asked ABC Sport journalist Samantha Lewis about all this. 'Perhaps one reason why it's more common for Australia's football teams is that the sport has traditionally struggled to secure major commercial funding compared to other sports, so that has perhaps made football's decision-makers more flexible when it comes to agreeing to this kind of advertising,' she told me, explaining that the women's national team previously had a deal with a shopping chain and was known as the Westfield Matildas at the same time that the top-flight women's league was known as the Westfield W-League. 'Nobody really batted an eyelid. If anything, people were excited by the arrival of CommBank, partly because Westfield had begun to noticeably reduce its investment in women's football, but also because CommBank already had a long history of supporting women's sport in Australia, primarily as the major financial backer of our national women's cricket teams, who became the best in the world thanks to their ongoing investment.' The bank dedicated money to grassroots schemes, just like Barclays bank – another mainstream financial sponsor – has done by sponsoring the Women's Super League in England.

It is perhaps unfair to go too hard on the Matildas for opting for a sponsorship deal with a high-street bank. This is a vanilla choice of partner compared to many other sponsorship deals mentioned in this book. Although this sort of naming arrangement is peculiar in football, it is not unheard of. Serbian team OFK Beograd, who were promoted to the top flight in 2024, adopted the name 'OFK Beograd Mozzart Bet' after signing a deal with a gambling website. These deals are more common in other sports. The England women's netball team is officially known as the Vitality Roses after a deal with the British health insurance company which also has a longstanding relationship with Premier League regulars AFC Bournemouth, who play at the Vitality Stadium. The Pakistan men's national cricket team is officially known as 'Pepsi Pakistan', while in South African club rugby, you can watch the DHL Stormers take on the Hollywoodbets Sharks. Of course, while commentators and media outlets may be mandated to use these official sponsored names, fans often do not do so in casual discourse, but the company name still gets a lot of publicity.

It is also hard to be too critical of sponsorship deals in women's football which is often starved of cash relative to the men's game. Many people involved in the women's game in England, and not only those on the commercial side, have credited the Barclays deal, signed in 2019, as helping supercharge the game in the country by giving it its first substantial injection of cash after decades in the wilderness.[6]

One of the most comprehensive sponsorship agreements in world football is between a club and a finance company: American Express's deal with Brighton & Hove Albion, which includes shirt sponsorship but goes far beyond just that. The club spent most of its history in relative obscurity in England's lower leagues, lacking a proper home stadium for fourteen years. In 2010, while on the verge of being promoted to England's second tier, the club was building a new stadium in Falmer on the city's outskirts and sold the naming rights. It would be known as the American Express Community Stadium when it opened the following year. Alongside the Emirates and the Etihad, 'the Amex' is now known as a geographical destination by its corporate name, a branding deal that seeps beyond sport and into the subconscious. This period has coincided with the best years in Brighton's history. It has almost become a cliché to say how well run the club is, developing a habit of unearthing gems at low prices, such as Ecuador's Moisés Caicedo and Spain's Marc Cucurella, before selling them on to other clubs at vast profit – often Chelsea – and reinvesting the proceeds wisely into new talent. Having an owner in boyhood fan Tony Bloom, who has been willing to lend hundreds of millions to the club in interest-free loans, is helpful too, many other clubs have spent more and achieved less. At the end of the 2022–23 season the club qualified for European football for the first time by finishing sixth in the Premier League.

A key part of Brighton being well run has been its long-running deal with American Express, renewed in 2019 for £100 million ($125 million) spread over twelve years, a huge sum for a club with little top-level pedigree.[7] Like all sponsorship deals that work well, the credit card company and the club have ties which go beyond one shirt deal; American Express has its UK headquarters in the south-coast city. Brighton's relationship with American Express appeared in an article I wrote for *The Athletic*, later cited in Parliament, which listed all the sponsorship deals that top-flight clubs had signed with cryptocurrency companies.[8] The article explained how lots of clubs had promoted speculative investments which had plunged in value. It turned out that every single club in the league had advertised a cryptocurrency product to fans which had crashed – apart from Brighton.

I first began learning about cryptocurrency in late 2020. I was studying for a part-time master's degree at Oxford University's Internet Institute, riding empty trains back and forth between London and Oxford to attend classes before the UK locked down completely and I was forced to study from home. Before immersing myself in studying the internet I had, of course, heard of Bitcoin, the mysterious virtual currency launched in 2008. I knew it had made a small number of people rich in ways I didn't fully understand but knew little beyond that. At that time, I was working for *The Athletic*, investigating the murky world of gambling in Asia, particularly in China, and how all this links back to Premier League football. Cryptocurrency kept cropping up in my research.[9] It turns out crypto, a new, digital form of money, is popular in China as a way of getting around the country's onerous gambling restrictions. It is also a way to avoid capital controls – the Chinese state limits citizens from moving more than $50,000 out of the country. Cryptocurrency is one of the ways for the wealthy to circumvent this.[10]

It is not necessary to know exactly how the technology behind cryptocurrency works to understand its wider impact, just as it's possible to have a good understanding of how Facebook, YouTube and TikTok are upending society without being able to read the lines of computer code that dictate all that. Essentially, cryptocurrencies are financial assets that can be bought and sold like stocks or bonds, but exist only in the digital world. Bitcoin was the first, but there are tens of thousands of others. The concept of digital money is a familiar one. We are all used to making payments on our phones or computers, money is transferred from one bank account to another without the need for tellers to move around gold coins or sacks of banknotes. The difference between cryptocurrency and conventional money, says technology journalist Geoff White, is the *authority* that sits behind the transaction. 'In the case of a bank or a shop dealing in traditional (so-called fiat) money, there is an army of employees running the computer systems and checking that transactions have really happened. If it goes wrong, you can complain to the bank or shop. If it goes very wrong, you can complain to the police. You could use the courts to try and sue for your money. And, of course, the ultimate guarantor of this fiat money is the government, so they have a hand in making sure it's stable and well regulated. In other words, traditional currency is under-girded by layer upon layer of officialdom.'[11]

With cryptocurrency there is no such tedious bureaucracy. Its lack of official middlemen means transactions can be anonymous, making cryptocurrency popular with criminals. Bitcoin first hit popularity as a method to buy drugs and other illegal items on the 'dark web' and cryptocurrency is popular for crime on a grander scale too. It is useful to money launderers, terrorist financers and gun-runners. Crypto can work in the absence of central authority because of a technology called blockchain which was invented in 2008 by the mysterious 'Satoshi Nakamoto'. A blockchain is a vast string of code called a 'distributed ledger'. 'Distributed' means it is public, and everyone can see it, and 'ledger' means a list of transactions. It is a 'chain' because each 'block' is added to the last – that is, it can be written to, but not deleted from. This means all transactions can be listed without anyone scrubbing them out later. For instance, if I have sent you $100, you can be confident I haven't sent that $100 to someone else as well, without the need for a bank in the middle to confirm this. Though the strings of numbers and letters recording these transactions are public, it is much harder to match the strings of numbers and letters to the humans behind it.

Cryptocurrency can be used for payment in this way, but the term 'currency' is misleading as it is not especially useful as a method of buying and selling things. The first reason is that the most common blockchains can only process a handful of transactions per second, while payment services like Visa and Mastercard can process thousands. Secondly, it is useless as an everyday currency because its price is so volatile. Conventional currencies like pounds, dollars and euros vary in value gradually over time but Bitcoin is far more volatile. A Bitcoin was worth a few dollars at first and you can watch YouTube videos of technology journalists in the early 2010s buying pizzas with a few Bitcoins, which would now be worth hundreds of thousands of dollars. After many years of gradual and uneven increases and rapid falls, one Bitcoin hit a value of $69,000 in November 2021. The total value of cryptocurrency worldwide had swelled to $3 trillion, ten times higher than the summer before. It then almost immediately crashed to half this. It rose again, passing $100,000 in the aftermath of the November 2024 election win by Donald Trump, who was perceived as friendly to the industry. All other cryptocurrencies follow similarly wild swings although plenty of less well-known tokens, often the ones promoted by footballers, have crashed to zero and never bounced back. With the value of cryptocurrencies changing daily, they are useless as a means of buying and selling everyday goods and services, unless secrecy is more important to you than all this fluctuation and hassle.

Rather than functioning as a currency, Bitcoin and other cryptocurrencies function chiefly as a *financial asset* – something to be bought now and sold later with the hope of making money. To some people, holding onto crypto has earned them a lot of money, especially those who were early adopters. Many others have lost out, especially those who got in late, perhaps when they heard about a crypto scheme on a footballer's social media feed. Importantly, the technology is 'zero sum' – every Bitcoin sold at the peak above $100,000 was bought by someone for the same amount. No tangible value is created at any point. Unlike the real economic growth that finance helped bring about during the Industrial Revolution, cryptocurrency is just numbers moving back and forth between people – fake internet money in exchange for real money.

Alongside Bitcoin, there are thousands and thousands of other coins or 'tokens'. Creating a new one on a new blockchain is relatively straightforward. Examples have included Dogecoin, a meme based on a cartoon picture of a dog boosted by Elon Musk that appeared on the sleeves of Watford FC during the 2021–22 Premier League season, while Floki, a bizarre cartoon Viking cryptocurrency, appeared on the sleeves of Napoli in Italy as well as Bayer Leverkusen in Germany and Nottingham Forest in England. Hilarious, if you're into that sort of thing.

From 2020 onwards, I have been documenting how football has been flooded by crypto-related promotions. These often take the form of non-fungible tokens or NFTs, which operate on similar principles to cryptocurrency and involve blockchain technology. Pounds, dollars or Bitcoins are 'fungible', which means my dollar bill can be swapped for your dollar bill or one Bitcoin for another

Bitcoin. They all represent the same value. One specific pound coin is not important compared to another pound coin. Non-fungible tokens do not work like this. Each has a unique identifying code. When the NFT hype began, this was cited as a method of bringing sporting collectibles into the digital world. NFTs are often attached to photos or images, the technology supposedly gives a provable uniqueness, meaning that although a photo of Cristiano Ronaldo or the Bernabéu Stadium may also exist on Google Images, the NFT of that photo is attached to a code demonstrating it is one of a kind or part of a small collection. To their advocates, they function a bit like rare sporting memorabilia, such as playing cards or rare shirts; only one numbered version can exist, making them valuable. Or so the story goes.

If you think you may have spotted a potential flaw in this, congratulations. A digital image can be instantly copied, pasted and sent around the world in seconds, unlike a physical matchday programme or a painting. The NFT works somewhat like a receipt – a string of numbers and letters that is associated with a purchase but has no tangible value on its own. Bizarrely, the most valuable NFTs often took the form of cartoon animals. Footballers and other celebrities became useful to those selling cryptocurrency and NFTs in generating hype for their weird products, one example being 'Bored Apes', NFTs which routinely changed hands for hundreds of thousands of dollars at the peak of the NFT craze in 2021. A grimly fascinating exchange between actress Paris Hilton and talk show host Jimmy Fallon saw the pair discuss their own 'apes' on national television, flaunting their cartoon monkeys supposedly worth hundreds of thousands of dollars.[12] Fun and games to people who can afford to lose that sum, and may not have even paid for their own apes, but less fun when advertised to the masses as a potential investment.

I became fascinated by all this and broke dozens of stories about NFTs promoted by footballers. I concluded that the whole thing was nonsense upon stilts, fake internet money designed to funnel cash from poor people to rich people. These schemes would often use whizzy buzzwords like 'metaverse' and 'web3', jargon designed to give these products an allure of something futuristic and exciting, rather than what it was: meaningless financial speculation.

The reason crypto money poured into football in 2021 and 2022 has a simple explanation which I understood following a conversation with Matt Slater, my former colleague at *The Athletic* and one of the best-connected journalists in football. A contact had given him a pithy reason why crypto firms were suddenly pouring money into football sponsorships: it is the cheapest way of advertising to young men. One study found that almost half of American males aged between eighteen and twenty-nine had owned or traded some form of crypto.[13] This demographic group, more inclined to financial risk than others, are often tricky for advertisers to reach, but one thing many of them do enjoy is live sport. Their eyeballs can be reached through advertising on the sleeves of a Premier League club or the commercials during an NFL game. Products can also be advertised via the social media feeds of famous players themselves.

One scheme I reported on involved former England and Chelsea star John Terry. After setting himself up on Twitter in December 2021, he quickly began sharing a bizarre scheme calling itself 'Ape Kids Football Club' with his new followers. This involved buying and selling virtual baby monkeys in the form of NFTs, an odd fit for one of football's hard men. I immersed myself in the details and a few months later broke the story that the tokens had lost around 90 per cent of their value within a few weeks, a figure that would soon be more like 98 per cent.[14] A person buying a token for

$1,000 at the time Terry was promoting them would now be able to sell it for around $20, if they could sell it at all.¹⁵ Terry never responded to my requests for comment, aside from blocking me on social media.

Another bleak example involved Michael Owen, the former Liverpool and England striker responsible for my first proper football memory with his sensational individual goal against Argentina at the 1998 World Cup at the age of just seventeen, which led to an irritating number of English people my age supporting Liverpool despite having no connection to the place. Owen promoted NFTs while making the bizarre claim that they would be 'the first ever that can't lose their initial value'. What this meant was that the NFTs could not be sold *at a loss*, effectively meaning if they plunged in value, which, naturally they did, holders would simply be unable to sell them at all.¹⁶ It would be like buying a house with the condition you could not make a loss on it. If there was a market downturn in which your only chance of a sale was losing a little on your initial purchase price, a contract would ban you from selling it. The difference in this analogy is that you would be stuck with a house you could live in, rather than a picture of Michael Owen that you can copy and paste for free on Google Images. He was later told to delete it by the UK's advertising watchdog and, separately, was later found to have broken UK laws by promoting another unlicensed cryptocurrency product.¹⁷

It was not only English players shilling these dubious schemes. Footballers and clubs around the world were making money from promoting crypto products to their unwitting fans. Alongside my own reporting on this, the journalist Martin Calladine has done brilliant work exposing countless schemes, documented in his excellent book *No Questions Asked*.

Over time, I concluded this stuff was the emperor's new clothes.

No level of cynicism is enough. Cryptocurrency tokens are just a meaningless vehicle for speculation. NFTs are not 'collectibles' and have no inherent value. This might seem obvious with the benefit of hindsight, but this was not the case at the time. I copped a lot of flak for criticising football cryptocurrency schemes on social media. Around this time I also attended a few sports business conferences, glitzy affairs where the food and wine flows freely and corporate attendees pay north of $1,000 a ticket, listening to executives talk about how best to 'monetise' fans. These things can be useful as a journalist, but felt far removed from the game I grew up loving. In 2021 and 2022, such events were full of people talking up NFTs and blockchain technology as things that would revolutionise sport through 'fan engagement'. I made few friends in this world by repeatedly calling it all out for what it was – a load of rubbish, shrouded in technobabble to try to throw people off the scent. NFTs and cryptocurrency products funnel money from poor people who are hoping to make money, to rich people who already have it.

In my reporting on this issue, I charted the rise and fall of countless coins and tokens, demonstrating that huge sums had been lost in schemes promoted by figures in the world of football, cash vanishing from people's pockets into the digital ether, likely hoovered up by a small number of vultures. Journalists always want to find the human impact of the issues they cover, elevating abstract numbers and charts into stories that engage readers. I had exchanged DMs with dozens of football crypto victims but most were reluctant to speak out. This was understandable. 'I can't tell my wife I've lost hundreds of pounds on this,' one told me. Another joked that if a relative queried him about the strange transactions on his bank statement, he would lie that they were for pornography. Far less embarrassing.

My conversations would usually go the same way. I would find someone on social media, usually Twitter/X, who was complaining about a particular cryptocurrency scheme that had lost them money, and I would message them. The person would almost always be anonymous, their username often a string of letters and numbers and their picture a default grey silhouette or something else, like a picture of a footballer or a cartoon character, perhaps even a Bored Ape. I once had a lengthy and highly technical discussion with a cartoon koi carp.

One day, though, I began talking to someone who seemed different. His username was Bernat Kurnaz, which seemed a real name, and his profile picture was a selfie – a Turkish man wearing sunglasses. We chatted over many weeks. He was happy to share his story, having no issue with me quoting him and using his name. What he told me was fascinating. I felt it was such an important story to tell that I managed to persuade my editor to let me fly to Turkey to hear his story in person, tying it in with a trip to the southern city of Antalya where I reported on how Russian clubs were playing friendlies against Serbian clubs in Turkey despite UEFA sanctions imposed following Putin's invasion of Ukraine. In the Istanbul suburb of Beşiktaş, a short walk from the eagle statue, we met in a cafe where it was warm enough to sit outside in January and drink black coffee. What he told me was horrifying.

A little more than a year before our meeting in Istanbul the cousin of Bernat Kurnaz had approached him with an unusual money-making scheme which he had heard about via the social media feeds of Paul Pogba. The midfielder, then playing for Manchester United, was a World Cup winner with France in 2018 and one of the world's most-followed footballers on social media. In November 2021 he made an unusual post. 'I am happy to announce that I'm partnering with a phenomenon, a project called

CryptoDragons,' said Pogba in a selfie video, which looked like he was relaxing at home rather than participating in a professional shoot. '[CryptoDragons] set the world record by selling an NFT for 35 Ethereum for primary sale in less than 10 seconds. This is huge.'[18] This essentially means that an NFT – a picture of a cartoon dragon with an electronic receipt attached – had been sold for an amount of Ethereum, a cryptocurrency like Bitcoin, worth around $162,000 at the time. Kurnaz told me the post appeared in his feed the same week that the Bitcoin price peaked before a dramatic crash. At the time there was huge hype that this strange virtual world was a place to make truckloads of cash. To Kurnaz and his cousin it sounded like an opportunity. If they could buy a CryptoDragon now for $2,000, they could potentially sell it for hundreds of thousands of dollars in the future, life-changing money in Turkey at a time of economic turmoil. The economic situation was the very reason cryptocurrency was so popular in the country. The Turkish lira was collapsing in value, meaning investments promising high returns were attractive, not to get rich but simply to stand still and maintain living standards, holding off the scourge of inflation. Cryptocurrency sponsorship was everywhere in Turkish football at the time, including on one of this chapter's two shirts: Beşiktaş's black-and-white home shirt sponsored by Rain, a Bahrain-based exchange which claims to be serving Turkey and the Middle East. As well as Turkey, with its inflation problem, I noticed many cryptocurrency victims were from Brazil and Vietnam, countries with similar economic issues. On one occasion I exchanged Instagram messages with Huy, a Vietnamese student who lost around $1,200 buying the nonsense 'Mini Football' token, which had been promoted by many top footballers, including Romelu Lukaku, Ivan Rakitić and Ronaldinho.[19]

You can probably now guess how Bernat Kurnaz's story ends.

MORE THAN A SHIRT

When he heard about CryptoDragons he was earning $600 a month as a courier and did not have $2,000 to 'invest'. So, he borrowed this sum from the bank, signed up to various apps to obtain the Ethereum cryptocurrency necessary to buy the NFT, and bought one. It did not explode in value and make him rich. The opposite happened. The amount of money traded on CryptoDragons fell from almost $50,000 per day when it launched, to virtually nothing a few months later. Pogba never tweeted about it again.[20] His representatives did not respond to requests for comment.

Kurnaz was left devastated. Where you live in the world will determine how big a sum $2,000 sounds; to a bike courier in Turkey, it is life-changing. I reached out to Kurnaz eighteen months later and most of his $600 monthly income was still going on interest payments. It will take him years to clear the debt. Kurnaz used to enjoy going out for drinks with his friends and taking the occasional trip to the coast on the motorbike he uses for his job but he was left unable to afford any of these simple pleasures. He was just working all the time to pay his debts, any downtime spent staying home and playing video games. 'The main reason we invested was Pogba,' said Kurnaz. 'It wasn't like someone was impersonating him online. He actually did videos for it. We thought he must know the people doing this. This must be legit.'

I spoke to other investors who preferred not to give their names but told me that much the same thing had happened to them. An American man I spoke to bought more than $10,000 worth of CryptoDragons jointly with his two brothers. The 'investment' became worthless. This man also cited Pogba's endorsement as a reason why he thought the scheme was legit. 'The main reason we invested was that Pogba is on there. He gave them validity. There is this guy who everyone knows who is famous and has a lot of influence and he is backing this project.' It may seem obvious with hindsight that this was all rubbish, but that doesn't lessen the human impact on people desperate to make a tiny fraction of the sum a top footballer earns in a week. Similar to Football Index, a particularly painful aspect of all this is the family connections between some of those who were persuaded to lose money, but Kurnaz does not resent his cousin. 'He warned me. He told me there are some risks, but I took the risk.'

This money did not vanish into thin air. It was sent from Kurnaz's bank account to someone else's. There is no reason to think Pogba personally profited from the scheme, and this is generally the case for footballers who promoted cryptocurrency products. The reasons they did were often more prosaic. Some get paid to do a promotional deal without understanding what they are doing. Others simply find it exciting in the same way someone with more limited means might buy a lottery scratchcard – you'll probably lose a small fraction of your income, but, hey, you might win lots! Others get asked to do it. I once spoke to the agent of a high-profile footballer who told me his client had recorded an endorsement for a scam crypto scheme because his teammate had asked him to do so on the long coach ride home from an away game.

I tried to trace CryptoDragons back to its foundations. The scheme's Twitter account repeatedly referred to a woman called Nari as the project's co-founder, and her location was listed as Canada. Interviews with her were once available on YouTube but have now been deleted. It is hard to know if she was truly responsible or merely a front person for others. Pogba, though, and the many other footballers to have promoted these schemes, bear responsibility as well. Some of the richest sports stars on the planet have been directly responsible for shilling nonsense products, inflicting genuine harm on people who can little afford it.

Telling Kurnaz's story shows how the crypto-football trend is not just bizarre but morally bankrupt. Though not every cryptocurrency project is a clear-cut scam like CryptoDragons, it is my firm belief that the whole industry is nonsense and anyone 'making money' from it is simply on the other side of a zero-sum transaction from which someone else is losing out.

Perhaps the most prominent crypto scheme in professional football in recent years has been Socios, which has signed major sponsorship deals with the likes of Barcelona, Juventus and Arsenal. Socios markets itself as a 'fan engagement' company through which fans can buy digital tokens which help them 'engage' in their club, such as by entering competitions or voting in polls, such as deciding what music should be played at half-time. This is relatively benign but all involves buying Socios's own cryptocurrency, Chiliz, which is used to pay for more cryptocurrency, in the form of tokens. The business model of Socios is to create tokens out of thin air, assign them monetary value by associating them with top football teams, and then sell them for real cash. My investigations into the company led me to the understanding that people trade these tokens not because they want to 'engage' in a particular club, but because they think they can make money from them as a crypto investment.[21] I unearthed confidential documents which Socios was using to pitch to football clubs, saying the average sum spent on tokens was £150 per user – a huge sum of money more consistent with an investment product than with 'fan engagement'.[22] I have repeatedly called this company out yet still it maintains a prominent position in a sport which is hungry for cash to pay ever-growing player wages. It signed up Lionel Messi as a paid ambassador. My research found lots of these tokens were being traded in places like Turkey where people became attracted to cryptocurrency investments because of the collapsing domestic currency. To be clear, there is no suggestion Socios has ever been involved in some of the fraudulent behaviour mentioned in this chapter. But I am extremely sceptical that it provides any value to football fans.

In December 2022, I was asked to speak in Parliament about cryptocurrency in sport in front of the Treasury Select Committee, an influential group of MPs. I would also speak to the Culture, Media and Sport Committee a few months later to talk about my reporting on Football Index. It is a fun thing to do putting on a suit and walking past police officers wielding machine guns into the vast atrium of Portcullis House, attempting to recognise politicians from afar before being guided into a large meeting room to be grilled by a bank of MPs, with the proceedings broadcast online. Addressing the MPs, I dismissed the idea that 'digital collectibles' were anything other than a speculative financial asset. From fan engagement tokens to monkeys in the metaverse, I said this was not about 'bad apples' in the cryptocurrency sector, but the result of a whole industry geared arounds selling people volatile financial assets while pretending they were in the business of 'technological innovation':

> Why do people buy (cryptocurrency tokens)? People buy them because they have heard stories about people who live on an island now because of some crypto investment four years ago – which did happen. These graphs went up before they went down. People buy them with the expectation of high returns. . . . Of course, these products will never say this to you. They will never say on the outside 'This is a financial investment that will go up', because that, of course, is very strictly regulated. They have stories to tell you. They will say, 'This is a piece of art. This is an exciting voyage into

the metaverse in six months' time' and 'There is a road map'. There are some very famous footballers who sold pictures of cartoon monkeys for hundreds of pounds, pictures that you could copy, paste and save on your computer for free, or you could pay £1,000 to a link posted by a very famous footballer.[23]

In Beşiktaş before I said goodbye to Kurnaz, he let me take his photo in front of the eagle and confirmed I could use his name and quote every word he told me. After we parted ways, he followed up with a message repeating his offer of assistance. 'I want to help people. There's nothing shameful about it. I just did it. That's what's happened to me.' Rather than being angry at the scammers he was fatalistic about the unfair world he lived in, an attitude I have often come across in people who lose money on cryptocurrency. Asked if he would like to send a message via the pages of *The Athletic* to Pogba and those ultimately behind CryptoDragons, he demurred. 'It doesn't mean anything. You can't do anything. In Turkey, it's too easy because people always need easy money. You will try to make easy money, so you lose again. It's the reason poor people are always poor. People always chase easy money.'

Easy money. That's also the title of a book subtitled *Cryptocurrency, Casino Capitalism, and the Golden Age of Fraud* by Ben McKenzie and Jacob Silverman.[24] McKenzie is an actor who shot to fame through his role as Ryan Atwood in US teen drama *The O.C.* I loved it as a teenager. The item of clothing I have owned the longest, even longer than any football shirt, is a brown T-shirt with the show's logo on it which I bought on holiday in California in 2007. It still fits me, just about. McKenzie, who went on to star in other shows such as Batman prequel *Gotham*, has an unusual background for a Hollywood actor. He studied economics before becoming a teen heartthrob, and has used his educational background to become a lonely voice in Hollywood sounding the alarm about celebrity cryptocurrency endorsements.

We struck up an unlikely friendship via Twitter DM, and I met him in November 2022 in the Portuguese capital of Lisbon when we both spoke on panels about cryptocurrency at an event called Web Summit. This huge tech conference was full of crypto evangelists including Italian football legend Alessandro Del Piero who was there promoting Socios tokens. The whole thing felt like stepping into the lion's den. We strolled around the vast conference centre together before McKenzie interviewed me in a side room for his own book, at times politely greeting fans who came up to him asking for selfies, generally women around my age who had been teenage fans of *The O.C.*

McKenzie may have lost friends in Hollywood writing his book which describes an industry 'divided into a few winners and a vast number of losers'. It names many actors who jumped on the crypto bandwagon. A notable example is Matt Damon, one of the highest-grossing actors of all time who in October 2021 announced a sponsorship deal with crypto.com, a cryptocurrency exchange that has poured huge sums into naming deals in sport including Formula One competitions, the home of basketball side the LA Lakers, and Italy's Serie A league. The VAR checks on Italian TV are accompanied by a commentator plug for *'crypto punto com'*. Damon's endorsements look absurd in hindsight. 'Fortune favours the brave,' he proclaimed, dramatically, in front of a space-age backdrop like he was starring in one of his films. Damon was effectively labelling those watching, with far less to lose than him, as wimps if they don't buy cryptocurrency. He says he gave the money to the clean-water charity he co-founded. 'We had a down year . . . I did that commercial in an attempt to raise money,' he later said.²⁵ This is laudable in isolation, but donating money earned by ripping people off rather defeats the purpose of charity. This advert was featured in the so-called 'Crypto Bowl' in early 2022, when the Super Bowl was deluged with crypto ads – the perfect way to find new young male targets.

McKenzie and Silverman write about other celebs who have shilled crypto. 'In addition to Matt Damon, many more movie stars got in on hawking various forms of digital "assets". Gwyneth Paltrow and Reese Witherspoon shilled NFTs, as did musicians Justin Bieber and Steve Aoki. Sports stars LeBron James, Tom Brady, Steph Curry and Aaron Rodgers pitched crypto exchanges and apps as the future of personal finance.'²⁶ Few celebrities faced repercussions. An exception was Kim Kardashian, who failed to declare she had been paid $250,000 to promote a nonsense token called EthereuemMAX, designed solely for speculative purposes, to her 328 million Instagram followers. She was fined $1.26 million by the US Security and Exchange Commission.²⁷ Football has seen plenty of these 'pump and dump' schemes, the values of meaningless assets jacked up through building hype via celebrity endorsements, then sold to dupes, making money for insiders and leaving the little guy 'holding the bag'. The Kardashian example is a rare case of justice being done in this world. While the celebrities who endorsed these products have moved on to other things, the identities of most of the victims will never be known, doubtless many of them people like Bernat Kurnaz who spent money they could little afford to lose in doomed attempts to speculate their way out of grim economic circumstances.

Looking back the whole thing feels obviously ridiculous. Crypto is not like investing in a company, where if the company becomes more successful and makes bigger profits, every shareholder benefits. It is not like investing in property, which gradually over time tends to become worth more as people get richer and there's more money chasing after a limited number of buildings. You can lose lots of money investing in companies or property, of course, but the opportunity for genuine profits is there. In cryptocurrency it is all zero sum. For every winner, there is an equal and opposite loser. The winners tend to be the athletes and actors being paid to promote stuff. The losers are the mugs watching in the cinema or stadium. That does not mean it is not possible to make money from cryptocurrency – a lot of people have profited from owning Bitcoin. But the people buying something promoted by an athlete or celebrity are likely on the wrong side of the trade. Donald Trump's second election win in 2024, after a campaign heavily backed by crypto-evangelist Elon Musk, ushered in a new era of crypto politics. In the campaign, Trump repeatedly talked up the industry and secured the backing of the most powerful people in crypto. He signed an executive order in March 2025 to create a 'strategic Bitcoin reserve' as well as issuing a Trump-branded 'meme coin' which netted hundreds of millions of dollars for the Trump family, according to CNBC.

'When you buy a share of Apple, you are effectively a portion of the revenue stream, as well as the brand equity, market share, intellectual property – all of that. But cryptos don't make stuff or do stuff,' McKenzie and Silverman write. 'The point is that just because a lot of people think that bits of computer code are valuable doesn't mean that they actually are valuable. During bubbles, folks often speculate wildly, hoping to sell a thing they see rising in price to someone else for even more money. In economics, this is called the greater fool theory. The price of an asset becomes uncorrelated with its actual value, and it ends up only being worth what you can convince the next person, the person more foolish than you, to pay for it.'[28]

Two years after meeting McKenzie in Lisbon, I followed up with him to ask for his reflections on cryptocurrency's ties to sport. 'The economics are depressingly simple,' he told me. 'Most of these athletes are paid in real money, dollars, pounds, euros, whatever, to convince these fellas to part with their real money and throw it into the opaque and often fraudulent world of cryptocurrency. These dudes almost always lose that money, but they're consoled by the fact that they've been told they were brave and trendsetting, and not just marks for the taking.'

Throughout my work investigating various football sponsors, I have always tried to strike the balance between criticising companies and bad actors where needs be, while supporting the general concept of sponsorship. Clubs raising cash from sponsors is no bad thing in itself. They essentially have three ways of making money: matchday, commercial and broadcast. If they can increase the commercial share of that pie, it means that in an ideal world they need to squeeze less out of fans on matchday and in TV subscriptions. Of course, it does not always work out like that but, still, money flowing into football from companies is a good thing, and the financial strength of the world's most popular game contributes to it being played and watched in more countries than ever. Still, the Matildas' training kit speaks to a world where more of football than ever is parcelled up and sold to advertisers.

Rain, the cryptocurrency exchange advertised on the shirt of the black-and-white stripes of Beşiktaş, is an example of how this weird digital money became such a big thing in Turkey in the early 2020s. Faced with financial issues of a conventional kind – high inflation, a lack of economic growth – many Turks sought out a risky financial product in their efforts to escape the squeeze. For many of them – like Bernat Kurnaz, the motorcycle courier from

Beşiktaş who took out a bank loan to buy a CryptoDragon promoted by Paul Pogba – this ended terribly. Football's dalliance with cryptocurrency shames many of those who participated in it who have used their platform to solicit money from those who didn't have it and funnelling it into the bank accounts of those who did.

Finance is not inherently bad. Without it, the world may not have seen the Industrial Revolution, which eventually helped billions of people out of the agrarian misery that most people lived in in the centuries before finance. Today, banks and insurance companies play a critical role in spreading risk and helping us to afford things. Finance of a relatively innocuous kind is widespread, from deals like Liverpool's with Standard Chartered, to the unusual deal where Australia's Matildas not only have their training shirts sponsored by CommBank but the name of the bank is incorporated into the team's official name too. The world is more financial than ever and football is too. The game has shifted from a pastime to an industry. The volume of cash flowing through it is getting ever bigger. This means the quality is higher than ever before and the broadcast product is slick and entertaining, but it can also make football feel dislocated from the game we learned to love as children.

POSTSCRIPT

On an industrial estate on the edge of Manchester in England is a warehouse containing one million football shirts. I visited the headquarters of Classic Football Shirts in August 2024, in between my research trips around the world for this book. After being welcomed inside by company staff I was taken for a walk beneath the huge silver roof and between giant aisles of corrugated cardboard, which contain those million shirts neatly folded, wrapped up in cellophane and stacked high into the sky. I tried to identify as many as I could while I walked along, my brain trying to process all the colours and badges before my eyes. I clocked the green and white of Real Betis from the Spanish city of Seville. Then there was the bright red of Jamshedpur FC from the city in eastern India associated with Tata Steel, whose logo is also on the shirt. I then spotted the black and red of Newell's Old Boys from Rosario in northern Argentina, the city that gave the world Lionel Messi. After walking past rows upon rows of shirts, I was shown the part of the warehouse which opens up onto a car park where vans come and go, picking up and dropping off the packages. Almost two-thirds of them were heading outside the UK, with the USA and South Korea the most common overseas destinations.

After the tour I met Doug Bierton who founded the company with two friends in 2006. They were students at the time and began the business by trawling charity-shop bins for shirts which

POSTSCRIPT

they then sold online. Things got bigger and bigger and, in March 2024, a US private equity firm invested $38.5 million in the company. In the lobby of the warehouse we sat on a sofa beside mannequins wearing recent shirts worn by English club Burnley as well as Parma in Italy, both shirts carrying the Classic Football Shirts logo. After years of selling football shirts the company had signed sponsorship deals of its own. I chatted to Bierton, a world expert in the meaning of football shirts, about how this humble garment has taken on new dimensions as both fashion symbol and historical artefact. Wearing one out and about is 'the ultimate ice-breaker', he told me. 'You can start a conversation with anybody. It could make someone instantly your best mate or get you your head kicked in ... Football shirts are very powerful. They can take you on a journey, just like listening to a piece of music.' As a Manchester United fan, his all-time favourite is the red shirt with the Sharp logo on it and a black zipper worn in the 1998–1999 season in which United won the treble. After our conversation, I left the office to catch my train home, walking through a nondescript car park, through the big metal gates, and then past the fish tank shop opposite. All the while vans were rumbling past, carrying football shirts to every corner of the world.

This book is not a warehouse of a million football shirts but is an overflowing drawer containing twenty-two of them, enough for two teams of eleven players. My travels to five different continents have reaffirmed my belief that football shirts can explain the world, giving a window into some of the biggest global issues of our time. First, the Gazprom-sponsored shirts of German club Schalke and Serbian club Red Star Belgrade. The story of Putin's invasion of Ukraine and everything that led up to it could fill thousands of pages. These two shirts are just a footnote to all this, alongside

Gazprom's sponsorship of the UEFA Champions League. But the role of football makes this topic feel a little more tangible than when told through oil statistics or lists of Russian names. Elsewhere in the world, the shirts of Parma and Envigado FC tell us how football and crime are often intertwined. Before carrying the logo of Classic Football Shirts, Parma was sponsored by dairy company Parmalat, but nostalgia for that era is now tempered by memories of one of Europe's biggest ever frauds. In Colombia, football was used by the cartels to launder cash and build the prestige of drug bosses, including one cartel leader whose silhouetted face featured on an actual shirt. These garments are more than just clothing, they are symbols that tell stories of culture, politics, and history.

On to Nottingham Forest in England and FC Goa in India. Football shirts do not merely reflect global forces, they can be an active part of them too. Online gambling is booming around the world and the wider consequences are unpredictable. A key part of this story is football sponsorship, and how obscure companies with opaque back stories have bought up prime real estate on the front of shirts of clubs around the world. One of the biggest global trends of our age is the mass migration from former imperial colonies to Europe and North America, a story told through the shirts of Changing Lives FC and the French national team. As millions around the world cross borders in search of a better life, football is often the only language they carry with them, with migrants washing up in boats frequently wearing the shirts of European teams despite not even speaking European languages.

Next there is Houston Dash and Inter Miami. A few decades ago football was the world's biggest game but could not claim to be loved, or even widely known, in some of the most populated countries. No longer. Like India, the USA is a place where football was once peripheral but things are changing quickly in a country that is unusual and exceptional in so many ways, as demonstrated by a club sponsored by a cancer hospital, to Messi's pink shirt of Inter Miami which may finally have made America a soccer-loving country, neatly coinciding with the 2026 World Cup.

Then there is Spain's big two, Barcelona and Real Madrid, which for two seasons was a direct clash between Middle Eastern airlines, based in Dubai and Qatar. The 2022 World Cup in Qatar changed football forever. Fans will remember the winter tournament for Lionel Messi's triumph in a thrilling final, but the event has been dogged by allegations of corruption and human rights abuses. Qatar's involvement in football went deeper than one tournament, as evidenced by Barcelona's shift from being 'more than a club', with no sponsor, to a team carrying the logo of the state airline of a Middle Eastern autocracy. Football shirts are often co-opted as moving billboards for power struggles playing out thousands of miles away, as oil states strategise for what they will do when the oil and gas run out. Barcelona's great rivals Real Madrid have long been sponsored by another Middle Eastern airline, Emirates of Dubai, alongside many of Europe's other top clubs.

Our next shirt is the green worn by Newcastle United since the club's Saudi Arabian takeover in 2021. This shows how football can be a tool used by oppressive regimes, alongside Saudi Arabia being awarded the 2034 World Cup. Thousands of miles away in South Africa, though, the football shirts worn by Robben Island prisoners tell a more optimistic story of how the game can have the power to bring about democratic change. Modern football can make fans feel weary but the game is so often a force for good – a unifying force and the one thing you are most likely to share with somebody on the other side of the world, with whom you may not share a culture or even language. Football can reinforce oppressive regimes but it can help bring them down too.

The shirt of West Bromwich Albion sponsored by an eco-town in China, and that of Guangzhou Evergrande, sponsored through its golden era by a doomed property company, show how football shirt stories do not all run in the direction of globalisation and deeper understanding between cultures. In the mid-2010s it looked like China was going to be a powerful force in world football but things swung sharply in the other direction. The rise and retreat of Chinese football neatly mirrors the rise and retreat of the country itself from the global stage.

China's retreat is notable because it is rare. Almost everywhere, football is on a relentless march, becoming ever bigger as a cultural force. Nowhere is this truer than when it comes to women's football which was banned in much of the world before its recent resurgence. Mary Earps's goalkeeper shirt, and one worn by Corinthians in Brazil, demonstrate this. This tracks wider shifts in women's rights which, though rocky and uneven, have been getting better around the world. The backlash to Earps's shirt's absence from shops, as well as the purple shirts of Corinthians in a country on women's football's new frontier, shows how the game is expanding at breakneck pace.

On to Rangers and CD Palestino. Football at the international level is defined by borders, those wiggly and confusing lines on maps that can be surprisingly stubborn. Rivalry in football is at its most juicy when there is politics behind it, like in Scotland where hundreds of years of history are distilled into the green shirts of Celtic and the orange away kits that Rangers have worn in recent years. The most contentious border in the modern world, between Israel and Palestine, can be understood through the prism of a shirt worn thousands of miles away in Chile.

Finally, the Matildas and Beşiktaş. Football these days is being upended by not just geopolitics but also the sheer volume of cash washing through it. A hobby has turned into an industry, mirroring broader global trends in which finance is a bigger and bigger part of developed economies. Football reflects this and teams now often carry adverts for financial companies. These range from the conventional, like the Australian women's team's deal with CommBank, to the strange cryptocurrency sponsors that I have spent so much time reporting on, like the one on the shirt of Beşiktaş in Turkey.

These twenty-two examples – a bursting drawer of football shirts – is just a tiny sample of those that can be used to explain the world. I hope this book changes the way you see the world in a small way. I hope that when you go about your life and spot football shirts, you now look at them a little more closely, equipped with the tools to understand things that may not be immediately obvious. Next time you spot a shirt in the wild have a think about exactly what you can see. Take it all in: the badge, the colours, the sponsor. The shirt may be one of the famous ones featured in this book or something more niche, perhaps a team local to you or one from a far-off corner of the world about which you know little. You might see a shirt and not know what team it belongs to at first, but you can always furtively look things up on your phone, or even ask the wearer.

These humble polyester garments contain multitudes. Every shirt tells a story. I hope you have enjoyed reading about a few of them. Good luck discovering more.

ACKNOWLEDGEMENTS

I am proud of this book but couldn't have done it on my own. I am especially grateful to my editor Tierney Witty for helping make the final product so much better than early drafts, for being hugely engaged and encouraging through the whole process, and putting up with the occasional rambling voice note. Thanks also to the rest of the team at Orion Books including Elizabeth Allen, Karin Burnik, Sarah Cook, Jess Hart, Tara Hiatt, Louis Patel, and Paul Stark.

I am also hugely grateful to my literary agent, Matthew Cole for having faith in me, and helping turn a half-baked idea about football sponsorship into this finished product, including helping come up with the device of using football shirts to tell bigger stories. Thanks also to the rest of the team at Northbank Talent.

A lot of people spared time and energy to help me with this book, which is the result of dozens of interviews with people scattered all over the world. Many are named in these pages, but others are not, in some cases because talking to me came with some risk. You know who you are and I am very grateful. Thanks especially to those who helped me on my travels, particularly to Fraser in Colombia.

Much of the reporting in this book was done while I worked for *The Athletic*. I owe a lot to Laura Williamson, my editor for most of that time, and the driving force behind several investigations

ACKNOWLEDGEMENTS

described in these pages. It was Alex Kay-Jelski who convinced me of the idea of going into football investigative reporting, a chat which changed my life. Thanks also to Amitai Winehouse, Luke Brown and Craig Chisnall and many others at *The Athletic* as well.

I changed jobs halfway through writing this book, which could have been tricky, but wasn't. I am very grateful to Tom Calver, my editor at *The Times* and *Sunday Times*, for being hugely supportive of this project. Thanks also to the rest of the data journalism team. Our conversations have given me a new way of looking at things and spared all sorts of interesting thoughts which had an impact on this book. Thanks too to other colleagues at *The Times* and *Sunday Times* for their support as well as others I have worked with in the past, particularly at the BBC where I spent three happy years.

I have always been someone who loves journalism without being completely consumed by it and am grateful to have lots of friends with other interests to keep me sane. This book is the product of many conversations with them, not just about football. Thanks to the Birmingham people, the Oxford people and the London people, among others, you know who you are. A few went above and beyond to provide detailed feedback in advance of this book being published — thanks to Marianna Spring, Dom Gilchrist and Will Hawkins. I have been lucky enough to make friends in the world of football too, and three of them, Miguel Delaney, Adam Crafton and Miles Coleman, gave this a close read and spotted some mistakes. Any that remain are all mine. A special thank you also to Sebastian Leape for the emergency loan of a laptop upon which much of this book was written, as well as Ollie Coombe, Annie Moore, Anuj Wali and Jane Rosenberg for being particularly helpful and engaged, at a crunch time for the book.

Lastly, my family – D'Ursos, Wises, Boyds, Taskers, Newells,

Clarks – and others, incuding Redmond-Greaveses and Greys, for always being supportive and kind. You are all great company. Perhaps you thought I would grow out of wanting to always talk about football all the time once I was well into my thirties. Here's to doubling down.

A special thank you to my brother, Peter, and sister, Lucy, whose company I enjoy more and more the older I get, and my sister-in-law Diana. Thanks to my Mum, Nicola, for always caring, and being supportive of everything I do. Lastly, my Dad, Paul, was the one who first got me interested in football, then politics shortly after that. He has not been with us for a long time now, but he is on every page of this book. Up the Villa!

ENDNOTES

Introduction

1. Ketchell M. The birth of the replica football shirt, 50 years on. FourFourTwo. December 25, 2023.
2. Kalt H. Soccer and Sponsorships. Soccer Politics. The Politics of Football. March 3, 2015.
3. Ibid.
4. Goldblatt D. *The Age of Football: The Global Game in the Twenty-First Century*. Macmillan; 2019.

1. Putin's Wars

1. Thimm K. Culture of Steel: Germany's Ruhr Valley Looks Back to Its Future. *Der Spiegel*. March 5, 2010.
2. Conradi P. *Who Lost Russia?: From the Collapse of the USSR to Putin's War on Ukraine*. Revised edition. Oneworld; 2022.
3. Ibid.
4. Short P. *Putin: His Life and Times*. The Bodley Head; 2022.
5. Ibid.
6. Belton C. *Putin's People: How the KGB Took Back Russia and Then Took on the West*. William Collins paperback edition. William Collins; 2021.
7. DW. Record Bundesliga Deal. DW. September 10, 2006.
8. Conradi P. *Who Lost Russia?: From the Collapse of the USSR to Putin's War on Ukraine*. Revised edition. Oneworld; 2022
9. Blumenau B. Breaking with convention? Zeitenwende and the traditional pillars of German foreign policy. *International Affairs*. 2022;98(6):1895-1913. doi:10.1093/ia/iiac166
10. Bennhold K. The Former Chancellor Who Became Putin's Man in Germany. The Ne York Times. April 23, 2022.

11 Sheahan M & Marsh S. Germany to increase defence spending in response to 'Putin's war' – Scholz. Reuters. February 27, 2022
12 Hummel T et al. The meat magnate who pushed Putin's agenda in Germany. A Reuters Special Report. Reuters. May 31, 2023.
13 Bennhold K. The Former Chancellor Who Became Putin's Man in Germany. The New York Times April 23, 2022.
14 Belton C. Putin's People: How the KGB Took Back Russia and Then Took on the West. William Collins; 2021.
15 Delaney M. States of Play. Seven Dials; 2024.
16 O'Donnell J. & Steiz C. Schroeder throws in towel as German industry clings on to Russian gas. Reuters. May 26, 2022.
17 Hummel T et al. The meat magnate who pushed Putin's agenda in Germany. A Reuters Special Report. Reuters. May 31, 2023.
18 Bennhold K, Solomon E. Shadowy Arm of a German State Helped Russia Finish Nord Stream 2. New York Times. December 2, 2022.
19 Delaney M. Chelsea facing 'totally uncharted territory' of life after Roman Abramovich. The Independent. March 11, 2022.
20 Robinson J, Clegg J. The Club: How the Premier League Became the Richest, Most Disruptive Business in Sport. John Murray; 2019.
21 Serbia unlikely to join EU before end of decade, says President Vucic. Reuters. August 31, 2024.
22 Bechev D. Hedging Its Bets: Serbia Between Russia and the EU. Hedging Its Bets: Serbia Between Russia and the EU. Carnegie Europe. January 19, 2023.
23 O'Connor R. Red Star Belgrade are paying a price for their defiance before Rangers Europa League clash. The Times. March 17, 2022.
24 Barlovac B. Putin Meets With Serbian President in Belgrade. Balkan Insight. March 23, 2011.
25 O'Connor R. Red Star Belgrade are paying a price for their defiance before Rangers Europa League clash. The Times. March 17, 2022.
26 Pancevski B. Exclusive | A Drunken Evening, a Rented Yacht: The Real Story of the Nord Stream Pipeline Sabotage. WSJ. August 15, 2024.
27 Entous A, Barnes JE, Goldman A. Intelligence Suggests Pro-Ukrainian Group Sabotaged Pipelines, U.S. Officials Say. The New York Times. March 7, 2023.

2. Criminal Connections

ENDNOTES

1. Bowden M. Killing Pablo: The Hunt for the World's Greatest Outlaw. Grove Atlantic paperback edition. Grove Press; 2018.
2. Gugliotta G, Leen J. Kings of Cocaine: Inside the Medellín Cartel - an Astonishing True Story of Murder, Money, and International Corruption. Simon & Schuster; 2018.
3. Ibid.
4. Harvey R. Colombian Sport Has Drug Crisis : Soccer: Cartels have been connected to four top clubs that produce most of the players for national team. Los Angeles Times. February 5, 1990.
5. Gugliotta G, Leen J. Kings of Cocaine: Inside the Medellín Cartel - an Astonishing True Story of Murder, Money, and International Corruption. Simon & Schuster; 2018.
6. Bowden M. Killing Pablo: The Hunt for the World's Greatest Outlaw. Grove Atlantic paperback edition. Grove Press; 2018.
7. Narcos (TV Series 2015–2017). IMDb.
8. Gugliotta G, Leen J. Kings of Cocaine: Inside the Medellín Cartel - an Astonishing True Story of Murder, Money, and International Corruption. Simon & Schuster; 2018.
9. Ingram S. The Dark Side of Colombia's Beautiful Game: Narco-Football, Money Laundering, and Mass Murder. Breaking The Lines. May 17, 2020.
10. Football and tobacco. Jogo Bonito. www.jogojogojogo.com/football-and-tobacco
11. Brodzinsky S. From murder capital to model city: is Medellín's miracle show or substance? The Guardian. April 17, 2014.
12. The Most Dangerous Cities In The World. WorldAtlas. June 18, 2024.
13. Chicago led nation in homicides for 12th year in a row in 2023, murder rate still 5 times higher than NYC's. Wirepoints. January 3, 2024.
14. Bowden M. Killing Pablo: The Hunt for the World's Greatest Outlaw. Grove Atlantic paperback edition. Grove Press; 2018.
15. Escobar JP. Pablo Escobar, My Father. First St. Martin's Griffin edition. Thomas Dunne Books, St. Martin's Press; 2017.
16. Evans M. USA 94: The World Cup That Changed the Game. Pitch Publishing; 2022.
17. Driver T. Two dead in fights following Medellín's soccer derby. Latin America Reports. May 2, 2023.
18. Treasury Designates Colombian Organized Crime Group La Oficina de Envigado for Role in International Narcotics Trafficking. U.S. Department of the Treasury. November 19, 2024.
19. Treasury Designates the Financial Core and Support Network of Colombian Criminal Group La Oficina de Envigado. U.S. Department of the

Treasury. November 19, 2024.
20. Reuters S. Colombian football club Envigado blacklisted by US Treasury department – video. The Guardian. November 20, 2014.
21. Upi. AROUND THE NATION; 4 Extradited Colombians Are Held Without Bond. The New York Times. January 9, 1985.
22. Several Serie A and Serie B clubs raided at dawn over tax affairs. Sky Sports. June 25, 2013.
23. Harvey R. Colombian Sport Has Drug Crisis : Soccer: Cartels have been connected to four top clubs that produce most of the players for national team. Los Angeles Times. February 5, 1990.
24. Goldblatt D. The Age of Football: The Global Game in the Twenty-First Century. Macmillan; 2019.
25. Jones, Tobias. The Dark Heart of Italy. Faber & Faber.
26. Sylvers E. New Report Widens Parmalat's Debt. The New York Times. January 27, 2004.
27. Rakes M. Parmalat. Financial Scandals, Scoundrels & Crises. Econcrises. November 29, 2016.
28. Horncastle J. Parma's new owner Kyle Krause on combining two passions: Italy and football. The Athletic. September 27, 2020.
29. Nolan K. Parma and the Parmalat scandal. These Football Times. January 15, 2015.
30. Zambia Hosts FIFA President Gianni Infantino for Historic Visit. Lusaka Times. June 14, 2024.
31. Nine FIFA Officials and Five Corporate Executives Indicted for Racketeering Conspiracy and Corruption | United States Department of Justice. Office of Public Affairs, US Department of Justice. May 27, 2015.

3. The Global Gamble

1. D'Urso J. Football Index crash: The whistleblowers – 'We were almost in denial.' The Athletic. March 23, 2021.
2. D'Urso J. Indian Super League final: Sunil Chhetri, £2 tickets and bags of whisky. The Athletic. March 19, 2023.
3. D'Urso J & Hay P. Simon Grayson's bid for glory in India: 'European players wouldn't enjoy playing in 35C.' The Athletic. April 7, 2023.
4. Contacts. ParimatchNews. January 25, 2021. https://parimatchnews.com/contacts/
5. Langella B, Pooler M. Brazil's growing gambling habit threatens to hit economy. Financial Times. November 10, 2024.

ENDNOTES

6 Davies R. Jackpot: How Gambling Conquered Britain. Guardian Faber; 2022.
7 Cassidy R, Ovenden N. Frequency, Duration and Medium of Advertisements for Gambling and Other Risky Products in Commercial and Public Service Broadcasts of English Premier League Football.; 2017. doi:10.31235/osf.io/f6bu8.
8 Organized crime and illegal gambling: How do illegal gambling enterprises respond to the challenges posed by their illegality in China? Request PDF. ResearchGate. October 22, 2024. doi:10.1177/0004865815573874
9 D'Urso J. Special report: How Premier League shirt sponsors 'facilitate illegal gambling'. The Athletic. February 3, 2021.
10 Ibid.
11 Ibid.
12 D'Urso J. Revealed: The obscure gambling firms with untraceable employees working with your football club. The Athletic. December 28, 2021.
13 Ibid.
14 Ibid.
15 Ibid.
16 Spapens T. Crime Problems Related to Gambling: an Overview. In: Brill | Nijhoff; 2008:19-54. doi:10.1163/ej.9789004172180.i-254.10
17 Davies R. Jackpot: How Gambling Conquered Britain. Guardian Faber; 2022.
18 Brown A. Who are ya? Josimar. November 16, 2023.
19 Ibid.
20 Auclair P. The Vanishing. Josimar. January 5, 2023.
21 D'Urso J & Bailey J. Norwich City's Asian gambling shirt sponsor criticised for using 'women as glorified sexual objects' in adverts. The Athletic. June 7, 2021.
22 Auclair P. Meet Mr Chau. Josimar. June 16, 2022.
23 Tsoi G. Alvin Chau: Macau gambling kingpin jailed for 18 years. BBC News. January 18, 2023.
24 Luck A & Harris N. MPs want investigation into links between jailed Chinese billionaire and clubs' betting partners. Daily Mail Online. January 21, 2023.
25 Nottingham Forest FC. Nottingham Forest announce landmark deal with BetBright. Nottingham Forest. June 13, 2018.
26 D'Urso J. The Football Index crash: 'More akin to a Ponzi scheme than a betting platform.' The Athletic. March 10, 2021.
27 D'Urso J. Football Index crash: The whistleblowers – 'We were almost in denial.' The Athletic. March 23, 2021.

28   Ibid.
29   D'Urso J. The Football Index crash: 'More akin to a Ponzi scheme than a betting platform.' The Athletic. March 10, 2021.
30   Ibid.
31   D'Urso J. Exclusive: Football Index owners spent £15m of customers' money on global expansion plan as company collapsed. The Athletic. October 7, 2021.
32   D'Urso J. Football Index cost users £90m – now co-founder is back with new 'trading site'. The Times. April 12, 2024.

4. World on the Move

1   Idris A. Charity minibus stolen and torched on fire found burnt out near Essex field. Essex Live. March 17, 2023.
2   Haas H de. How Migration Really Works: A Factful Guide to the Most Divisive Issue in Politics. Viking, an imprint of Penguin Books; 2023.
3   Patel IS. We're Here Because You Were There: Immigration and the End of Empire. First published. Verso; 2021.
4   Enoch Powell's "Rivers of Blood" speech. The Telegraph. June 12, 2020.
5   Goldblatt D. The Age of Football: The Global Game in the Twenty-First Century. Macmillan; 2019.
6   Men's Football | Black Footballers Partnership. www.bfporg.com/mens-football/
7   Euro 2020: FA review on Wembley final disorder finds series of crowd "near misses" which could have led to fatalities. Sky Sports. December 4, 2021.
8   D'Urso J. The role of 'football hooligans' in political protests. The Athletic. November 16, 2023.
9   D'Urso J & Crafton A. Kylian Mbappe, his complicated relationship with Paris and a showdown with his dream club. The Athletic. November 25, 2024.
10   Les Bleus Une Autre Histoire de France. Black Dynamite Production; 2016.
11   Thompson CS. From Black-Blanc-Beur to Black-Black-Black? L'Affaire des Quotasand the Shattered Image of 1998 in Twenty-First-Century France. French Politics, Culture & Society. 2015;33(1). doi:10.3167/fpcs.2015.330106.
12   Les Bleus vs the far right: Three decades of attacks and counterattacks. Le Monde. June 18, 2024.

13. Smith R & Panja T. The Erasure of Mesut Özil. The New York Times. October 26, 2020.
14. France-Algeria: can football be a diplomatic tool? Afrique Chronique. September 7, 2022.
15. Sutherland B. Desailly urges anti-Le Pen vote. BBC News. April 26, 2022.
16. Thompson CS. From Black-Blanc-Beur to Black-Black-Black? L'Affaire des Quotasand the Shattered Image of 1998 in Twenty-First-Century France. French Politics, Culture & Society. 2015;33(1). doi:10.3167/fpcs.2015.330106.
17. Smith C. World Cup 2018: The Black and White and Brown Faces of Les Bleus. The New Yorker. June 22, 2018.
18. Fraser C. France's World Cup 'disaster' prompts soul-searching. BBC News. June 21, 2010.
19. Ibid.
20. Thompson CS. From Black-Blanc-Beur to Black-Black-Black? L'Affaire des Quotasand the Shattered Image of 1998 in Twenty-First-Century France. French Politics, Culture & Society. 2015;33(1). doi:10.3167/fpcs.2015.330106.
21. Arfi F, Hajdenberg M, Mathieu M. Exclusive: French football chiefs' secret plan to whiten "les Bleus." Mediapart. April 28, 2011.
22. Thompson CS. From Black-Blanc-Beur to Black-Black-Black? L'Affaire des Quotasand the Shattered Image of 1998 in Twenty-First-Century France. French Politics, Culture & Society. 2015;33(1). doi:10.3167/fpcs.2015.330106.
23. French coach cleared in football racism row. France 24. May 10, 2011.
24. Chrisafis A. France football heads mired in race row over alleged quotas for ethnic players. The Guardian. April 29, 2011.
25. Hytner D. Benoît Assou-Ekotto and Sébastien Bassong attack France race quotas. The Guardian. May 11, 2011.
26. Anelka - Racism in France. Sky Sports. December 7, 2010.
27. Dubois L. Another France Is Possible. Look at Its World Cup Team. The New York Times. December 10, 2022.
28. Gheerbrant J. Kylian Mbappé needs this World Cup more than ever. The Times. November 18, 2022.
29. Ibid.
30. Equipe de France: la mère de Mbappé explique ce qu'il s'est passé avec celle de Rabiot à l'Euro. RMC Sport.
31. Straus B. Kylian Mbappe Takes on the Weight of His World. Sports Illustrated. December 29, 2022.

32 EPSN. French football president claims racism does not exist after Neymar incident. ESPN. September 16, 2020.

5. American Exceptionalism

1   Tocqueville A de. Mélanges, fragments historiques et notes sur l'ancien régime, la Révolution et l'Empire: Voyages--pensées entièrement inédits. M. Lévy frères; 1865.
2   Reagan R. Message to the Nation on the Observance of Independence Day. Ronald Reagan Presidential Library& Museum. July 3, 1983.
3   Goldblatt D. The Age of Football: The Global Game in the Twenty-First Century. Macmillan; 2019.
4   Devine K. Tom Hanks suffers a rollercoaster of emotions while watching Aston Villa lose out 2-4 to Arsenal. Daily Mail Online. February 18, 2023.
5   What did Harry Hotspur look like? A new portrait gives us an idea... Tottenham Hotspur. September 5, 2024.
6   Romero S. What's in a Brand Name? Houston just found out. The New York Times. January 27, 2006.
7   West P. How the Houston Dynamo got their name. MLS Soccer. July 9, 2016.
8   Why you're more likely to die of cancer in Europe than America. POLITICO. April 9, 2019.
9   Burn-Murdoch J. Why are Americans dying so young? Financial Times. March 31, 2023.
10 Yang S. Dash GM explains Maris Sanchez trade, says there's 'buy-in and belief' as team searches for results. The Athletic. May 2, 2024.
11 Montague J. The Billionaires Club: The Unstoppable Rise of Football's Super-Rich Owners. Bloomsbury; 2017.
12 Kellison T, Orr M. Climate vulnerability as a catalyst for early stadium replacement. International Journal of Sports Marketing and Sponsorship. 2021;22(1):126-141. doi:10.1108/IJSMS-04-2020-0076
13 Ibid.
14 Ozanian M. The World's 50 Most Valuable Sports Teams 2023. Forbes. September 8, 2023.
15 Scholes T. Stateside Soccer: The Definitive History of Soccer in the United States. Pitch Publishing; 2019.
16 Once in a Lifetime: The Extraordinary Story of the New York Cosmos. Passion Pictures, Cactus Three, ESPN Original Entertainment; 2006.
17 Dickinson M. David Beckham: how I brought Lionel Messi to Miami. November 22, 2023.

18 Newsham G. When Pele and Cosmos were kings. The Guardian. June 10, 2005.
19 Scholes T. Stateside Soccer: The Definitive History of Soccer in the United States. Pitch Publishing; 2019.
20 Ibid.
21 French S. The Shot Heard 'Round the World: 25 years later, Paul Caligiuri recalls goal that changed US soccer forever. MLS Soccer. November 19, 2014.
22 Delaney M. States of Play. Seven Dials; 2024.
23 1994 FIFA World Cup (USA '94). History. US Soccer.
24 Searcey I. 'Soccer, the game? I've never heard of that' (1994). Channel 4 News. June 10, 2014.
25 Evans M. USA 94: The World Cup That Changed the Game. Pitch Publishing; 2022.
26 Robinson J, Clegg J. The Club: How the Premier League Became the Richest, Most Disruptive Business in Sport. John Murray Publishers; 2019.
27 Menicucci P. Calderón's candid criticism finds national audience. The Guardian. January 17, 2007.
28 Wahl G. The Beckham Experiment: How the World's Most Famous Athlete Tried to Conquer America. Three Rivers Press; 2010.
29 Tenorio P. How Beckham's transformative MLS contract paved the way for Messi. The New York Times. July 10, 2023.
30 Isos. Soccer's Growth in the U.S. Driven by Young, Diverse Audiences. Sports Business Journal. March 23, 2023.
31 Dickinson M. David Beckham: how I bought Lionel Messi to Miami. The Times. November 22, 2023.
32 Draper K, Smith R. The Stratospheric Rise of Lionel Messi's Pink Jersey. The New York Times. October 23, 2023.

6. Beyond Oil and Gas

1 Goldblatt D. How to Get on TV. London Review of Books. 2022;44(22).
2 Panja T & Smith R. Qatar 2022: The World Cup That Changed Everything. The New York Times. November 19, 2022.
3 D'Urso J. Exploring Qatar's eight World Cup 2022 stadiums and what fans can expect in November. The Athletic. November 19, 2022.
4 Cholewinski R. Understanding the Kafala Migrant Labor System in Qatar and the Middle East at Large, with ILO Senior Migration Specialist Ryszard Cholewinski. Georgetown Journal of International Affairs. February 1, 2023.

5 Leaders Special Report – BeoutQ: an unprecedented piracy story. Leaders. October 4, 2019.
6 Soriano F. Goal: The Ball Doesn't Go in by Chance ; Management Ideas from the World of Football. Palgrave Macmillan; 2012.
7 Delaney M. States of Play. Seven Dials; 2024
8 Horncastle J. Milan CEO Giorgio Furlani on battling Premier League spending and the future of San Siro. The Athletic. May 10, 2023.
9 D'Urso J. The Premier League in India: It's just not cricket. The Athletic. March 23, 2023.
10 Press A. Barcelona agree €150m shirt sponsor deal with Qatar Foundation. The Guardian. December 10, 2010.
11 Hunter G. The price of success. ESPN. December 20, 2010.
12 Hughes R. Barcelona Changes Jerseys and Its Values. The New York Times. September 28, 2011.
13 Kuper S. Barça: The inside Story of the World's Greatest Football Club. Short Books; 2021.
14 Ibid.
15 Ibid.
16 Hughes R. Barcelona Changes Jerseys and Its Values. The New York Times. September 28, 2011.
17 Rutzler P. How Michael Jordan helped make brand Paris Saint-Germain cool. The Athletic. December 26, 2023.
18 Dettmer J. Qatar influence campaigns need much greater scrutiny. POLITICO. December 13, 2022.
19 Jenson P. Barcelona under pressure to tear up record sponsorship amid terrorist fears. Mail Online. December 21, 2010.
20 Conn D. How Qatar became a football force: from Barcelona to PSG and World Cup. The Guardian. November 18, 2013.
21 Ibid.
22 Hytner D, Romano F. Lionel Messi leaving Barcelona after 'obstacles' thwart contract renewal. The Guardian. August 6, 2021.
23 Al-Sayeh, KM. The rise of the emerging Middle East carriers : outlook and implications for the global airline industry. Research Gate. September, 2014.
24 Krane J. Dubai: The Story of the World's Fastest City. Atlantic Books; 2015.
25 Hawley D. The Trucial States. Allen & Unwin; 1971.
26 Yergin D. The Prize: The Epic Quest for Oil, Money, and Power. Simon & Schuster; 1991.

27. Krane J. Dubai: The Story of the World's Fastest City. Atlantic Books; 2015.
28. Ibid.
29. Interview with Boutros Boutros, Senior Vice-President, Emirates Airlines - Sport360 News. December 4, 2013.
30. Delaney M. States of Play. Seven Dials; 2024.
31. Krzyzaniak J. The soft power strategy of soccer sponsorships. Soccer & Society. 2016;19:1-18. doi:10.1080/14660970.2016.1199426
32. Lawrence A, Ingle S. Arsenal's Henrikh Mkhitaryan to miss Europa League final over safety fears. The Guardian. May 21, 2019.

7. Democracy's Limits

1. Simpson T. Date with history: the arrest of Nelson Mandela. Chatham House – International Affairs Think Tank. August 3, 2022.
2. Korr CP, Close M. More than Just a Game: Soccer vs. Apartheid : The Most Important Soccer Story Ever Told. 1st U.S. ed. Thomas Dunne Books; 2010.
3. Williamson M. The D'Oliveira Affair. ESPNcricinfo. June 24, 2008.
4. Korr CP, Close M. More than Just a Game: Soccer vs. Apartheid : The Most Important Soccer Story Ever Told. 1st U.S. ed. Thomas Dunne Books; 2010.
5. Ibid.
6. More countries are now democratic than at any point since World War Two. World Economic Forum. December 11, 2017.
7. Saudi Arabia Population, 1950 – 2024. CEIC Data.
8. Saudi Arabia: Events of 2023. World Report 2024. Human Rights Watch.
9. Whitehead J. Yasir Al-Rumayyan: A life of power, privilege and risk for golf's most powerful man. The Athletic. March 29, 2023.
10. Hope B, Scheck J. Blood and Oil: Mohammed Bin Salman's Ruthless Quest for Global Power. First edition. Hachette Books; 2020.
11. Ibid.
12. Ibid.
13. Saudi Arabia's sovereign wealth fund swings to $36.8 bln profit in 2023. Reuters. July 1, 2024.
14. Hope B, Scheck J. Blood and Oil: Mohammed Bin Salman's Ruthless Quest for Global Power. First edition. Hachette Books; 2020.
15. Taylor L. Almirón stunner sinks Crystal Palace and takes Newcastle to 40-point mark. The Guardian. April 20, 2022.

16 Rudd A. Eddie Howe struggles will show if Saudis are romantic or ruthless. The Times. December 31, 2023.
17 Whitehead J. Saudi Arabia at St James' Park and Newcastle United's new commercial reality. The Athletic. September 12, 2023.
18 Saudi Arabia: Mass Execution of 81 Men. Human Rights Watch. March 15, 2022.
19 Newcastle manager Eddie Howe hits back at critics over Saudi ownership: "My specialist subject is football." Sky Sports. March 16, 2022.
20 Shearer A. Ashley's Newcastle was a shell of a club – now he's gone I'm excited…but conflicted by Saudi involvement. The Athletic. October 8, 2021.
21 Shearer A. Dear Eddie… Thank you, for all of it. The Athletic. May 22, 2023.
22 Whitehead J. Saudi influence in Newcastle: A story of property, prosperity and power. The New York Times. October 6, 2023.
23 Ibid.
24 Hewitt M. Newcastle United's key takeover powerbrokers and what happened next. Chronicle Live. October 14, 2024.
25 Saudi Arabia: Events of 2022. World Report 2023. Human Rights Watch.
26 League, Newcastle and St James Holdings settle dispute over takeover of club, which has been sold. Premier League Statement. October 7, 2021.
27 Crafton A. Newcastle's Saudi takeover: The UK government's emails revealed. The Athletic. April 6, 2023.
28 Caulkin G. Amanda Staveley interview: 'Why do Keegan and Shearer get so little recognition from our club?' The Athletic. October 10, 2021.
29 D'Urso J. Newcastle takeover: Why PIF and the Saudi state are the same thing. The Athletic. October 14, 2021.
30 Media PA. Court document describes Newcastle chairman as 'sitting Saudi minister.' The Guardian. March 1, 2023.
31 Hope B, Scheck J. Blood and Oil: Mohammed Bin Salman's Ruthless Quest for Global Power. First edition. Hachette Books; 2020.
32 Saudi Pro League clubs spend US$957 million in record-breaking football transfer window. Deloitte. September 9, 2023.

8. China's Rise and Retreat

1 Slater M. Wycombe to purchase Reading's training ground Bearwood Park. The New York Times. March 13, 2024.
2 Reading training ground: Wycombe put purchase of Bearwood Park "on hold." BBC Sport. March 18, 2024.

ENDNOTES

3 Palm Eco-Town Development Co Ltd 002431.SZ. Stock Price & Latest News. Reuters.
4 Population: Guangdong: Guangzhou: Usual Residence | Economic Indicators. CEIC.
5 West Brom takeover: Who is Guochuan Lai? Express and Star. August 5, 2016.
6 West Brom: Company owned by chairman Guochuan Lai misses deadline to repay £4.95m loan. BBC Sport. December 31, 2022.
7 Burke E. West Brom secure £20m loan from MSD Holdings. The New York Times. December 29, 2022.
8 Wright D. West Brom biggest shareholders may be Chinese state. West Brom News. June 8, 2023.
9 West Brom takeover: Guochuan Lai completes £175m deal. Express & Star. September 15, 2016.
10 Manchester United: Sir Jim Ratcliffe's £1.25bn deal for 27.7% stake is completed. BBC Sport. February 20, 2024.
11 Robinson J, Clegg J. The Club: How the Premier League Became the Richest, Most Disruptive Business in Sport. John Murray Publishers LT; 2019.
12 Birmingham City owner Carson Yeung jailed for six years. BBC News. March 7, 2014.
13 Crafton A, Whitwell L, James S, et al. Special investigation: Birmingham City on the brink. The New York Times. November 25, 2024.
14 Tan TC, Bairner A. Globalization and Chinese Sport Policy: The Case of Elite Football in the People's Republic of China. The China Quarterly. 2010;(203):581-600.
15 Burnton S. Silent fans, black eggs, 90-hour trip: recalling West Brom's tour of China. The Guardian. October 8, 2018.
16 Elton John's Watford in China in 1983, watched by Xi Jinping. Wild East Football. December 17, 2018.
17 Goldblatt D. The Age of Football: The Global Game in the Twenty-First Century. Macmillan; 2019.
18 Ibid.
19 Legge J. The 'May 19 Incident': When Hong Kong football sparked a riot in Beijing. The China Project. August 26, 2020.
20 Goldblatt D. The Age of Football: The Global Game in the Twenty-First Century. Macmillan; 2019.
21 Ibid.
22 Pidd H & Perraudin F. Ex-Man City Chinese player's hall of fame honour "a grubby little fix." The Guardian. October 23, 2015.

23 icade. Read Chinese Football's 50-point reform plan in full - exclusive translation. Wild East Football. April 9, 2016.
24 Fifield D. Chelsea's Antonio Conte: Chinese Super League is a danger to all teams. The Guardian. December 16, 2016.
25 May T. China Evergrande's Founder: From Rags to Riches to Under Investigation. The New York Times. October 2, 2023.
26 Communiqué of the Seventh National Population Census (No. 7). National Bureau of Statistics of China. May 11, 2021.
27 Shum D. Red Roulette: An Insider's Story of Wealth, Power, Corruption and Vengeance in Today's China. Simon & Schuster; 2021.
28 Ibid.
29 Buckley C & Wu A. Ending Term Limits for China's Xi is a Big Deal. Here's Why. The New York Times. March 10, 2018.
30 Explainer: How China Evergrande's debt troubles pose a systemic risk. Reuters. September 14, 2021.
31 How Evergrande's downfall signaled China's property crisis. Reuters. November 25, 2024.
32 Explainer: How China Evergrande's debt troubles pose a systemic risk. Reuters. September 14, 2021.
33 China should stick to 'houses are for living, not speculation' – state media. Reuters. August 23, 2023.
34 Rajah R & Leng A. Revising down the rise of China. Lowy Institute. March 14, 2022.
35 Kirton D. Disgruntled China Evergrande investors crowd headquarters in protest. September 13, 2021.
36 Brown D & Lewis C. Tycoon faces £30m loss on Hyde Park mega-mansion. The Times. October 8, 2022.
37 Oi M. Evergrande: Crisis-hit Chinese property giant ordered to liquidate. BBC News. January 29, 2024.
38 Cooper M. Fallen giants have abandoned 100,000-seater stadium as debts rocket to £220bn. The Mirror. September 8, 2023.
39 Campbell C. China's Real Estate Crisis Has No Easy Fix–Just Ask Chinese Soccer Fans. TIME. October 5, 2023.
40 D'Urso J. 'Li Tie: Confessions of corruption, at risk of time in jail – so what has happened? The Athletic. February 20, 2024.
41 Ibid.

9. The Other Half

1 Wrack S. A Woman's Game: The Rise, Fall, and Rise Again of Women's

Soccer. Triumph Books LLC; 2022.
2. Dunn C. Unsuitable for Females: The Rise of The Lionesses and Women's Football in England. Arena Sport; 2022.
3. Wrack S. A Woman's Game: The Rise, Fall, and Rise Again of Women's Soccer. Triumph Books LLC; 2022.
4. Dunn C. Unsuitable for Females: The Rise of The Lionesses and Women's Football in England. Arena Sport; 2022.
5. Lily Parr. National Football Museum Hall of Fame Profile. National Football Museum.
6. Wrack S. A Woman's Game: The Rise, Fall, and Rise Again of Women's Soccer. Triumph Books LLC; 2022.
7. Anstiss S, Grey-Thompson T. Game on: The Unstoppable Rise of Women's Sport. Unbound; 2021.
8. Wrack S. A Woman's Game: The Rise, Fall, and Rise Again of Women's Soccer. Triumph Books LLC; 2022.
9. Williams J. A Beautiful Game: International Perspectives on Women's Football. 1. publ. Berg; 2007.
10. Anstiss S, Grey-Thompson T. Game on: The Unstoppable Rise of Women's Sport. Unbound; 2021.
11. Wrack S. A Woman's Game: The Rise, Fall, and Rise Again of Women's Soccer. Triumph Books LLC; 2022.
12. Brisbane MH. Women's World Cup: Mary Earps hits out at Nike in shirt row. The Times. July 20, 2023.
13. Mary Earps: Nike will sell "limited quantities" of England World Cup goalkeeper shirt. BBC Sport. August 24, 2023.
14. Hayes E. It's not sexist to call for smaller pitches and goals for women. The Times. August 29, 2024.
15. Harpur C. Spain's glory, Renard's stand, Earps vs Nike – the moments that defined the year in women's football. The Athletic. December 27, 2023.
16. Sheldon D. Marys Earps: Goalkeeper, brand, icon. The Athletic. December 19, 2023.
17. Wrack S. A Woman's Game: The Rise, Fall, and Rise Again of Women's Soccer. Triumph Books LLC; 2022
18. Christenson M. & Kelso P. Soccer chief's plan to boost women's game? Hotpants. The Guardian. January 16, 2004.
19. Tumin R. Title IX Gave Women Greater Access to Education. Here's What It Says and Does. The New York Times. June 22, 2022.
20. Hunter L. Future of Football: Why ACL injuries have been on rise in women's game – and the technology and solutions to fix it. Sky Sports. February 20, 2024.

21. Saini A. The weaker sex? Science that shows women are stronger than men. The Guardian. June 11, 2017.
22. Criado-Perez C. Invisible Women: Exposing Data Bias in a World Designed for Men. Vintage; 2020.
23. Brazil named as hosts for 2027 Women's World Cup. BBC Sport. May 17, 2024.
24. Jones D. Nike Launch Corinthians 21/22 Third Shirt. SoccerBible. September 27, 2021.

10. Borders

1. D'Urso J. 'War and sport have never been so close': Our podcast following Shakhtar Donetsk is out now. The New York Times. November 7, 2022.
2. Reus-Smit C. Struggles for Individual Rights and the Expansion of the International System. International Organization. 2011;65(2):207-242. doi:10.1017/S0020818311000038
3. Diener AC, Hagen J. Borders: A Very Short Introduction (Very Short Introductions): Amazon.co.uk: Diener, Alexander C., Hagen, Joshua: 9780199731503: Books.
4. Ibid.
5. Scotland has highest per capita crowds in Europe. BBC Sport. September 18, 2024.
6. Maguire K. The Price of Football: Understanding Football Club Finance. Agenda Publishing; 2020.
7. Adetunji J. Hooligans jailed for causing "worst violence in Manchester since the blitz." The Guardian. September 3, 2010.
8. Moffat C. Helicopter Sunday: Rangers' last-gasp triumph, 15 years on. BBC Sport. May 22, 2020.
9. McMillan F. Rangers Tax Case. Oracle Law. July 10, 2017.
10. McGuirk B. Celtic FC: The Ireland Connection. Black & White; 2009.
11. Woodham-Smith C. Ireland's Hunger, England's Fault? The Atlantic. Published January 1, 1963. Accessed November 25, 2024.
12. McGuirk B. Celtic FC: The Ireland Connection. Black & White; 2009.
13. Ibid.
14. Murray WJ. The Old Firm in a New Age. First Edition, First Impression. Mainstream Publishing; 1998.
15. Baker L. Remembrance Sunday tribute stopped after nine seconds as Celtic fans sing and boo through silence. The Independent. November 11, 2024.

16 Diener AC, Hagen J. Borders: A Very Short Introduction (Very Short Introductions): Amazon.co.uk: Diener, Alexander C., Hagen, Joshua: 9780199731503: Books.
17 The Project Gutenberg eBook of The Jewish State, by Theodor Herzl. Accessed November 25, 2024. https://www.gutenberg.org/files/25282/25282-h/25282-h.htm
18 Newman MK. Why Chile has a Palestinian football team – the bigger history. The Conversation. May 21, 2024.
19 Rueckert P. When Palestinians Crossed the Chilean Andes by Mule, a New Diaspora Was Born. New Lines Magazine. March 22, 2024.
20 Newman MK. Why Chile has a Palestinian football team – the bigger history. The Conversation. May 21, 2024.
21 Elsey B. Citizens and Sportsmen: Fútbol and Politics in Twentieth-Century Chile. 1. ed. Univ. of Texas Pr; 2011.
22 Ibid.
23 Al-Arian AA, ed. Football in the Middle East: State, Society, and the Beautiful Game. Hurst & Company; 2022.
24 Chile bans Palestino football club "anti-Israel" shirt. BBC News. January 21, 2014.
25 Edwards DAJ. Statement by the UN Special Rapporteur on torture and other cruel, inhuman or degrading treatment or punishment on one-year anniversary of the October 7th attacks. The Question of Palestine. United Nations. October 7, 2024.
26 Duerr GME. Playing for identity and independence: the issue of Palestinian statehood and the role of FIFA. Soccer & Society. 2012;13(5-6):653-666. doi:10.1080/14660970.2012.730768
27 Diener AC, Hagen J. Borders: A Very Short Introduction (Very Short Introductions): Amazon.co.uk: Diener, Alexander C., Hagen, Joshua: 9780199731503: Books.

11. Financial Times

1 Swarup B. Money Mania: Booms, Panics, and Busts from Ancient Rome to the Great Meltdown. Bloomsbury Publishing USA; 2014.
2 Ibid.
3 Tran, H. Financialization has increased economic fragility. Atlantic Council. December 1, 2023.
4 Zuckerman G. Meet the New King of Subprime Lending. Wall Street Journal. August 11, 2015.
5 Andrew T. CommBank to replace Westfield as naming rights sponsor of

Australia's Matildas. SportBusiness. April 13, 2021.

6   Anstiss S, Grey-Thompson T. Game on: The Unstoppable Rise of Women's Sport. Unbound; 2021.

7   Naylor A. Brighton's record £100m Amex deal will transform club – for men and women - The Athletic. August 8, 2019.

8   D'Urso J. How the crypto crash has impacted each Premier League club. The New York Times. June 28, 2022.

9   D'Urso J. Special report: How Premier League shirt sponsors 'facilitate illegal gambling.' The Athletic. February 3, 2021.

10 McKenzie B, Silverman J. Easy Money: Cryptocurrency, Casino Capitalism, and the Golden Age of Fraud. Abrams Press; 2023.

11 White G. Rinsed: From Cartels to Crypto: How the Tech Industry Washes Money for the World's Deadliest Crooks. Penguin Business; 2024.

12 Paris Hilton, Jimmy Fallon Show Off Bored Ape Yacht Club NFT. Vulture. January 25, 2022.

13 Dellatto M. Crypto's Super User: Young Men. 43% Of U.S. Males Aged 18 To 29 Have Bought The Currency. Forbes. April 21, 2022.

14 D'Urso J. John Terry's NFT collection plunges 90% in value. The New York Times. March 9, 2022.

15 D'Urso J. How the crypto crash has impacted each Premier League club. The New York Times. June 28, 2022.

16 D'Urso, J. Explained: Michael Owen's claims about his NFT collection - The Athletic. May 11, 2022.

17 D'Urso J. Michael Owen breached UK law by promoting unlicensed cryptocurrency casino. The New York Times. June 8, 2022.

18 D'Urso, J. Losing three months' wages in Paul Pogba crypto scheme: 'The main reason we invested was him' - The Athletic. March 1, 2023.

19 D'Urso J. MiniFootball: The strange story of a cryptocurrency players and legends 'pumped' on social media. The New York Times. September 12, 2021.

20 D'Urso, J. Losing three months' wages in Paul Pogba crypto scheme: 'The main reason we invested was him' - The Athletic. March 1, 2023.

21 D'Urso J. Special investigation: Socios 'fan tokens' – what they really are and how they work. The New York Times. August 18, 2021.

22 D'Urso, J. Special report: Socios expects to make £150 from each fan who buys a token - The Athletic. April 29, 2022.

23 Non-fungible tokens (NFTs) and the blockchain - Committees - UK Parliament. October 11, 2023.

24 McKenzie B, Silverman J. Easy Money: Cryptocurrency, Casino

Capitalism, and the Golden Age of Fraud. Abrams Press; 2023.
25 "Fortune Favors the Brave": Matt Damon Reveals Why He Starred in THAT Crypto.com Advert. Yahoo Finance. April 12, 2023.
26 McKenzie B, Silverman J. Easy Money: Cryptocurrency, Casino Capitalism, and the Golden Age of Fraud. Abrams Press; 2023.
27 Kim Kardashian pays $1.26m over crypto "pump and dump." BBC News. October 3, 2022.
28 McKenzie B, Silverman J. Easy Money: Cryptocurrency, Casino Capitalism, and the Golden Age of Fraud. Abrams Press; 2023.

PICTURE CREDITS

1. Raúl celebrating a goal at FC Schalke 04, who's shirts were sponsored by Gazprom. (Getty Images)
2. Luka Jović playing for Red Star Belgrade, another club sponsored by Gazprom. (Getty Images)
3. The 2012 shirt of Envigado FC featuring the face of founder Gustavo Upegui. (Sentimiento De Chanca)
4. Hernán Crespo in the yellow-and-blue of Parma FC, who were bankrolled by Parmalat, a local diary company later implicated of fraud. (Getty Images)
5. The home stadium of Goa FC, the pitch ringed by advertisements for Parimatch News. (Joey D'Urso)
6. Brennan Johnson at Nottingham Forest, sponsored by Football Index between 2019-2021. (Getty Images)
7. The red shirt of Changing Lives FC. (Changing Lives FC)
8. Kylian Mbappé in the French national shirt, which embodies worldwide migration patterns. (Getty Images)
9. Veronica Latsko of Houston Dash, sponsored by a local hospital, the MD Anderson Cancer Center. (Getty Images)
10. The pink shirt of Inter Miami, worn by Lionel Messi, the visual symbol of the USA finally embracing football. (Getty Images)
11. Messi and Cesc Fàbregas in the shirts of FC Barcelona, sponsored by Qatar Foundation, the first signs of Barcelona falling to commercial pressures. (Getty Images)
12. Cristiano Ronaldo at Real Madrid, sponsored by the UAE's Emirates of Dubai. (Getty Images)
13. Joelinton at Newcastle United, the shirt reminiscent of Saudi Arabia's green and white flag. (Getty Images)
14. The pitch which the prisoners of Robben Island played on, wearing whatever shirts they could acquire. (Getty Images)
15. Gareth Barry broke the all-time Premier League appearance record at

PICTURE CREDITS

     West Bromwich Albion, sponsored by Palm, the company of club owner Guochuan Lai. (Getty Images)
16. Paulinho, one of the many stars who moved to the Chinese Super League in the 2010s, playing for Guangzhou Evergrande. (Getty Images)
17. Mary Earps at the 2023 World Cup in the England Goalkeeper's shirt that Nike originally refused to sell. (Getty Images)
18. A purple kit worn by Brazilian club Corinthians. (Alamy)
19. The green-and-white kit of CD Palestino in Chile. A symbol of the country's Arab community. (CD Palestino)
20. Alfredo Morelos, wearing the orange away kit of Rangers. (Getty Images)
21. Dele Alli playing for Beşiktaş, sponsored by Rain, a website selling cryptocurrency. (Getty Images)
22. The Australia women's team, sponsored by CommBank. (Getty Images)